ROUTLEDGE LIBRARY EDITIONS: EARLY YEARS

Volume 15

I0083816

PARENTS AND PLAYGROUPS

PARENTS AND PLAYGROUPS

A Study by the Pre-school Playgroups Association

LADY PLOWDEN

Routledge
Taylor & Francis Group

LONDON AND NEW YORK

First published in 1981 by George Allen & Unwin Ltd

This edition first published in 2023
by Routledge
4 Park Square, Milton Park, Abingdon, Oxon OX14 4RN

and by Routledge
605 Third Avenue, New York, NY 10158

Routledge is an imprint of the Taylor & Francis Group, an informa business

British Library Cataloguing in Publication Data
A catalogue record for this book is available from the British Library

ISBN: 978-1-032-34369-3 (Set)
ISBN: 978-1-032-34376-1 (Volume 15) (hbk)
ISBN: 978-1-032-34383-9 (Volume 15) (pbk)
ISBN: 978-1-003-32182-8 (Volume 15) (ebk)

DOI: 10.4324/9781003321828

Publisher's Note
The publisher has gone to great lengths to ensure the quality of this reprint but points out that some imperfections in the original copies may be apparent.

Disclaimer
The publisher has made every effort to trace copyright holders and would welcome correspondence from those they have been unable to trace.

In 1975 the Pre-school Playgroups Associations in Scotland, England and Wales came together to analyse and record some of the experience gained in the previous fourteen years and to assess the stage of development which the associations and playgroups had reached by the late 1970s. Parental involvement had become the keystone of PPA's philosophy of enabling parents to become actively involved with their children in community situations. In these studies some of the full implications are explored in a frank and open manner. Much of what is revealed and debated is relevant to any community venture seeking to provide opportunities for involvement.

The spectacular growth of Mother and Toddler Clubs (often parent and toddler clubs in reality) in the late '70s was largely an uncharted area until PPA's working party completed its survey. These clubs are a major factor in helping many young parents come to terms with the problems of isolation felt in bringing up a family today. The study contains much solid information not only in recording past development but in providing pointers for the future. Both the report on parental involvement and the report on Mother and Toddler Clubs were prepared by working parties of grass roots people.

The inquiry into patterns of playgroup oversight and support was on a larger scale than the other studies and involved more than thirty researchers covering England, Wales and Scotland. The growth in the number of playgroups since the early 1960s has presented many challenges to social services departments and this enquiry looks at the differing patterns of oversight and support that have emerged and attempts to assess their effectiveness as seen from the playgroup angle. It is invaluable reading for anyone interested in statutory support for voluntary organisations.

This book presents some aspects of the playgroup movement which make it one of the most exciting developments in the United Kingdom in the last twenty-five years.

Also published by Allen & Unwin in conjunction with the Pre-school Playgroups Association:

THE PLAYGROUP MOVEMENT by Brenda Crowe

PARENTS AND PLAYGROUPS

A Study by the Pre-school Playgroups Association

With a Foreword by LADY PLOWDEN, DBE

Published in conjunction with the
Pre-school Playgroups Association

London
George Allen & Unwin
Boston   Sydney

First published in 1981

GEORGE ALLEN & UNWIN LTD
40 Museum Street, London WC1A 1LU

This edition © Pre-school Playgroups Association 1981

British Library Cataloguing in Publication Data

Pre-school Playgroups Association.
  Parents and playgroups.
  1. Play groups – Great Britain
  I. Title
  372'.216   LB1140.25.G7   80–41790

  ISBN 0–04–372030–7

The three reports included in this volume were originally published in booklet form by PPA: *Mother and Toddler Groups* and *Patterns of Oversight and Support for Playgroups* in 1978 and *Parental Involvement in Playgroups* in 1980.

Set in 11 on 12 point Baskerville by
Typesetters (Birmingham) Ltd.
and Printed in Great Britain
by Biddles Ltd, Guildford, Surrey

'Playgroups arose from a meeting of a need and an idea, evolved through a continuing exploration of purpose, achieved an identity and grew to become an organisation to promote learning and to support its members. It found a national role. This set of papers reveals the quality of the playgroup thought, the dynamism of a movement which has brought ideals and practice into an endeavour which challenges tradition while seeking the elusive partnerships of parent with professional, voluntary with statutory. It merits study and response – without prejudice.'

MAX PATTERSON
Past President of Scottish Pre-school
Playgroups Association

Acknowledgements

PPA would like to pay tribute to the many people who have helped in the compilation and writing of the three reports published in this book. We are indebted to those who answered the questionnaire and to Barclays Bank whose grant made the three reports possible. We are also deeply grateful to PPA members and friends in regions, branches, and County Associations who assisted in the survey work and to all the other PPA members who contributed to our thinking.

Contents

Foreword

by LADY PLOWDEN, DBE

President of the Pre-school Playgroups Association

Five years ago, in 1975, Barclays Bank made it possible for the Pre-school Playgroups Association to mount studies in areas of major interest to the playgroup movement, its admirers and critics. PPA is an association of families with young children which puts its energies into servicing its vast membership.*

Although PPA receives welcome and essential grant aid from national government, it has not attracted charitable funding for an exercise which would include resources to explore either the successes or the problems of the movement.

Lack of research is a matter for concern: it is seventeen years since a Report, *Children and their Primary Schools*, urged that education 'will only succeed in full if it carries parents into partnership'. The playgroup movement was then in its infancy (PPA was formed in 1961); since then, the nature of the experience enjoyed by millions of pre-school children in playgroups and their parents calls for in-depth evaluation of the work and potential of the playgroup movement, so that there can be an assessment of what has been learnt in the process, what support is needed and what the implications are for future family orientated policies.

Barclay's imaginative gift of £10,000 has enabled PPA itself to begin evaluating these concerns. Three working parties were set up; their respective briefs were *Elements of parental involvement and growth*, *Mother and Toddler groups* and *Patterns of local authority oversight and support for playgroups*. Meeting from 1976/79, their reports were produced just before, during and after the 1979 International Year of the Child.

Among the many pronouncements in that year, scant attention was paid to the work of the PPA, its member playgroups and mother and toddler clubs. Yet at the Athens

---

*September 1980: 11,750 group members, meaning approximately 420,000 children; 390 local branches and 40 county associations.

Conference in June 1978* held to launch the Year of the Child explicit and complimentary references were made to the 'experience of the vast pre-school playgroup movement in great Britain' as well as to kindred organisations in Yugoslavia and Italy and much of the English-speaking world; there was also a wealth of statements from the gathered experts regarding the importance, not only of parental involvement, but of partnership and responsibility, the key philosophy of the playgroup movement.

The three studies carried out by the PPA and presented together in this volume will serve as an introduction to the developed thinking of the association, and point to areas for further research. They describe something increasingly vital in our present society, which is so often rootless and purposeless; as the group studying parental involvement says (p.36), 'one of the greatest strengths of the playgroup movement is that overall it is a positive force in a largely negative society'.

The experience of *Parental growth and involvement* is felt by PPA to be as significant, where it occurs, as the young child's experience of play in the company of his peers. The group decided to record the corporate experience of parental involvement within the playgroup movement; as they explored the nature of this involvement, what factors caused it to flourish and what diminished it, they became convinced that 'Parental involvement in playgroups can lead to a unique enrichment of children's early lives through play'. This ties in with the views of Mann, Harrell and Hurt in *A review of Headstart Research since 1969* (Social Research Group, George Washington University, USA). The group warn that parental involvement is not a magic formula easily attained; it has to be sought, fought for and preserved.

In the 1980s, society seems to be moving slowly away from consumerism towards shared responsibility and participation

---

*The edited papers and discussions are published in the UK as *The Child in the World of Tomorrow*, general editor Spyros Doxiadis, Minister of Social Services, Greece (Pergamon).

in decision making – for example, parents as governors and representatives of voluntary organisations on such bodies as community health councils. The playgroup movement has shown some of the potential which is waiting in the community.

The First Report of the Select Committee on Violence in the Family (1978) referred to the increasing involvement in the management of their own playgroups of individuals and groups described as 'deprived' and 'socially incompetent'; they remarked that participation in pre-school activity engendered a wider interest in neighbourhood affairs; they urged greater encouragement by central and local government in the setting up of pre-school playgroups. The purposeful activities of the playgroup mothers described in this report contrast with the depression in mothers with a low self-image recorded in 1978 by Brown and Harris.*

The rapid growth of mother and toddler groups or clubs in the last ten years demonstrates their popularity with today's young mothers, many of whom are denied the back-up of the extended family and the practical experience of child care gained in such a family. In the main, these groups spring from perceived needs of companionship for both mothers and children, whether they are begun by mothers themselves or by others aware of their plight. The mutual support of the peer group is their spin-off and their strength. The needs of non-earners in a wage-oriented society are too often overlooked. The Select Committee commended these groups, which play a significant role in combating depression in mothers of young children. The comments of various mothers can be found on p.18.

One working party conducted a survey of mother and toddler clubs, the first attempt to look nationally at these groups. Since the survey relates to the winter of 1976–7 the

* *The Social Origins of Depression* – *a study of Psychiatric Disorder in women* (Tavistock). See also 'The Rag Rug', in *Adult Education*, 1980.

present finances of mother and toddler clubs are even more stretched. Many rents for premises have doubled or trebled at a time when family finances are equally affected; yet growth and enthusiasm continue unabated wherever premises can be found.*

The working party was impressed by the great desire of these groups to retain their independence and freedom from regulation. I would underline their final paragraph: 'here is an investment not only in mother and child but in society and its future which the working party recommends to policy makers and those who carry through the implementation of policies at various levels. It has inestimable value.'

The oversight and support of playgroups by local authorities is a comparatively new role, developed out of their responsibilities under the Nurseries and Child Minders Regulation Act of 1948. The working party on this subject produces much of interest for future liaison between local authorities and playgroups in particular and voluntary organisations in general. Unfortunately there were not sufficient resources to explore fully relationships with education, health or recreation services. The report identifies the dual system of oversight and support which affects playgroups – the formal local authority responsibility which is often much more than a mandatory interest and the informal system supplied by the PPA network of voluntary fieldworkers and branches. It is noteworthy that the local authority appears to be most valued for the visits of its adviser, where one has been appointed, and the PPA most valued for the personal support, bulk buying, informal course and branch meetings. The branch is a different expression of the mutual help characteristic of playgroups identified by the Wolfenden Report on Voluntary Organisations. It is essential that the two systems of support from within PPA and from local authorities

*Of 8,229 groups responding to the PPA membership survey in 1979, 1,524 were PGs with an attached MT Club, and 322 were independent mother and toddler clubs, so 22 per cent of the membership appeared to have a mother and toddler connection.

should be complementary and that neither should frustrate the other.

The report further emphasises that it takes time for joint consultation between local authority departments and voluntary organisations to be effective. Informal meetings may lead to genuine consultation once mutual confidence has been established.*

The new towns continue to attract much interest; the contribution of playgroups to the development of these new communities, and the nature of help received is discussed.

The views of directors of social services departments were sought by the working party and they present contrasting views: 'a middle-class luxury' or 'a preventative resource'. Perhaps I may refer the exponents of both views to the work of the *parental involvement* working party and suggest as further reading *The Child in the World of Tomorrow*, mentioned earlier, with special reference to the papers of K. Luscher, E. Grotberg, B. and J. Tizzard, T. B. Brazelton, E. J. Anthony, S. Sjolin, A. Petros-Barvazian and M. G. Wagner.

There are many lessons and hopes for the future in this volume. In collaboration with its Scottish counterpart, SPPA, PPA has performed an invaluable task in collating their joint experience of involvement with the various arms of local authority departments; they have not, I believe, shirked the responsibility of pinpointing problems, hoping that if problems can be identified, solutions may be found.

What Next? PPA's greatest strength is that it is and must remain a grass-roots organisation; the members' first duty is to their local groups and branches. The families of those who give time willingly should not be penalised by having to find the expenses from their housekeeping money; unless this is accepted, only those who can afford to do so will become involved. Playgroups and the supporting network of the

---

*See also *Facts & Figures 1979* (PPA).

association cannot exist without financial support from central and local government; news that in some areas local authority support is being reduced as part of overall strategies of financial retrenchment, together with vastly increased costs, places intolerable burdens on families who make up the playgroup movement.

PPA values the contribution of parents of all backgrounds; it now needs to experiment by taking new initiatives as well as offering its traditional support to those who express an interest in forming groups or encounter difficulties once established. All this costs money; it also calls for evaluation and the work itself needs recognition in the form of more generous and more widespread grant aid to the playgroups and mother and toddler clubs themselves. In its 1979 survey of grants to playgroups, 28 per cent of the responding playgroups had received a grant. Of these, 82 per cent were less than £100.

Since PPA cannot continue without financial support from public funds it must be accountable for their use and accept some supervision. I do, however, believe most strongly that PPA must remain a voluntary body, a loose and rather lumbering organisation with a head organisation the size of a pin in relation to its total membership. It must adapt to the changing conditions of the 1980s whatever they may be; it must adapt to the needs of mothers of young children, a constantly changing group. It is their voices that must be heard. No bureaucratic government department can move swiftly enough or keep in touch with the insistent voices that come, and will continue to come, from the PG and M and T club mothers. They must remain the foundation on which PPA continues to build, for whom it is responsible. PPA is a remarkable organisation deserving not only financial support from statutory and charitable bodies, it also merits the encouragement and support of individuals, the media and the decision makers – councillors and MPs. This volume will, I hope, broaden the knowledge of those who believe playgroups to be concerned 'only' with the play of small children, valuable as that is: it should introduce them to the complex and exciting society of a democratic organisation of parents which has pioneered 'parents' lib – not by shelving their responsibilities but by sharing them. As Professor Bruner remarks, 'No country in the world has achieved anything like it.' The country cannot afford to allow this miracle of the post-war years to wither through lack of public interest and essential financial back-up.

The aims of the PPA are encapsulated in the following:

PPA exists to help parents to understand and provide for the needs of their young children. It aims to promote community situations in which parents can with growing enjoyment and confidence make the best uses of their own knowledge and resources in the development of their children and themselves.

The three parts of this book explain how this is being put into effect.

BRIDGET PLOWDEN

July 1980

Relevant Reading

The Playgroup Movement, Brenda Crowe (Allen & Unwin).
Who Cares, Penelope Leach (Penguin).
Facts & Figures 1979 (PPA).
Under-five in Britain, Jerome Bruner (Grant McIntyre).
Cogs & Spindles, Maude Henderson (PPA).
PPA Coming of Age in the 80s – Thoughts of the President and Vice President (PPA).
The Child in the World of Tomorrow, ed. Spyros Doxiadis (Pergamon).

Glossary

Names and titles of organisations are generally written out in full but the following abbreviations are occasionally used for brevity and clarity.

AO	Area Organiser (PPA)
ATO	Area Training Officer
CDO	Community Development Officer
CHC	Community Health Council
CQSW	Certificate and Qualification in Social Work
CSS	Certificate of Social Service
CVS	Council of Voluntary Service
DES	Department of Education and Science
DHSS	Department of Health and Social Security
LA	Local Authority
LEA	Local Education Authority
MT	Mother and Toddler Club or Group
MY	Mother and Young Club or Group
NEC	National Executive Committee
NISW	National Institute for Social Work
NNEB	National Nurseries Examination Board
NUT	National Union of Teachers
OU	Open University
PG	Playgroup
PCO	Pre-school Community Organiser
PPA	Pre-school Playgroups Association
SAAUFF	Scottish Association of Advisers for the Under-fives and their Families (formerly SAPA)
SAPA	Scottish Association of Playgroup Advisers (now SAAUFF)
SCF	Save the Children Fund
SEC	Scottish Executive Committee
SPPA	Scottish Pre-school Playgroups Association
SSD	Social Services Department
TDO	Training and Development Officer
VOLCUF	Voluntary Organisations' Liaison Committee for Under-fives
WEA	Workers' Educational Association
WRVS	Women's Royal Voluntary Service
YMCA	Young Men's Christian Association

Part One

Parental Involvement in Playgroups

Introduction

In 1975, the Pre-school Playgroups Association decided that there was a clear need to study and document some of the elements of parental involvement in playgroups. The National Executive Committee appointed a working group whose members met together over a period of three years. There were representatives from PPA in England and Wales; the Scottish Pre-school Playgroups Association produced a series of link persons who joined the group at a later date. The working group remembers with gratitude the contribution to its thinking by the late Maureen Huntley, National Adviser.

Early in the discussions, we decided that we could make a contribution only by trying to record the collective experience of parental involvement within the playgroup movement. For this reason, the report does not contain a critical review of the literature on the subject, although that would be valuable and might commend itself as a worthwhile future project. Neither is it an assembly of facts and figures – not only because to do this would have taken more money than was available, but also because it was demonstrated that certain qualities of parental involvement are not yet amenable to such analysis.

We started by thinking about involvement as an experience common to everyone. Then we tried to describe as honestly as possible what is meant by parental involvement in playgroups, and to note how it arises and what does and does not nourish it. We sought to explore its benefits and drawbacks to the child, the family and the wider community. In the course of our study, questions arose to which we could give no final answer; we have included them so that individuals may seek their own solutions.

The report is a collection of papers written by different individual members, as is evident in the differing styles and the fact that the same topic may be referred to more than once. But each reflects the corporate thinking of the group.

From the beginning, it was clear that it was necessary for the thinking of the working group to reflect the grass-roots experience in playgroups. There were a great many informal exchanges of views, and each of the eleven regions of PPA was asked to convene meetings which would bring members together to discuss the issue. This was followed by talks with members of the Scottish PPA, who have been exploring a similar theme for several years.

Nine regions arranged meetings which a member of the working group attended. It was quite clear that there is a huge ground swell of feeling and care within the playgroup movement for parental involvement and its resulting authority and responsibility to be given its rightful place in playgroups, and also for that involvement to be accepted as the basis of all pre-school provision in the coming decade.

We are convinced from our observations, as well as from our understanding of current research in the pre-school field, that parental involvement in playgroups can lead to a unique enrichment of children's early lives through play.

It can bring a deepening of the mother-child relationship; an awakening of parental confidence, care and insights; and the release of those qualities into the community as a whole.

We hope that this document will cause people in playgroups, and all those concerned with pre-school provision, to think again about the role of the family as the cradle of our future generation.

Moiya Codling	Brenda Crowe	Marjorie Dykins
Maureen Huntley	Joanna Matthews	Edna Salsby
PPA		

Nita Brown   Mary Henderson   Barbara Ritchie
SPPA link persons
December 1978

1

Involvement as a Common Experience of Living

'Parental involvement' is a fashionable term used to describe different ways in which parents are drawn into activities to do with their children. So often is it used for different practices that it has become a cliché.

The trouble with clichés is that they are so obviously true that they trip thoughtlessly off the tongue and very few people bother to question them. 'Parental Involvement' is now referred to and advocated so often, and so glibly, and in such a wide variety of contexts, that we felt we had better begin our task by exploring the word 'involvement'.

The root of the word is the Latin *volvere*, to roll

So far so good, and personal experience leads the thinking further:

    involvement is rolling in
    devolvement is rolling out(wards)
    evolve is rolling out(of)
    revolving is rolling round
    convolve is rolling round in twists.

There is a sense of energy in all these words, but also a feeling that the words could be transposed to mean that much more. Just think of all that the word 'evolution' implies!

Let us start with the rolling-in definition, and look at it in the context of playgroups. How easy it is to stand in the doorway saying in effect, 'Roll in, roll in! Straight into the kitchen please, to make the coffee and mix the paint.'

Is that what involvement is all about?

If not, could it be 'Roll in, roll in and be done good to?' Or, 'Roll in, roll in and save us paying another helper?' Or, 'Roll in, roll in so that we can qualify as a committee-run playgroup with charitable status, for then we shall be eligible for a grant?'

All these are familiar cries, only instead of the honestly flamboyant fairground language they are apt to be couched (with varying degrees of honesty or self-deception) in such terms as 'Would you like to come in and help us? We'd love to have you.'

All this somehow implies that one person, or group, is firmly settled in, and other individuals are invited to do all the moving (rather like players moving chessmen?). Only in a playgroup the chessmen are flesh and blood, with feelings, and they don't want to be master-minded (or if they do it is particularly important that the pattern is changed).

But we can interpret 'roll in' rather differently: if someone's clothing is on fire the first aid directive is 'Roll in a blanket or a carpet.' A variation on this theme is the comment on two people in love, that 'they're wrapped up in each other'.

Once we begin using terms of mutual involvement, other examples come to mind:

- 'Have you heard about Tom's Gladys? She's got herself involved with that chap who took over from Bert.'
- 'John's very involved with the scouts; he's taking a party abroad during his summer holiday.'
- 'Our neighbours fight like cat and dog, and keep coming to us for sympathy, but we just don't want to get involved.'
- 'We thought hard about having one of the children from the Home down the road for the weekend, but we felt he might get too dependent on us, and we didn't feel we could get that involved.'
- 'My sister's in a terrible state. Her boy got in with the wrong set and now he's involved with the police.'
- 'I'll help you if I can, but what exactly does it involve?'
- 'There isn't time to tell you now; it's a terribly involved story.'

All these people have found their lives caught up, or about to be caught up, in the lives of others.

Some have been swept off their feet unexpectedly; some were

already seeking a new involvement in their endless search for happiness-ever-after; some seek only to give happiness (and forget that they also need to be gracious enough to receive); some give a bit, and then pull back when it gets uncomfortable; some stand firm, at great cost, when the crisis comes because they count the outcome to be more important than their distress; some can look ahead to gauge the likely impact of their involvement, and will give or withhold according to the need of others; some are willing to give a stated amount only; some can be the still centre of a stressful involvement, identifying helpfully with everyone. Every playgroup is likely to be familiar with every one of these motivations and reactions to involvement. Involvement is a costly business in time, effort and emotions – especially the latter.

No wonder it isn't easy to 'involve parents', especially since playgroup leaders, volunteers and staff are themselves struggling with the same motivations and reactions as the parents. There are no 'experts' in the playgroup movement: from parents to the National Committees, from supervisors to tutors-to-tutors, from office staff to National Advisers, we are all incomplete human beings trying to grow up through our relationships with children and each other.

Back once more to the roll-in theme. If we reject the idea of 'roll in and mix paint' as true involvement because it implies that one person is merely inviting another person to be useful, then we must replace 'roll in and pass me by' with 'roll in and meet me'. But that isn't easy either. Do we stand at the door and wait for the other person to advance towards us? Or do we go out to meet them with such determination and/or enthusiasm that we frighten them into retreat? Or do we meet them half-way? Judging the half-way mark calls for sensitivity: the roller-in may be a strong and dominant personality and an apparently half-way gesture may still be overwhelming. *It is the one about to roll in who needs to feel that she has something to contribute.*

Even when someone has rolled in, and settled in, there is never any guarantee that the involvement will deepen, ripen and produce fruitful feelings, actions and reactions within the group.

As part of this inquiry we have listened to playgroup parents, staff and helpers; voluntary and statutory visitors; playgroup course tutors; teenage boys and girls in playgroups; committee members and field workers; caretakers and professional spiritual caretakers; and others who feel that they have been truly involved, or wish they had been but weren't, or were and wish they hadn't been.

There are three areas in which it is particularly important that we learn:

> First, many of those who are most thankful for their involvement try to pass on the experience by asking others to adhere to the outward signs (mother rotas, committees, membership forms) to which they attribute all that 'happened'. We need to understand more about the invisible dynamic that underlines the visible symbols.
> Second, there is a type of involvement which hooks people on their own personal growth, often aided by those whose protégés they are, to the detriment of those who are standing in the wings waiting to roll in to join the play on the stage.
> Third, PPA believes itself to be a caring association, but this word 'care' needs careful scrutiny.

Sometimes the word 'care' is taken to be synonymous with 'not hurting anybody', but there are times when we all need to be told a thing or two, and we surely hope it will be our friends who tell us. Failure to do so denies the opportunity of growth to everyone, particularly if the professed desire not to hurt is a euphemism for moral cowardice.

But 'inflicting' pain on others needs to be thought about deeply too, for the cry 'I did it for her own good' can be as misguided as the not telling. One way or another, each of us has been hurt, but the hurt often leads to new growth: hurt isn't to be confused with harm.

It isn't so much that others hurt us, but rather that we feel hurt within ourselves as we see ourselves more clearly in the mirror of our relationships, and in self-knowledge there is growth.

The working group's experience of involvement is that it begins with a 'feeling', leads on to action, and at every stage carries with it responsibility – responsibility in personal relationships, responsibility for undertaking and carrying out tasks, and shared responsibility for decision making.

2

What is Meant by Parental Involvement in Playgroups?

Whenever parents and children are happily involved together, this strengthens the bond between them and helps each towards his and her own maturity: this is the rock on which the playgroup movement is built.

Love and concern for children have always existed and have found expression in the different customs of child rearing down the ages. For many, the continuity of family life flowed on from grandparents to children and grandchildren, relatively untouched by outside influences. Then two world wars at a twenty-year interval disrupted two successive generations with a devastating effect on the inherited pattern of family life.

The extended family has scattered. Some family groups move across counties, sometimes even countries, for work, for a home, for asylum. Some cope. But for others there is the hell of living in one room; or the strain of living in a over-large house with a garden, trying to maintain desired standards in the face of inflation and the physical and emotional stress of a growing family; or the unexpected difficulties and the hurt of rebuff that are summed up in the old fashioned phrase 'being out of your class'; or the totally unshared responsibility of being a one-parent family; or the loneliness and unshared responsibility of the mother, left with young children from early morning until late at night, while her husband commutes; or the feeling of fear and inadequacy in mothers faced with the responsibility of a new human life, often with no experience of babies or young children and sometimes even without memories of a happy childhood on which to draw. Many statutory and voluntary bodies are aware of and are trying to meet these needs in various ways. Mother and toddler clubs and playgroups are among them but, unless this whole background of family stress is understood, the idea of parental involvement is interpreted as parents having a series of jobs that have 'got to be done' – instead of each job being seen as an opportunity to encourage someone to come forward to contribute their time and skills, thereby taking the first step towards involvement and responsibility that will not only help the playgroup but open up their own lives.

Many parents need playgroups and playgroups need parents, and children need play and parents who are ever growing in confidence, happiness, and understanding: a playgroup at its best can meet these needs simultaneously.

Although many parents are capable and confident, others are shy and cautious or just plain tired, and some are at screaming-point or beyond with frustration. A playgroup needs to be small enough in numbers, friendly enough and local enough for it to be accessible to all these mothers and fathers.

Right from the start parents should feel that they are as welcome as their children, and that the continuing happiness and welfare of the children is as dependent on them as on the playgroup leader and committee. Parents should feel confident that their ideas will not only be listened to but acted upon, if others agree. For example, sometimes the existing pattern of the playgroup calls for all children to listen to a story 'to get them used to sitting down ready for school', but if some parents say that their children are not interested in stories, or are more interested in something else, and if some say that the playgroup should be enjoyed in its own right rather than getting ready for the next stage, then in direct response to these expressed thoughts it may be agreed to hold story-time only for those who want to listen, whilst the other children continue to do what they want to do as long as it does not interfere with the enjoyment of the listening children. Another example of established playgroup routine being changed by the parents has occurred in areas hit by unemployment, where the opening time has been delayed by as much as two hours because they have agreed that 'having a lie-in in the morning' is one of the few bonuses of being out of work.

In a playgroup where parents are truly involved in helping

with their children it is inevitable that each new wave of parents will come in with their own inherited ideas and attitudes and therefore it is almost inevitable that they will wish to change the playgroup to conform to 'their' way – and some of their ideas may be temporarily detrimental to the children's play. But if the parents continue to learn from the children and from each other, and to adopt and modify their decisions in the light of experience, then in the long term the children can gain far more than they lose.

At every stage of learning it is important that the parents have access to those who have more knowledge and experience than they possess, but this expertise should be offered in such a way that it is relevant to the experience of each group at the time of asking. It is worth repeating that if the 'standard' of the playgroup is fluctuating it is often a sign that a new wave of parents is making changes in accordance with their present beliefs; but with help, and in each others' company, their set ideas and attitudes can be gradually modified by their growing understanding of children's needs and abilities.

This modification of attitudes is doubly important: first, the quality of play improves for the children; and, second, the sheer excitement and success of letting go and re-learning flows into the home in the nature of this learning. In addition to all the practical learning, it is learning to see children as people, with specific needs at each stage and age; learning how to get on with other adults, and that no one has all the answers; learning that there is no one way or quick solution to problems, and that problems are not 'wrong'; learning that the reality of family life is a far cry from the glossy image, but that it is still possible to pull yourself up by your own bootlaces; learning to strike the balance between undervaluing and overvaluing your contribution to the group; learning not to withdraw from the painful part of learning. It would be foolish to pretend that these benefits are experienced by everyone. Some people are 'there' already; some don't want to change; some are unable to change; others are so busy 'doing' that they give themselves no time to learn about 'being'.

When it does happen, all this learning has repercussions in the home: a husband and children may respond to this more alive mother, and the family unit becomes more positive and the marriage begins to grow up. But sometimes there is fear and resentment, resulting in withdrawal and counter-attack.

It cannot be overstressed that in the playgroup movement the real impact of the action takes place in homes. Playgroups need to be seen as extensions of the homes, rather than as an entity in the centre of the picture.

Nevertheless, it is in the playgroup that the learning starts by the parents accepting the responsibility for the group. Even in an established playgroup the learning of the new parents should still be concerned with basic decisions that it is their right to question. The learning tends to come in recognisable stages:

1 **The Practicalities**
Choosing the new playgroup leader.
Deciding the starting and finishing time and working out each family's share of the total cost (this 'share' is not a 'fee').
Sharing the management of the group (some elect a committee and strive to make it work democratically, but in other playgroups the parents 'en bloc' are the committee).
Arranging a rota of help, before, during, and after the play session.
Mending, making, painting, sewing, doing the laundry, etc.
Encouraging individual skills and making the opportunity for these gifts to be used.

2 **The Dynamics**
Usually it is only after the above practicalities have been thought through and put into practice that the parents feel ready to give their full attention to what is happening in the group. Learning comes about as they:

Watch the children, the playleader, each other, the playgroup equipment, and the relationships between them all.
Negotiate within the playgroup, and between the

playgroup and the local community.
Reconcile, grumble, inspire, compromise.

3   The Children

Many parents have never really watched their children before and they begin to learn as they:

Provide for their children's play in the group.
Watch, recall their own childhood, and talk about play (both in the playgroup and on playgroup courses).
Choose and buy equipment.
Bring ideas, and suggestions, experience and values in the group.
Seek to improve and widen the opportunities for play, following their observations of children.
Discuss problems that are common to parents and behaviour that is common to children.
Discover that it is taken for granted that their children will probably cling or misbehave when parents and children are at first in the playgroup together, and that it is a stage that passes.
Discover how difficult it is for a child to learn to share his mother and to part from her (and for some mothers to part from their children).
Watch the playleader and other parents cope with behaviour that they find so difficult at home, and then go home and try it out for themselves.
Learn to relate to other children with growing confidence and respect.

When the expectations of the group do not positively encourage every parent to choose to do these things, or any others which arise from natural concern for their child, then the group cannot be said to give parental involvement a real chance to reach its potential.

3

The Results of Parental Involvement in Playgroups

Why do people in the playgroup movement want parental involvement? Do the results justify the efforts to bring it about? In a playgroup's early days, parents may provide the adults required to meet the requirements of registration by social services departments. But, as enthusiasm of the founder members is lost, the practice of involving the parents may decrease. We know that it is much easier to run a playgroup with one, two or three people having the authority and responsibility; it's more convenient to have all the helpers regular and paid; and it's far easier to tell the parents about the activities of the group rather than have them take a share in all the planning and doing.

So why is it that this parental involvement is still sought? Why is it seen to be crucial to the life of the playgroup movement? Is there any difference between the parental involvement as practised in many nursery schools and that possible in playgroups?

It is true that there are problems relating to parental involvement, and these are described in Chapter 5. But the advantages seem to outweigh the disadvantages, especially when the learning of the pre-school child is seen in context as part of the united learning of the family in the community.

In the inquiries and discussions that the working group undertook in many parts of the country, it was clear that parental involvement was the linchpin of the movement. Without it, the strengths and advantages of a playgroup could disappear; with it there came not only a new way of looking at the needs of pre-school children and their families in the community but also a fresh approach to meeting those needs. What, then, are these strengths and advantages?

The Child

Think first of the child in the playgroup. Does the three-year-old boy or girl benefit from having his or her mother and father closely involved in the life of this new group at which he or she spends up to eight or ten hours a week? This playgroup is a new experience for the child: the room is bigger than any at home; there are more children there than he has been used to; the noise is greater; there is a wonderful, often bewildering, variety of playthings to choose from; there is milk-time, singing-time, wait-your-turn-time. The adults are different too: one or two seem to be in charge, and the child quickly sees that here are new people to obey, to try to please and to ask for help. And, in all this new and exciting world, he might be expected to be happy and secure without his parents.

Remember that up until then Mum and Dad have been the centre of the little one's life: from complete dependence, there has come a slow growth, but, at rising-three, how far has it gone? Mum and Dad are the bosses in one's life at home: they decide what one shall eat and wear, at what time one goes out, comes in, has a wash, goes to bed. They set the behaviour patterns; their talk is the child's language; their tastes and style set the pattern of living.

It is hardly sensible, let alone practical, to expect a child at the age of about three years so to change and mature that, often without preparation, he can easily leave the presence and influence of parents and gain maximum benefit from a new and perhaps strange group.

There are children who will clearly show playgroup parents and leaders that they need their mother or father physically present at the playgroup session: they cry, or are withdrawn, or show signs of unhappiness at home. The vast majority of parents want to help their children to be happy and fulfilled through new experiences, and yet some may not be able to use words to describe how they feel.

Over and over again in our discussion we heard that, given the opportunity, most parents welcomed the chance to stay in the playgroup until their child settled, and to stay on other days when necessary without feeling it was a 'special occasion'.

Here is how a supervisor described one parent starting her involvement in a playgroup:

Mary stays during playgroup mornings settling her children: it takes many months before they feel secure enough for her to leave them. Mary does her turn on the rota duty, but takes no part in committees, or helping organise fund raising; if she has money to spare she'll come to the coffee morning; if not, she and the children don't come that morning – she just says 'I forgot'.
I try telling her of the whys and wherefores of playgroups, but stop when she says she's enough problems without taking on the cares and responsibilities of other mums and children. She is a loving mother, giving and receiving cuddles and kisses, both she and the children, supporting and caring only for each other. She cares what happens to their feelings, and is sensitive to their needs as they are to hers.

This is another description of how a mother responded to the needs of her child in the playgroup:

Stephen started at the playgroup a week before he was three. He seemed stunned by the experience, and although he appeared to enjoy the activities and raised no objection when his mother left he had a tendency to withdraw into a private world where he did not relate to adults or children, so I asked Jan to stay all the time for about a month (two mornings a week). She managed this despite the difficulties imposed by the younger child and Stephen soon began to emerge from the cocoon. Jan spent most of this time sitting quietly nursing Alan and watching the other children, and Stephen. She then introduced the break gradually to ensure that he could manage on his own and when she was confident that he could do so stayed occasionally to help.

It cannot be denied that there is a danger of instability for the children if there are many changes in adults during the play session. But, if the parental involvement is functioning well, parents come to understand the needs of their children. They can arrange that the active involvement of a large number of people during the session is balanced by the presence of one or two to provide the continuity and security of environment so necessary to the young child's growth and development. But it is not only having Mum and Dad staying during the session that the child can appreciate. A mother or father who feels comfortable in the playgroup room is likely to pass it on to the child; parents who understand the programme of the session and share in the plans and aspirations of the leader can breed confidence in their children; the time at the playgroup can become a focus for renewing and extending the experience into the home. This parent spoke for many when she described how her involvement enriched her home life with her child:

> I do not find mothering comes naturally. It often goes against all my instincts. I would ten times prefer to have my head in a book than care for young humans. Luckily, with my fourth child I encountered a playgroup, and through it I learned to see small children with entirely different eyes. Playgroup revealed to me the fascination, even enjoyment, of time spent with undeveloped minds. And now, even though our children are much older, I still, daily, make use of the principles learned then. Constantly I find myself thinking: 'Now, this is how they would have handled this in the playgroup', or, 'Yes, that is regressive behaviour, and I think I know why', and, 'that is blackmail by child (deal very firmly!)', or, 'that child is needing more attention, or something more testing'.

> And then playgroup gives one so many ideas for so richly supplying these needs, and always by such simple means.

> The immediate result, of course, is a much more relaxed relationship between me and the children (hence, between me and my husband too!) and we all enjoy each other more.

Take it a stage further. The parent who is involved in the playgroup's life, not only by being present at the sessions, takes part in many of it activities.

The choosing of equipment can be a learning experience and the observations of why certain toys help children learn through play is surely remembered at birthday or Christmas time. The choice of a person to be a supervisor or leader means that parents have to think deeply about what qualities they look for in someone to take care of their own children. We know how that kind of thinking is remembered when a parent is trying to cope with the tiresome, demanding, lonely time that marks a toddler's growing up. Looking at other people responding to one's own child, and seeing different behaviour patterns fitting in to the whole development of the child, helps a parent to cope with rearing the under-five. The workshop learning which happens all the time in the playgroup can be reinforced when the parents join together for a course on any one of a number of subjects to do with running a playgroup. Over and over again, the working group heard from parents that the variety of experience in playgroup and on courses had helped them come to a deeper understanding of the effects on children of interrelationships between adults. This allowed them to see that disagreement or friction within the playgroup could affect all the children. One mother said:

What about the children? They are like sponges, and I do believe that they react when the adults are not working well together. A strained, anxious, unhappy atmosphere can have very bad effects on the children. I think such an atmosphere can exist anywhere – homes, schools, hospitals. I just feel it needs to be said more clearly, or perhaps people will think we neglect the children or are unaware or don't care.

The working group heard many times of long, hard, committee meetings,

We had to get the problem sorted out before we went back to the playgroup.

Their involvement also gave opportunity to deepen and enrich their relationship with their children – not only with the under-fives, but also with older and younger children. Here are a few of the comments:

- 'The doorstep course helped me – where I would once have said ''No'' to most things, I now think, maybe we could do that in a minute. I used to hate those TV programmes (e.g., *Playschool*, *Rainbow*, etc.,) when they would say ''Paint a stone'', ''Make footprints with paint'', etc., 'cos the kids would ask ''Mum, can we do that?'' and I couldn't face the mess. After the course, we did it together. I gave them more time and it brought us closer.'
- 'My Jane asked me, ''Why aren't you a playgroup Mum at home?'' This made me think and I feel it has helped us.'
- 'I find most mothers talk to their children and for the first time make time to play with their children.'
- 'Playgroup gives me a bit more time to spend with my new baby.'
- 'I must say I would have taken an interest in their education anyway and tried to help them forward. I think I'd have had little success. My response if the child hadn't immediately understood my explanations would have been irritation and impatience. I know, because these emotions still rise in me at times. But playgroup experience comes to the rescue. The child receives help now. Before he'd have just been shouted at for his ''stupidity''. I even find it helpful with our eldest, a thirteen-year-old daughter. Many a potential confrontation between adolescent and parent has developed instead into warmth and even laughter. We have tussles, but without the danger of frustration from a misreading of a growing child's needs.'

The Parent

Think next of the parent. Although an increasing number of fathers are being drawn in, it must be admitted that it is the mother, or mother-substitute, who takes the major part in the life of the playgroup. This is mainly because of the present division of labour which decrees that fathers go out to work while mothers stay at home and look after the children.

We know, however, that the close involvement of fathers can be encouraged, and we are sure that it is a good thing, for it brings strength to the shared adventure of rearing children. Here are mothers talking of the effect of their playgroup involvement on their life with their husbands:

- 'Could I have done it without an understanding husband? No – he's put up with phone calls, masses of jumble, chaos at bazaar time and people everywhere.'
- 'In this village, the whole family is usually involved, and much of the equipment is made by dads and grandads.'
- 'I have more time to spend with my husband, because I am more active.' (That is, she did not push her husband away, or take three hours to do the washing-up.)
- 'My playgroup has been running for over a year now; I am the local branch secretary, and my confidence has grown. I have a full, rich and very rewarding life. Not the least of my support comes from my husband who, on one occasion, took the group on his day off to enable me to attend a study day. My young son now attends his sister's playgroup once a week and my husband signs on the mothers' – sorry, parents' rota.'

The working group heard that the support of fathers is often necessary if a mother's involvement is to reach its full flowering. But this is one area where much deeper thinking is needed. We are aware that because of playgroup experience a mother's expectations of her child may be different from her husband's, and this may cause difficulties. Here is how one worker in PPA described the dilemma:

The problem is 'mother involvement' which excludes fathers. It comes sharply to light in the 'Child in the Family' part of our Foundation Course and needs our due thought and consideration. More important than good play experience even is *family stability* for the young child. We all know this, yet in some ways we are usurping it.

An example is given by a mother on a course. She tells how her child explores his cake with his fingers, a lovely experience for him. Mother understands his need; father is repulsed and flies into a rage. Mother is torn between what she knows is normal behaviour for a three-year-old – she helps in playgroup and has been on a course – *she knows*, but what about Dad?

Several students expressed anxiety about this and stated that their playgroup experience had not helped their relationship with their husbands in the upbringing of the children. Some treated their children differently on week-days, when Dad was at work. Two sets of behaviour from Mum must be frustrating for the child.

Are we really facing this problem? What can we do?

There is, perhaps, a need for greater awareness of family and community learning which does not exclude either mother or father, but emphasises that if both parents are involved there can be increased possibilities for the whole family. It is heartening that the Scottish Pre-school Playgroups Association is giving special attention to the role of fathers in the playgroup movement.

A playgroup is usually started and run by a group of mothers. Collectively, they are responsible for every action arising from the activity. If all these jobs are shared, then each parent needs to shoulder some responsibility. Many mothers do this when their under-fives are most demanding of their time and energy. It's a time marked in a mother's life by feelings that the house will never be tidy, meal times never orderly and the washing never done. Time and again, the working group heard remarks like these:

- 'If I hadn't had the playgroup, I'd have gone crazy.'
- 'I just felt like a cabbage until the playgroup made me get off my backside and do something outside the house.'
- 'What did it [the playgroup movement] do for me? Well – it gave me back my confidence, I'd lost it totally. It gave me an individuality I could have lost at my daughter's birth and early childhood.'

● 'Before we came here we lived a long way from the playgroup and I couldn't help – I was lonely – so I went screaming up the wall. I am fairly new in the village, but I am accepted because I help with the playgroup. I have met lots of people and made friends – now there is not enough time for all I want to do.'

Why, you may ask, does the playgroup do this for a mother in a different way from another group activity? Involvement in any group brings mutual support. But it seems that joining a playgroup is particularly helpful. It may well be that this is because, when time is precious, the activity which has to do with their child's welfare is more acceptable.

The model playgroup is a home from home. The supervisor is more like a mother having lots of kids to play in her own home than anything else we know.

The playgroup is a place where a mother's time and effort can be seen to bear fruit for her child's welfare; it is where other mothers are keen to know the details of another child's habits – where everyone is in it together and where one's own bit of effort is essential.

Mothers in a community playgroup enjoy each other's company while working for the group, and the activities and times of happiness and some disappointments can bring support to each individual life. The playgroup can be the extended family that modern living conditions have destroyed.

This support brings confidence and can open vistas of opportunities to mothers who felt that their own lives had ended with the birth of their child. Some mothers go on and find themselves wanting to learn more about children, and themselves, and the society in which they live. They go on courses, take new jobs, do O levels. They are not easily put off from making their voice heard when the needs of families are in question, and they can, if supported, challenge local and national public authorities and private firms.

Here is one former playgroup mother describing her experience. In doing so, she confessed that she was not 'as self-confident as I was when I left playgroup'. Nevertheless, the evidence of her personal growth and development shines through her words.

I first became involved in playgroups about five years ago and was introduced to committees and their make-up and function. I became chairman of our particular playgroup and joined the branch. I also set up the mother and toddler group and ran it for some years.

I found my self-confidence growing, was less self-conscious and was able to speak in public. I found that in playgroup I became more aware of people and their problems and therefore more politically aware, in the broadest sense of the word. I left playgroups in order to have another baby.

I have since joined the parent-teacher association and find there other mothers like me, who have come up through playgroups and who otherwise would have lacked the confidence to come forward to join a committee. At present I am setting up an information centre on 'provision for the under-fives'.

On the whole I think that playgroups give ordinary mothers the opportunity to expand as people and therefore become more aware and better members of the community.

Another mother describes her growing confidence:

Why did I do it? Because I was *pushed* and having been pushed I found I loved it. I had no confidence to begin with – but when your committee job is fund-raising you've got to find confidence somewhere! And having found one's feet within playgroups it leads on to other things – with me it's led to me offering myself as a candidate at district (unsuccessful) and at county (hopeful) council elections – mostly because I heard so many mums wondering why 'they' didn't do something. I decided to try to represent our feelings to 'them'.

The growth in confidence comes slowly, as this account shows:

Wendy, the chairwoman, asks Mary if she would keep an eye on the first-aid box, make sure the plasters and Germolene are always replenished. Mary agrees, she feels she wants to help now, she's too erratic in moods and time-keeping to take on heavier responsibility.

And a supervisor describes another mother's experience:

I suspect that this is only the beginning of the changes that playgroup involvement will make to Jan. I am sure that if the opportunity to attend a course were there, she would take it and make a valuable contribution. As the younger child becomes less demanding of time and attention, I hope she will be able to do more playgroup sessions. I see her as a potential future supervisor, though I don't think she has recognised this yet. Her concern for her children has now received a focus, and family life in general has improved as a result. Above all, she is regaining confidence in herself after a major upheaval in life. She is by nature a giver, and she is finding that what she has to give, which is herself, is valuable and valued, and that this enables her to give more.

This confidence is sometimes delicate, easily destroyed by bad times, and by the heavy hand of oppressive statutory support. But in the growth and development of the playgroup movement in Great Britain today we have been persuaded that parental involvement in playgroups can result in succeeding generations of more confident, better informed and happier mothers.

The Community

So let us think now of the wider community. We have already explored in some detail the good that comes to a child and its parents when parental involvement occurs in the playgroup. The whole family can be active in the community venture – instead of delegating the job to the expert, mothers and fathers have to do it themselves. As one playgroup person put it,

In playgroup we have parents actually planning what they need in their own particular area. Sometimes parents do not want to be involved, and this is their own choice. I hope by watching the 'growth' of friends through being involved in playgroups they may feel they are missing something!

I think a person 'grows' with involvement in playgroups. They question much more what goes on within their community at first, and this then grows to include area, region, etc. I don't just mean playgroup things, I mean all things which matter to parents.

Parents, of course, ask the experts for help – the health visitor, playgroup adviser, schoolteacher. But, when the chips are down, the authority is theirs: they can (and do) decide when to open or close the playgroup; they make their own rules and decide when to bend them; justice and mercy are the parents' prerogative; authority, decision-making and responsibility are laid firmly at their door.

In these days when many troubles in our society are being blamed on a lack of parental responsibility, it is easy to see why the dimension of parental involvement in playgroups is precious.

It may be easier to cope with a three-year old than with a teenager, but, if parents are not encouraged to take full responsibility for the three-year old, how will they have the confidence and experience to take the right amount of responsibility for the teenager?

In addition, parents grow in understanding of the needs of the wider community and vice versa. There can be a change in attitudes towards families of all ages. Here is a young man talking about the growth of his awareness of children's needs by involvement in a playgroup:

This experience was good for me, as I didn't have much knowledge of children. Just like any other bachelor, I saw no reason for young kids to run around the shops bumping into those nearby. To me there was a simple solution and that was for the mother to take more care with her children. Travelling on the bus with a screaming child was one of the worst things that could happen. The mother didn't seem to care as it continued to howl. In both cases my playgroup experience gave me an understanding of these situations and many others.

The feeling and practice of responsibility for others is taken up into the community. That is what can bring into being hospital playgroups, opportunity groups for handicapped children, playgroups in prisons, together with unnamed ventures sparked off by parents. Here is an example of that kind of spread – a sort of horizontal diffusion effect from the playgroup:

> I spoke to the mother who was doing her turn at the after-school club with me. We had not met before and she did not know my background. I asked how she enjoyed the club. She replied that she was very happy to come. She had been a part of the playgroup and the mothers took turns there so she knew that if everyone took turns like this then it was the right amount to cope with. It was noticeable in the area that this club did not get started properly until mothers who helped at playgroups 'grew on' with their children.
>
> Out of a small playgroup which my son attended there grew a baby-sitting circle. The circle extended beyond the playgroup and I would see that as community involvement.
>
> One of the nearby playgroups used an old school house which the village community renovated. Vandals were damaging the structure last year when the parents wanted to repaint the inside of the building. One night the vandals were caught in the act – young teenagers. The parents invited the lads in and asked for their help in improving the building. The lads did help and protected the building until this year when they left school and started work.
>
> Unfortunately, now the vandalism has started again, with younger children involved.

Workers on the board of directors, parents as school governors, patients on hospital committees – these are just three areas in which our society is moving towards giving greater participation to users of services. Through parental involvement in playgroups, the users are the direct providers of the services for pre-school children. There need be no intermediate layers of representatives or staff here, and the links between the service provided and those in authority are clear and simple. There are, we think, some guidelines in the principles of parental involvement in playgroups which could point the way to greater understanding of the dynamics of participation by consumers.

There are many movements against further fragmentation and compartmentalisation of the structures of our society. Because of the effects of parental involvement within the community, the playgroup movement has become one of these movements. The results of our exploration have shown that parents can take a greater share in their children's learning; families can learn and enjoy the world together; the community can respond to the needs of its members without setting up impersonal, expensive structures.

Through parental involvement, playgroups can show one way to bind people together.

4

How Can Parental Involvement Be Encouraged?

In the preceding chapter, parents have offered their own accounts of how they became involved in playgroups, and what it has meant to them. If, then, involvement and its results are welcomed as worthwhile experiences, it makes sense to ask how involvement comes about, and what kind of environment makes it easy for parents to become involved.

The vital factors seem to be the people concerned: the parents, the supervisor, the group of parents (and it may be all of them) who make up the committee and the rules by which they work, and finally the wider community that serves and is served by the playgroup.

Parents

In the early days of a playgroup's life, it often happens that groups of parents come together to plan and work towards the opening. The active involvement of the parents is something that arises naturally and spontaneously; there is a free flow of information on all details. The expectation of the group is that parents will give what they are best able to contribute. To meet the pressing needs as they arise, people are challenged beyond their own view of their abilities, and, supported by the group, they are given strength to undertake tasks which they would have felt unable to tackle themselves. So their involvement is rooted in their own personal growth as the playgroup flourishes.

A Welsh group tells about its beginnings:

It all started with our toddlers' birthday parties. We would talk, as mothers do. One day someone asked whether we had heard about playgroups. One of us was a teacher; she'd heard about them. Next came a gathering in a home in the street. All young wives were invited, including those who didn't have any toddlers. We decided to try and form a playgroup. Where should we meet? One of us knew the secretary of the community centre, and promised to inquire. How should we enrol the children? A notice in the post office. The community centre didn't want us. We had to do some hard canvassing, stand up in a public meeting and plead our case. For this, we did our first literature search. And we learned for the first time, a few phrases about the needs of the pre-school child. The community centre relented and gave us our room. It was time to gather the mothers together. We had twenty children enrolled.

There were only six chairs in the house, so a few dads raided their dining-rooms, and carried more chairs to the meeting-place. It was midnight when we broke up; midnight when the furniture removers collected their chairs! Everyone thought we were mad. We had a fund-raising event. Every mother had a stall. We were getting to know each other and the community. In the early days, we knew everyone – their joys and sorrows. We had a supervisor, chairman, secretary and treasurer, but everyone joined in everything.

We didn't expect anything else to happen.

Some features of the involvement were:

It arose from a corporate need. Because of the need, all kinds of people were involved at different levels, for example, mothers, wives, husbands, councillors.

The degree of involvement matched the individual's need to be involved, so that it grew naturally. Individual efforts were accepted and equally valued.

The activities were aimed at starting the playgroup, not at involving the parents, and this gave a spontaneity, a naivety, to our actions.

Pioneering is hard work. But what of the parents in an established group, and the new parents who come to join them? The playgroup has, perhaps, to take a different view of the words like 'successful' and 'professional' from that taken in – say – a thriving business concern.

● 'Nothing, they say, succeeds like success.'

Yet success, measured by our society's current standards, can spell death to parental involvement in playgroups.

Take the standard measured by a good sum in the bank. Maybe a group of parents has worked hard and raised enough money to put a good bit in the deposit account. It's enough to cushion the group against any foreseeable crisis, so there's no need to have the usual rummage sale. That means that those parents who feel they can help effectively only at such an event don't have the chance of doing so. It also means that the surrounding community is not asked to help, and therefore does not get to know about the group, its life, and its problems. Isolation has begun.

Consider the standard of success measured by continuity in staff or leaders. It's much easier and more acceptable for the school, the social services department or the health visitor not to have to deal with new people. The parents have confidence in a stable staff pattern; no one wants the bother of finding new people to act as leaders; it's much easier for the group to carry on with someone who knows the routine. So parents forget that they, themselves, set the routine – it's not decided by any other authority. Times and days of opening can be changed to meet needs. But is it not difficult to challenge the knowledge and experience vested in long-serving staff? Rigidity is taking hold.

Or think of the group which has no difficulty in getting a committee. It has a reputation in the community, and it's considered an honour to be one of the inner circle of those parents making decisions. What time is given to talking about what the playgroup is trying to achieve? Are all the choices made by the inner group? What sort of people are on the committee? Do they all come from the same estate or area? Is there someone representing the shy, incompetent, retiring? If not, how can the playgroup reflect the views of all the parents? Successful playgroups can sometimes forget parents.

Yet because of the accepted meaning of 'successful' – which we all, as part of our culture, willy-nilly accept – it can be almost impossibly difficult to reject 'success' for an alternative which opens up (for good or ill) possibilities of involvement, of taking responsibility for our own and our children's future.

My daughter goes to a very good playgroup. The supervisor (who has been in post for five years and has attended several courses) sets out a wide range of activities, and the committee runs everything smoothly. So perhaps I have no right to niggle about little things – rules like 'no dough in the home corner', or 'stop for milk the minute you're told', or the fact that I don't know the committee members' names. And if I want to change things, how do I go about it, without looking like a grumbler? If I, as branch secretary, find this difficult, it's probably harder for some of the younger, 'newer' mothers.

At the playgroup which my older son attended, groups of mothers used to argue frequently and acrimoniously about everything, and we went through five supervisors in two years. It was hell – but it was alive!

Must we say that playgroups can't involve parents unless they have continual problems and worries? No, for many groups flourish without trauma.

A mother:

It's nice to go somewhere to meet people, lovely for 'D' to have somewhere to play safely – he loves it here! I hope there's always a playgroup – I'd like another baby and I'd like to think 'she' could come here.

A mother points out the importance of continual friendly interaction between all parents:

My playgroup is a large one, involving some 110 children per week – but with size comes an almost de-humanising efficiency which means close contact is cut down unless people (especially committee) are overtly friendly and almost garrulous. Mums don't get to know us – *we*, the volunteers, almost become the dreaded 'them' of the establishment. How to get around this? Simply by talk – to be prepared to chat, *anywhere, anytime, anyhow* – and have an ever-open door at playgroup. We at our playgroup insist on mothers (with certain exceptions) doing rota duty and this definitely helps – if only to make them realise that supervisors and committee *do* do work outside playgroup hours. Also I think that a *newsletter* helps. A calendar of events is informative but sterile. Chat and joke, get your point over that way – they take far more notice.

Some large playgroups have found it useful to divide into sub-groups, to make things more friendly and manageable.

And a parent from the other end of Britain comments on the simple fact of being needed:

I wasn't looking for a job, but somebody had to be treasurer.

What does seem clear is that if the involvement and growth of parent and child together is the priority in playgroups we must be prepared to accept (at least temporarily) less than perfect play provision – something that is not apparently 'successful' or 'professional'. A mother who moved to a new home and a different playgroup recognises this:

She can almost pinpoint the 'stage' the playgroup is at and recalls her own feelings and ideas of three years ago. She wants to hurry it all up. There isn't enough water, natural materials, books, creative activity, adult contact and communication. If only they would make her playleader. But that's not right either. The playgroup belongs to the families, in this case to the mothers. Boozy dances and smoky meetings feature. The playgroup is full of children. They, and their parents are growing in their own way.

People have to recognise and grasp this thing for themselves, we can only let them know that it is there.

Each new generation of parents must have opportunities to discover for themselves what a playgroup is about, and be convinced that they, themselves, need to play a part if the aims are to be reached. Only then can their involvement become meaningful. One of PPA's national advisers teased out, from her understanding and from what she learnt from the experience of others, pointers towards the kind of playgroup that continues to include, to use, and to value all its members. These constitute the rest of this section.

1 It is necessary to make sure that parents know that the playgroup exists in their community. Posters and information can help bring this about. In addition, members of the existing playgroup will want to tell other parents about the opportunities offered. Formal notifications are often a hindrance to some. Think of the experience of the mother who described herself thus:

> 'There is a malady called "new town blues" which hits most mothers. Diagnosed, it means: I miss my Mum. I could rattle and shake my kids, murder my husband, and run to the North Pole away from the whole blooming lot, if I had the spunk (which I seem to have lost), or the money (which I haven't got) – so I sit in my own four walls and go steadily bonkers.'

Would that mother have become involved if presented, coldly, with a playgroup prospectus? She would more likely need a friend to help her, and to go with her to the playgroup for the first time. Mothers who are naturally friendly, or who have been alerted to other people's needs, are often the best people to introduce the idea of a playgroup to a lonely or diffident parent.

2 When a mother first comes to playgroup with her child to put the child's name down, the person who warmly welcomes her is one of the existing mothers; she invites her to come in and join *us*. She explains how the group is run by the parents and the different opportunities available to each mother and father.

3 The first week of term is kept for existing playgroup parents and children to settle down and re-establish the relationships and links of the previous term. The first two new families are invited to join the playgroup. As the playgroup is the responsibility of the parents there will always be some of them present at each session alongside the regular helpers, helping with the children's play, tidying up or just enjoying being there, and they will welcome and include the new parents and children coming to join the group which would have from eighteen to twenty four children per session. Only two families would be invited together at once so that enough time is given for them to feel comfortable, welcome and immediately part of the group. The new parents would also have the support of each other in this new venture. It is important for those who welcome new members to accept each family as they are, including the props they may need to make it possible for them to come. This could mean a fur coat, a grandmother, sometimes other children in a pram, even the family dog for a couple of sessions. The door of the playgroup may need to be closed for safety reasons but it should always be metaphorically open. Because our expectations of how people will behave strongly influences what they do, it is important that existing parents in the playgroup understand this.

4 The playgroup is an extension of home for the child – and for the mother. Because she moves from *her* doorstep to the *playgroup* doorstep there is a doorstep course available.

A doorstep course is a natural extension of the activities of the playgroup which takes place in the playgroup and is organised by a group who will seek out, with the help of the supporting PPA structure – for example branch or area organiser, or branch visitor or tutor – someone who understands what a playgroup is and can lead discussions on this and any other needs of that particular group.

5 Gradually, small responsibilities are offered to the mother, not necessarily in the playgroup setting, building up into close involvement. She has the opportunity to share the responsibility, not just the tasks.

6 When as many parents as possible have been tempted to

participate in the playgroup, it would be run by small groups taking responsibility for different aspects of the work, for example courses, fund raising, play provision, cleaning – all sharing the responsibility for the whole. Each group could choose its own leader, who, after a certain period of time, would move on so that someone else could take her place. The areas in which these groups could operate would possibly be along the following lines:

(a)   provision for the children's play, including arrangements for leaders to receive small remuneration, to relinquish leadership at a time decided by the parents and other terms of service;

(b)   fund-raising and social events;

(c)   organising courses and meetings;

(d)   liaison with local schools and other 'outside' bodies;

(e)   maintaining, cleaning and mending playgroup equipment and materials;

(f)   producing newsletter;

(g)   obtaining PPA and other publications;

(h)   liaising with the body that runs the premises on which the playgroup operates;

(i)   liaising with local PPA branch and other levels of the structure (county, etc.).

The Supervisor

(N.B.: It is recognised that groups may use the terms 'supervisor', 'playgroup leader' or 'playleader' (or even 'teacher') for the person who is required by the regulations of social services departments to be in charge of the group. None of these names is ideal – they all carry the notion of this person having a role which gives him or her a function above that of the parents. But, since these names are generally used, and no other has yet been suggested, we have adopted the practice in this report of using 'supervisor' or 'playgroup leader' according to the custom of the writer.)

Over the years different models of playgroups have evolved; the name can be used by anyone or any group of people and there are wide differences in how groups are organised. Many, however, involve parents in various ways as part of their organisation and aims. The bringing in of the parents is either part of the whole way the group is run, with elected parents themselves involving the other parents, or it can be organised by one or two individuals who take responsibility for the group but believe in the value of parents helping.

Where playgroups hold to this dual purpose of (a) offering play opportunities for children and (b) offering opportunities for helping, learning, social events and responsibilities to parents, then the role of the regularly attending supervisors or playgroup leaders needs to be thought through carefully if these aims are to be reached. When a prospective playleader comes to an interview or meeting, what is she told is her job? What does it include? Traditions in other fields don't always help us to think through radically and for ourselves. In the traditional (and still often practised) approach, people with skills and experience are appointed to do a job, and expected to get on with it themselves. The 'best' candidate is chosen, and it then behoves this person to prove her worth through her own achievements.

Thus, a playleader appointed with the kind of thinking shared by the interviewing group will most likely think it her duty to be the 'best' and to prove her worth at knowing 'most' about the children's play. These are crude words, but may put across a meaning. If she feels she should interpret her job in this way, then what happens to the curiosity, the eagerness (often unexpressed) of those around her? It often depends entirely on the personality of the supervisor whether the wish to learn of the helpers, the parents, the committee, is satisfied or blunted and turned to apathy – 'The mothers in our playgroup don't want to help.'

Society is full of 'experts' in all the professions (the 'priesthood' of the lawyer, the doctor, the nurse, the teacher; the mystique or mystery of these jobs as seen by the layman). It is not surprising then that this was the model that many of us in playgroups initially sought after in our wish to do the 'right thing', the best. Today, both within and outside the professions there are many who question the use of authority and knowledge, and some efforts are being made to demythologise jobs, particularly those concerned with working with people. In the recent past, another kind of working or professional role has emerged – one where knowledge and experience are still valued and sought for, but combined with the capacity and intention of working through and with other people, giving and taking from the common resource of knowledge and experience and recognising skills in others.

This approach to a job does in fact require new dimensions of skill; in no way is it a lessening or denigrating of a person's experience and knowledge, but an adding to them.

In the case of the playleaders, then, their job would include their knowledge of play and of children's growth and needs and of family life (and this knowledge is always incomplete, always being added to) plus a capacity to recognise existing or innate skills in others, and to facilitate the use and development of these skills, outside their own. The supervisor's rewards, her 'success' if measurement is made, would lie not only in the children's growth, enjoyment and learning but in the development of group skills and individual expertise within the group, put to the use of the children's play and the total environment of the playgroup for children and parents alike. It seems likely that over the years of playgroup development the job of playleader or supervisor has frequently been modelled on the role of the teacher – a benevolent and loving teacher but nonetheless in the traditional mould of the expert around whom the rest cluster as best they can.

It is interesting that other jobs or roles within the total playgroup movement, such as area organiser, playgroup visitor or adviser, have been subject to more debate and scrutiny than that of the playleader. The enabling or facilitating aspect of the fieldworkers' job has been explored, questioned and painfully practised despite unsureness and stumbling-blocks. From this approach to the job has resulted growth and renewal in the form of the development of branches, courses and people to help with courses, as well as other fieldworkers. Aren't there many parallels between the approach to the work of a supervisor and the way an area organiser or adviser works with a group of playgroups and a branch?

'Working yourself out of a job' is a well used phrase; it doesn't usually mean finishing work, but that parts of one's work gets taken on by other people, and this happens when new aspects of the job emerge as needing to be done. There is an ebb and flow in this approach to playgroup work: what one person does depends upon the other people around, at various stages of interest and growth, often doing or wanting to do similar work.

For example, at times one is busy with certain aspects of the job: it may be the mixing of paints in the playgroup, or visiting all the local playgroups as an area organiser. A few months later other people may well have taken on these two jobs (in fact with mixing paint it may have passed from the playleaders to the helping mums to the children!) and the focus would be on another aspect of the playgroup or the area organiser's job.

There are some aspects in common in playgroup work, whether one is a playleader, a visitor, an area organiser or chairman.

(a) Whatever job we do there will be others able to learn it and do it in their way.

(b) In many situations one's own work can be greatly enhanced if done in a group, even if the group is only two people sometimes.

(c) Most of the playgroup work benefits from planning and talk beforehand. (If we say we have parent involvement, if parents are seen as partners, though not necessarily all giving the 'same', then doesn't planning become very important?)

(d) Whether we like it or not, we grow and change from one year to the next as our experience grows; this affects how we are in relation to others, also changing and growing, and it affects how we do our job.

A change of emphasis in the role of the playleader would not make the job an easier one, and it would need trial and error on the way. A changed playleader's role would entail changing roles in the playgroup committees and among the helping parents. Time would need to be set aside regularly for talking and thinking, and on playgroup courses much more time would need to be allotted for discussion of these matters. It follows then that the working out of the helping rota would need more thought:

- In how many playgroups is it enjoyable and meaningful?
- Does the frequency of turns in each term matter?
- Could there not be much more flexibility about turns, according to willingness, stage or family?
- Is the parents' help really needed, especially in long-established playgroups?
- Is it a personalised form of helping, or is it just one name on a list?
- Is helping too optional, too peripheral?
- Do playgroup courses give enough time and thought both to acquiring helping skills (what it's like to be a rota mum) and how, as a supervisor, to learn about this new dimension to the job? Ten weeks wouldn't be too much to discuss parent involvement!

Incidentally, a thought on the hoary question of the 'rising-fives' in playgroups. Could it be that only when the helping parents bring more partners, when the playleaders' role changes to incorporate parents more, will there be enough resources and thinking time to give to the delightful, creative and exhausting talk, questions and activities of those children whose development demands 'yet more'? The questions in this section are not really optional ones for the playgroup movement, though they could well be better phrased and rethought. They are urgent questions if playgroups are to stay alive as learning, growing and joyful places for children and parents – places where mother and children *choose* to come.

Do you remember the beginning of the playgroup, the vitality and excitement, with everybody involved and learning and needed? Do you rememberr the enjoyment, the using of many skills in the making of the group, the problems, the difficulties which had to be overcome?

Institutionalisation creeps up on every organisation: 'We do it this way because we always have. The play-room is always arranged like this. We depend on Mrs X, we couldn't do without her.'

The questions 'Why?', 'How?' and 'What?' become fainter and fade away – and there comes the cry, 'Our mothers don't want to help.' Would you?

The Committee

'**Committee** – body of persons appointed for special function by (and usually out of) a (usually larger) body.' (*Concise Oxford Dictionary*).

Some committees, especially those which act on behalf of small playgroups, can be a source of enjoyment and learning for their members, and can be an appropriate use of time and energy for the good of the playgroup. But in a playgroup the role of the committee is often seen in very different lights by parents, mothers particularly, at different stages of their involvement.

1 The beginning

In the early stages, when a playgroup is just starting, 'The committee' as an idea is often seen as an organisational nuisance. The mothers involved in trying to provide for their children's needs may well see a committee structure as something imposed on them from outside. (And this may well be true, of course.) The previous knowledge of committees may be nil, based on hearsay, second-hand from other bodies, actual or theoretical. Reactions vary from enthusiasm through boredom to hostility.

- 'They're a clique, all friends of the supervisor.'
- 'They are the "posh" ones.'
- 'It's decided beforehand, not at the meeting.'
- 'I learned about committees in Business Studies.'
- 'We want all the mothers to be involved. Why do we have to have a committee?'

The committee idea is often not welcome, and may indeed be rejected. But there are jobs to be done. The group, in practical mood, assigns them to specific people. Someone has to be in charge of the play sessions (supervisor/playleader). Someone needs to write the letters (secretary), to look after the money (treasurer), to keep track of what has been decided and what has been planned (minutes secretary), and so on.

These jobs are often assigned to the most active members of the group, those who saw the need to start the playgroup in the first place. But they may also be taken on unilaterally, or by self-assumed right, and in many cases the initiators have not involved others at this stage anyway. They may be so determined to accomplish the practical task that they fail to see the need to involve others, who acquiesce in allowing the small group the control and decision making. Once begun in this way, control remains with the small group.

> I won't go on the committee, but I'll help whenever you need me.

2 The new playgroup
The practical task of getting the playgroup sessions going may take some months, and the committee survives the strains and setbacks impelled by ambition to get going at last. Once the play sessions are established, and the playgroup is 'opened', the ongoing tasks may seem more routine and less exciting. Activities such as fund raising are still important, but are at one remove from working with the children. The committee may have 'jelled' or not, and often momentum is lost, never to be regained.

Fairly typical of this stage of development is the playgroup with a committee composed of the most articulate parents, those with the know-how, a professional background or qualifications, the teacher or solicitor's wife, the older ones who have more confidence in their own abilities. They were chosen or came forward for their ability to get on with the job, running and perpetuating the committee structure, and controlling and organising the rest of the group. It is seldom at this stage that anyone is chosen by the whole group for his or her skill at involving others who do not already have the know-how.

The only hint the committee will get that change is inherent and must be planned for is in the constitution clause that states that committee members, or officers, may serve only for a limited number of years. The clause is often ignored when the time comes, because it is viewed as a blocking mechanism for continued involvement rather than seen as a built-in guard against stagnation and an indication that the group must be self-replacing, not self-perpetuating:

- 'Just when the treasurer knows the job, she has to give it up, because she's done her time on the committee.'
- 'We have to train some-one for the job every year, because their children grow up and leave playgroup.'

The playgroup is in danger of being run by a small, unchanging group, and no longer run on behalf of all the members. How do new mothers coming into the group feel now – welcomed, ignored, put off, scared?

There are two jobs in the committee which hold particular difficulty: chairman and supervisor.

Chairman: Often the most difficult office to fill. There is a formality about the position, implications of authority, leadership, control and responsibility. The chairman is often seen as the ultimate arbitrator, settling difficulties, keeping the peace, preventing factions, being impartial, being the spokesman, initiating action. During committee meetings she has to try to have everthing done by agreement, producing a consensus from the group, stopping members gossiping or getting off the point, but getting them to contribute to the discussion. Like every other job in the playgroup movement, it is a process of mutual confidence-giving, encouragement, learning and taking it easy.

Supervisor: If the supervisor is paid by the committee, and the playgroup has charitable status, she cannot be a member of the committee, with a vote. The rule seems to put her outside the committee, although she may attend and advise. She knows all the children, and their parents, which the committee members may not; she may well have been part of the playgroup longer than anyone else, and yet cannot take a full part. Many playgroups find this a difficult situation to accept, and so do many supervisors, who find it very frustrating. Without an active committee, and the ability to involve others in her part of the playgroup, it is very easy for her to become a block, and then to take over.

3   The established playgroup – arrival of new members

The inexperienced new mother approaches an established playgroup with a certain amount of anxiety. She may see the playgroup as an institution, much in the same way as she would approach a school. The responsibility for getting the relationship right at the beginning must lie with the playgroup. The playgroup needs to explain itself to the mother. The way this is brought about must be decided by the committee, or the group as a whole. It may be a prospectus, written and reconsidered from time to time by the committee, or it may be a friendly smile at the door from another mother.

Often bits of papers get in the way of the welcome. An officious, daunting prospectus may be far worse than nothing at all.

> When I got that prospectus, I just went along with it. I felt so insecure I couldn't have done anything else.

Too much pressure may be put on new mothers to participate, to join in, to conform; the committee may be too informal or too big. There is often a need to make the steps, in which a mother joins, smaller, more manageable, and more likely to succeed. Mothers need to feel they are wanted and that they have something to give which is necessary to the group, but they also need to feel that enjoyment and having fun are part of the playgroup as well.

4   Ups and downs

A playgroup that has run into the doldrums may find that unexpected events get them out of trouble. An unexpected crisis may arise which threatens the existence of the playgroup, or a long-standing member may suddenly have to relinquish her job. The hall rent is increased, or the supervisor's husband gets a new job in another town. The new situation means a re-evaluation of the problem, and the group's activities suddenly seem much more important and central to the parents.

Money matters often seem to figure in the crisis. Fund raising can be a source of satisfaction to some people but an unbearable burden to others. It is often seen as the only important task for parents.

- 'We've had more bother through fund raising than anything else.'
- 'Not the nicest side of playgroup.'

The problem of whether to have a Christmas party or not may lead to heated debate, or it may be accepted as a natural, unquestioned activity. All the parents can have an opinion on a matter like this. But if involvement is to be real, parents' views need to be sought on all matters relating to the life of the group.

The Wider Community

If we look around at the structures in our society today, it is clear that there is always a move towards stability. Constant change of teachers or policy in schools, of doctors or principles in the health service, of police or the law, of the government and the Civil Service would create uncertainties and confusions which the majority would find frightening. It is not surprising, therefore, that many people inside and outside playgroups find a constant change in people concerned in the details of activities and the general flux of the group's life neither desirable nor manageable. Yet, if there is to be real involvement by succeeding generations of parents with the accompanying potential for change that goes with it, there must be a move away from stability. Many playgroups have felt under stress when local authority staff or community workers remark, 'A new chairman, again?' – as though it were a rebuke, and not a matter for satisfaction that the cycle of involvement was rolling well.

It is important, therefore, that playgroup people take time to explain the dynamics of involvement to those in the wider community so that their efforts at involvement are not undermined by false expectations.

They will need to make it clear that:

1   An annual change of committee or officers is due to the parents of the children in the playgroup taking responsibility for the running of the group. It indicates success in involving parents.

2   A change in supervisor or leader does not necessarily mean that the parents are dissatisfied with her work, but that she herself has seen the need to give other parents a chance to undertake her role. As she herself has grown and developed she needs for her own and the playgroup's sake to move on, inside or outside PPA.

3   Continuous fund-raising efforts do not mean that the group is insolvent, but that the parents so finance the group that their costs are only just met by the sum of the charges to the group. Moreover, they see the benefit of the activity arising from fund-raising efforts.

4   A grant of money direct to the playgroup can have a disastrous effect on the level of the involvement. In a group where money raising is the main area of involvement, the need for parents to continue their efforts is removed. But in a group where decision making includes making choices about all the activities of the playgroup, including purchases of equipment, a grant can lead to an even higher level of participation, in understanding what is required and why. A sum of money raised for some special items for the playgroup may lead also to the need to participate in their selection and purchase.

5   If a playgroup closes, it is not necessarily because it has failed, but may be because it has done its job for the parents and children in that community in that area. New groups may open as the natural shift of the population with under-fives moves from one part of the town to another. This constant renewal may indicate a strength, not a weakness.

In order to cope with the difficulties of these situations where statutory and other bodies in the community are concerned, the playgroup organisation, at whatever level of branch or county is more convenient, will need to be the source for information of changes in the details concerning the running of the playgroup. This means that resources must be available to branches and counties so that they may undertake these back-up services.

5

Some Hindrances to Parental Involvement in Playgroups

Habits of speech deeply ingrained in society are slow to change and in the still young playgroup movement it is sometimes difficult to differentiate between what people say and what they are trying to convey. One of the biggest barriers to understanding is the indiscriminate use of the words 'fee', 'salary' or 'wage', 'staff', 'training' and 'rota duty'.

In a truly cooperative playgroup (as distinct from one that imposes the structure and rules upon uncomprehending parents) there are no 'fees': the money that each family pays is quite simply their *share* of the total running costs involved in coming together to plan and provide play for their children.

Similarly there is no proper 'salary' or 'wage' for the supervisor and any regular helpers, for the very simple reason that, if there were, the daily costs would be so high that families could no longer pay their share. The very small amount of money that each receives (the average amount for a supervisor was £1·91p per session of 2½ hours from a 1977 survey) is only a token of appreciation contributed by the parents in recognition of the fact that a commitment is made to be at every play session, as distinct from the parents occasional days with the children.

Neither should these regular supervisors and helpers be thought of as 'staff', for that word implies to most parents someone in authority who is above them, whereas these regular attenders are very much of them, and they have been chosen by them because of a recognised ability to work with the children and parents together for the mutual benefit of everyone concerned. These regular supervisors and helpers are not 'trained' for the work, any more than the parents of the children are 'trained' when they express the desire to come together to share and extend their learning and understanding. The skill needed by the tutors of playgroup courses is not that of direct teaching (let alone training) but an ability to help their students to learn through their observations of children, practical work, and the discussion that links the two and transcends it to become self-awareness.

'Rota-duty' is another instance of ill-chosen words. Many parents haven't the slightest idea of what a rota is or does or looks like – the word just leaves a blank in their minds. Duty, on the other hand, registers as something vaguely forbidding in this context, and the two words together in no way convey the happiness of being with their children in the playgroup two or three times a term: they could think of it as their turn for a play day.

It bears repeating that if the words 'fee', 'salary' or 'wage', 'staff', and 'training' continue to circulate in the playgroup community then parents will continue to presume that a playgroup is somewhere to 'send' their children. And if the words 'rota duty' persist then some parents will continue to think of it as an imposition and others will try to evade it through dread of the unknown.

Even if these quite major changes are made in the use of words, there are still many other gaps in communication that need to be bridged. Broadly speaking, there are two directions from which the problems of involvement need to be studied in some detail: from inside the playgroup looking out, and from outside the playgroup looking in. At the moment there is still much talk of 'us' and 'them', and if this gap is to be bridged there has to be a greater sympathy between the outsiders and the insiders.

From the inside looking out

What prevents some supervisors from involving parents? Even in cooperative playgroups there are still some supervisors who are appointed to be responsible for the children's play. At no time in her interview is it clearly explained (nor is it written into her terms of appointment) that she is required to work with the children and parents together.

If a supervisor feels that she is to be fully responsible for the children, and then finds that 'parents are supposed to help' or that 'they have to do their rota duty', then understandably she may be dismayed on the following grounds:

1   She loves being in charge of the children, and now her joy is marred and she feels she has been misled. The appointment starts with false expectations on both sides and this can lead to disappointment and resentment affecting relationships in ever-widening circles.

2   She cares passionately about the children and can't bear them to be subjected to a relationship or experience that is different from, or less sensitive than, her own relationship with them. If parents are allowed in they may be corrected and criticised in such a way that they feel like children themselves.

    If they are not allowed in they are denied the opportunity to copy her best points and to learn from the children and each other – let alone to discover that they have something to contribute.

3   She can manage perfectly well without help; in fact she prefers it because other adults break into her relationship with the group as a whole.

    Parents sense that they are not needed by the supervisor and lack the confidence to believe that they might be needed by those children who would welcome individual attention and the stimulation of fresh adults, each with time to give.

4   She may feel that the children behave so much 'better' (by which we generally mean more quietly) when their parents are not with them that it is best 'for the children's sake' (also for her sake?) if parents are excluded. She hasn't seen that one of the 'best' things for children is to have parents who can remain calm in the face of the emotional blackmail that children can bring to bear by their anger, distress or showing off. The playgroup offers unique opportunities for parents to learn to relate to their children with an integrity that is not influenced by fear of what the neighbours will say – but this can only happen if they feel

supported by all the adults in the group.

5   She may only feel confident when she is alone with the children, and fear that parents would criticise her. She would find it particularly daunting to deal with a rebellious child in front of his mother.

In shutting out the parents she doesn't see that she may be perpetuating her own experience of rejection, which will in turn deny them confidence to cope with their children in front of other adults.

6   She may have little understanding or appreciation of family patterns of child-rearing that are incompatible with her own. In particular she may be impatient with parents who bring their children beautifully dressed and then warn them 'not to get dirty'.

How can such parents feel welcome when their efforts to be good parents are consistently undervalued? They may have bitter memories of being physically, emotionally and socially uncomfortable throughout their childhood in an endless succession of passed-down and ill-fitting clothing. In remembering the discomforts, and in their determination that their children shall not suffer in the same way, they may have forgotten the freedom to play that was also conferred by those old clothes.

In any case, in this materialistic age it takes a very confident parent to walk along the road and deliver a child to an initially unkown group in real playclothes.

7   The supervisor may want to hug to herself the delightful feeling of importance that is a right and proper stage in the growth and development of us all.

Very often this sense of importance experienced by new supervisors (many of whom never dreamed they would attain such heights of recognition) overflows with a warmth and happiness that is infectious and, generously, the experience of 'feeling important' is handed on to others. But sometimes it is jealously guarded and there is no room for others to give because the supervisor wants to do all the giving herself. Some people need to help to encourage others to 'feel important', and to perceive this as success.

8 She may be unappreciative of the thought and effort that lie behind apparently simple actions. A mother may make a special bus journey with two children in order to find sticky buds like those referred to in a story, and when she hands them over the next day the supervisor just says, 'Oh thanks! Put them on the nature table.'

9 She may be unaware of the different anxiety levels in different parents. One said, 'She gave me the towels to wash and I dreaded taking them back. I didn't know if they would be clean enough or whether I ought to iron them or not.'

10 She may be a taker rather than a giver. Some supervisors have the unfortunate effect of making parents feel clumsy, ineffectual and anxious just as surely as others make them feel wise, witty, clever and comfortable. One mother said of an older supervisor, 'No matter how rough you feel, when you see her you feel that everything is going to be all right, and by the time you go home you're fine.'

It doesn't have to be the supervisor who reassures every parent, but she needs to be capable of making a warm relationship with each one even if the individual befriending of new parents is shared between many.

11 She may not be able to recognise the unique gifts of each parent because she is still bound by traditional thinking or because she is on the look-out for her own particular gifts in others.

When an anti-parent supervisor comes through her own experience to be pro-parent, this change of heart can bring its own problems.

1 Pendulums usually swing too far and new converts can often be spotted by their reference to 'my parents': this is a far cry from 'the parents', but there is another long haul of learning before arriving at 'we parents', which falls between the extremes of non-involvement and over-maternal involvement.

2 New converts sometimes have strong principles about 'parents who are made to do menial jobs', and instead of

being banished to the kitchen or lavatory there is an insistence upon their being in the playroom with the children. This swing needs adjustment, too, for some parents may need the security of making coffee before venturing into a roomful of children. More important still, parents may come to see some jobs as 'menial', but if we are truly involved with each other in a joint venture then every job is part of the whole. Taking children to the lavatory is no less an act of personal involvement, caring, and learning than taking them on our laps for a story. It may well be that the supervisor needs to demonstrate this by the way in which she does it, but that is not at all the same thing as 'doing the menial jobs on principle'.

From the outside looking in

What prevents some new parents from being involved?

1   Some don't feel any warmth or real friendship offered to them on their first approach to the playgroup, so they take their cue from this first meeting and keep the relationship on an impersonal level.

2   Some don't feel that they have anything to offer, and if they do stay in the playgroup initially it may only be because that was a condition of entry for their child. They neither receive nor give, they just stay. One of the challenges and joys of involvement lies in helping such parents to discover talents that they had no idea they possessed.

3   Some promise to do their 'rota duty', but as the day draws near they can't face the thought of their child playing them up in public. They often invent excuse after excuse as they effectively duck the issue each time.

   Their guilt is then twofold, guilt at letting the playgroup down and the deeper guilt of feeling that they have failed as parents since they can't be sure that their child will behave beautifully. Many supervisors and committee members write off such parents as being unreliable and the personal relationship deteriorates, which speeds up the vicious circle.

The more helpful course is for someone to explain well in advance that almost all children cling, show off, or 'act silly' when their mothers are helpers for the first time or two. They need to know that this is natural, expected and accepted, and that it is a stage that will pass.

4 Some are intensely shy and will try to evade involvement rather than risk the blushing, stammering, sweating, shaking, tummy-ache, headache or other physical symptoms that engulf them at the very thought of going into a strage room and having to talk to people.

5 Some cannot read or write and are afraid of being found out. When notices are pinned up on boards it is helpful reinforcement anyway to make sure that parents are told about the new notice; it makes the impersonal request more personal, and therefore more likely to lead to involvement.

But the real stress cannot be lessened until the non-reading cat is out of the bag, followed by the discovery that it simply doesn't matter or make any difference – except that people will go out of their way to be particularly helpful to make sure that newsletters and notices are shared verbally.

6 Some mothers aren't maternal and do not enjoy being with under-fives, though they may be deeply involved with guides or youth club work. They may enjoy being involved on the organisational side and will often pick up enough knowledge and understanding in general conversation to feel less alien with their under-fives at home.

7 Some want a break from their children and beg to be let off rota duty. This often leads to their being excluded from taking turns to help, or to the punitively expressed attitude of 'They ought to do their share'. Very few supervisors or committees explain that all parents need time to be away from their children, and that is one of the advantages of the playgroup system of sharing supervision. If there are twenty mothers, and a different two are in the playgroup each session, then every parent has nine sessions free to do as she likes for every one session in the playgroup. This

simple logic so often fails to get through to parents.

8 Some can be embarrassed or diffident if they feel that their speech, mode of transport, husband's job, home or ideas put them at a disadvantage. This is one of the reasons why parents choose supervisors from their local community: some supervisors emphasise cultural gaps instead of bridging them, particularly in the matter of attitudes towards bringing up children. Every parent should find familiar memories of their own childhood revived in the playgroup, such as Rupert Bear and Enid Blyton in a corner of otherwise unfamiliar books.

9 Some sum up the supervisor as standoffish, bossy, prim, immature or just inadequate to meet their own personal needs; since there is no rapport, there is no point in pursuing the relationship. And if the supervisor is the only gateway to the other parents and children in the playgroup, then the gateway is effectively barred.

10 Some feel too tired to be involved. This may be genuine physical over-taxing, lack of sleep, or a condition that could be diagnosed and put right by a visit to the doctor (only they are often too tired to make the effort to go to the surgery), or it may be the exhaustion of depression or boredom - in which case involvement is often a dramatic cure.

11 Involvement may be frozen in the very early stages because someone inadvertently reinforces failure. This is particularly damaging if memories of school are unhappy. Why stick your neck out to be told off all over again?

12 Some, perhaps the majority of those who are reluctant, say that they 'don't want to be involved'. This shouldn't be taken at face value for, since many of them may never have experienced happy involvement in anything, they don't know how much they could enjoy themselves if they dared to take the plunge.

13 Some are put off by observing what involvement can lead to in the way of workloads and family disruption. We all need to remember that we may be less of an advertisement than a warning to others if we dash about laden with files and brief-cases, tear off after bath time to a chorus of 'Are

you going to another meeting?', complain (albeit cheer-
fully) that we haven't got a completely free day for the
next fortnight, agonise that there is *so* much work to be
done – and try to press others on to committees.

Who wants to be on a treadmill?

It is comforting for those on the brink of deeper
involvement to hear those immersed saying 'No' so as to
protect themselves and their families when necessary.

The charitable committee

Ironically, the committee that is required (by the playgroup
constitution giving charitable status) to ensure that the parents
are fully involved in the playgroup can sometimes become so
uncharitable that it defeats its purpose.

1 The committee can become such a close-knit group, with
   everyone on such familiar terms with each other in the
   playgroup or social life revolving round it, that everyone
   else feels excluded.

2 The committee can exclude not only the parents but the
   playgroup supervisor, which either leaves her isolated or
   causes her to 'join' the mothers 'against' the committee.

3 The committee can come to have such power that even an
   annual general meeting is useless as a vehicle for change,
   especially if none of the other parents knows how to use the
   rules to beat such a committee at its own game.

4 The committee can be so warmly united to protect the
   playgroup, and to prevent any unpleasantness, that no one
   else has a chance to grow up.

5 The committee can become so competent that no one dares
   to follow in their footsteps.

6 The committee can be so determined not to become an in-
   group that they pressure others into putting their names
   forward for election – it isn't unknown for someone to be
   swept on to the committee at their very first meeting – so
   others stay away rather than risk being pounced upon.

7 Committee members can become so addicted to feeling
   'somebody' that they hold on to their office even if they are
   too busy to do the work or even to attend the meetings.

The deepest involvement and shared responsibility often occurs when all the parents want to be involved in the decision making at every level. Not all parents avail themselves of their right to attend meetings and to vote (or to agree, or usually disagree, without any vote), but at least there is the possibility of attending – and no possibility of being rejected.

Perhaps the Charity Commissioners (who register charities in England and Wales) may rethink their ruling in time, and widen the scope of the constitutions not only so that *everyone* is eligible to be the committee but so that the work and responsibilities can be broken down into manageable proportions without the need for a formal secretary or treasurer at all – and even the chairman's job can be shared by two or three people being responsible for seeing that the decisions are implemented between meetings.

The already involved parents
We all assume too much.

We assume that those parents who have been warmly welcomed and become deeply involved will 'naturally' extend a similar warm welcome to the new parents. Some do, but most just seem to assume that whoever befriended them will go on doing it, or that 'they' will, or the supervisor, or the committee will do it. It begins to look as though arrangements need to be made at the end of each term to see who lives near the new families about to start, and that the responsibility for visiting is given to someone definite.

The old-fashioned idea of introductions needs to be revived, even in the informal setting of the playgroup, for the established members can be just as shy of the new ones as vice versa. We need to say clearly to each parent, 'What have you received? Pass it on!'

From the depth of involvement
What causes people to draw back?
1 Some wives come to life quite dramatically through involvement, only to find that great happiness outside the home is counterbalanced by growing unhappiness inside it. Traditionally, husbands have had their own circle of friends

through business or hobbies. But, when wives begin to dash off to sparkle with the friends made through their new interest, it can lead to friction. (On the other hand, this may be the strengthening of home life.)

2   Sometimes the stresses and strain of involvement are too great to be borne. When people come together to work for a common cause there is bound to be a conflict of interests or personalities from time to time. Some can't cope with this, and letters, messages, phone calls, whispering, accusations and lobbying behind the scenes make life a sleepless misery: withdrawal is sometimes the only way to self preservation.

Sometimes husbands will move in to back their wives, and a marriage that appeared under stress will spring into new life. Sometimes the opposite is true and it is the last straw that leads husbands to say 'Pack it in or else.' (And sometimes this works positively too.)

3   Sometimes there is a particularly distressing decision to be made about involvement when a mother and child have been very happy in their playgroup for a long time, and then through a course or a visit or hearsay the mother suddenly realises that her child is in a 'bad playgroup'. The first reaction is usually guilt and anxiety – guilt that she was enjoying herself too much, and that she didn't know the difference between a 'good' and a 'bad' playgroup, and anxiety lest the playgroup has done him any harm. Some set about trying to change the playgroup, and several have said, 'I tried to do it too quickly and they turned against me.' Sometimes this brings a long and happy relationship to a bitter end, and more than one mother has had a breakdown.

Sometimes the other parents agree with her and there are new stresses and strains as they try to find the courage, and the know-how, to get rid of the supervisor and find another.

Sometimes the parents will set to work slowly and carefully to help the group to grow and change. Some have done it triumphantly; some get so far and can't go any further; some have to get out and leave it for the others to go ahead as they decide.

Some have to opt out if their own marriages are under

stress and the dual areas of nervous expenditure too much to tolerate.

4   Sometimes the growth of insight is too dramatic in its consequences to be tolerable: it is the deeply disturbing, but rewarding, learning about themselves as they really are, questioning everything they were brought up to believe, and either holding on to it with renewed certainty or painfully letting go in order to follow the evidence of their own eyes and experience backed by increasing knowledge. This is a particularly difficult process for parents involved with their under-fives, for they are torn between loyalty to their own parents; loyalty to the playgroup tutors, leaders and contemporaries that they have come to trust; loyalty to their own inner feelings that are in a sudden state of flux; and above all loyalty to their precious children. Perhaps playgroup people must learn not to fan the flame of individual learning too single-mindedly, but rather to start with the children's needs and then to see (with empathy rather than judgement) how everyone in the family and playgroup perceives these needs and feels about meeting them.

5   Some parents can't combat the down-drag of negativism. It is as though some people are positive poles and others are negative poles. The positive poles expect to see, and therefore do see, the good in individuals and the possibilities in events. The negative poles expect to see, and therefore do see, the weaknesses in people and the snags in events. In between these two extremes come the majority of people with a propensity to be drawn either way: if they become involved with a positive individual or group they light up and their latent talents begin to grow and multiply; if they become involved with a negative individual or group then their interest isn't roused and their talents remain buried.

Despite all the hindrances described in this chapter, the working group perceived that the particular contribution of the playgroup lay in its being able to build on parents' insights, knowledge and experience, through their active involvement in their children's early learning. In this way, the support of those professionals which society appoints to do certain jobs – for example, teachers, health visitors, and community workers – can enhance rather than weaken the role of parents and all those within the community with a positive role to play in helping families with young children. It is this approach that marks the playgroup movement as a positive force in a largely negative society, and it is one of the greatest strengths of the playgroup movement.

6

Some Questions for Further Discussion

1 How does PPA consciously take the elements of parental involvement into its thinking, planning and activities? What if anything should PPA do to ensure its implementation in member groups?

2 If we accept that parental involvement leads to opportunities to accept responsibility and authority, are we being careful to ensure that children have these same opportunities for learning through their play:

- Is the atmosphere of the playgroup sufficiently accepting, stimulating and peaceful for the children to become deeply involved in their self-chosen play?
- Are they able in their own good time to become involved with the other children and adults?
- Are they encouraged to develop a sense of responsibility for their play material, and for each other, and towards the group?
- Are they involved in choices, decisions, and in making suggestions that are always considered and accepted as often as possible?
- Are they allowed sufficient time to explore materials and practise skills until they come to feel a sense of authority?
- Are they listened to seriously when they talk with the authority of their own 'knowing', and are they helped to accept the authority of those responsible for them?

3 How does the present structure of PPA, hedged around as it needs to be by constitutions and standing orders, affect the growth of parent involvement?

4 How can we ensure that there are enough people and resources to give the support and information on all aspects of parental involvement to members of the play-group movement?

5 What means are used to feature parental involvement as a core in PPA courses to distinguish them from other similar courses?

6 Many professional bodies offer courses relating to the needs of pre-school children and their families. What steps would PPA have to take to explore with them how their training programmes could be modified to include learning the enabling skills of relationships with parents?

7 How can PPA contribute to the present debate on allocation of human and material resources for pre-school children, so that the benefits of playgroups with parental involvement are given proper recognition?

8 What resources does PPA need so that every opportunity is taken in the pre-school field to enable professionals to see their task as one of shared responsibility with parents?

9 How can PPA be involved in ensuring that any new legislation (relating to pre-school groups) should advance, and not hinder, opportunities for parental involvement?

10 Should PPA be working with other bodies representing parents to pursue the advantages of parental involvement in fields other than pre-school provision?

11 How can we retain our sensitivity so that people can grow at a pace that is right for them, and encourage people with the time and understanding to support community play-groups when asked?

Part Two

Mother and Toddler Groups

Introduction

PPA – the Pre-school Playgroups Association – began in 1961 and is registered as an educational charity. It exists to help parents understand and provide for the needs of their young children. It aims to promote community situations in which parents can with growing enjoyment and confidence make the best use of their knowledge and resources in the development of their children and themselves. About 10,500 playgroups and some 1,500 individual members belong to the Association and this involves almost 400,000 pre-school children and their families.

The Mother and Toddler Working Party was formed towards the end of 1975 and was part of a natural trend in the Association towards interest and involvement with mothers and their young children who met together in groups. From the early 1970s groups were starting up (15 per cent of those in the survey began before 1972) and by 1973 some areas (for example, Inner London and Sussex) were undertaking wider discussions and deeper thinking about the growth of this comparatively new phenomenon.

PPA's national committees had 'mother and toddler groups' (MT) as a recurring item on agendas and in 1974 the Training Committee was asked to consider a course for those running MT groups. A small working party collected together existing information but found itself recommending that any formal guidelines would be premature and suggested that the first task should be to set down what was already known about such clubs and by means of a survey, if possible, to try to discover the size of the movement and the real needs for support. Training Committee and Communications and Media Committee budgets carried the work through 1975 and the PPA booklet 'Mother and Toddler Clubs – A basis for discussion' was published in the spring of 1976. The timing proved opportune. PPA received a grant from Barclays Bank to undertake a limited number of projects and the study found the necessary funding. £3,000, to be spent over two years, was the sum allocated and the working party was enlarged to become more representative of the whole country.

The working party met on fourteen occasions in either Birmingham or London between October 1975 and June 1978. In addition members visited many groups and reports were made on over sixty visits. Meetings and conferences on mothers and under-threes and young family support as well as MT groups were attended and addressed by members in many different parts of the country.

Helen Blythe (Chairman)
West Midlands member,
National Executive Committee PPA
June 1978

1

The Mother and Toddler Club

By definition the working party was to consider the growth, style, potential and needs of clubs run by or for mothers and their young children where the majority of the children were under three years of age and remained in the care of the mother (or mother substitute, for example, father, grandparent or minder). This report is not concerned with groups providing a service which enables a mother to leave her child in the care of someone else while she takes part in some other activity.

A 'typical' club

To begin to examine this rapidly growing movement we conducted a survey. While the independence and distinctive individuality of each club are among the joys of the movement we uncovered, a generalised profile can be built up from the returns to our questionnaire. This 'typical' club meets in a community/church hall for up to two hours one afternoon a week, except in school holidays. Mothers sit and chat in the same rooms as the children and play with the children at activities which probably include some kind of 'messy play'. There is probably not a regular play leader, though there is an organiser who may include this among her roles. Families pay up to 15p* per session, which is primarily used for rent (over £1 per session*) and refreshments. Fees are supplemented by fund raising. Some, if not all, mothers take some share in organising the group and in the running of the session.

*These figures refer to winter 1976/77.

2

The Survey

With advice from PPA's Research Committee a set of twenty-four questions was drafted. After a pilot run and re-drafting, the questionnaire was printed and issued in October 1976. Working party members channelled the forms out through existing PPA networks of county associations and branches, with the help of volunteers in the field who have many contacts and links with unattached groups. Nationally almost forty organisations which might also be interested in young family support were asked to assist. All this gave access to a wide range of groups throughout England, Scotland and Wales and 4,400 questionnaires were distributed.

Returns were collected regionally until 31 March 1977. They were then analysed in regional bundles to give an initial picture. 1,702 questionnaires returned were then assembled and we were fortunate to be able to have them processed by computer at Birmingham University at the end of 1977.

Nearly half the groups were linked to playgroups. In both Wales and Northern regions MT are more likely to be connected with a playgroup than not. It does seem reasonable to assume that more of the playgroup-linked groups will be members of PPA and this is borne out by our survey, although only 42 per cent of respondents said they were PPA members. The working party felt this to show satisfactorily the success of the survey in reaching wider than just PPA membership. The Welsh result of 61 per cent members of PPA and 58 per cent linked with playgroups might simply indicate less contact with groups outside the PPA network; while in Eastern and South East regions, the higher percentage of PPA-member MTs would indicate that a higher proportion of MTs than average were PPA members in their own right. From PPA's annual

Regional areas with number of actual returns and percentage of total, playgroup links and PPA membership

Region	No. of Returns	% of total (1,702)	% linked with PG	% Members of PPA
Northern	118	7	59	45
North West	101	6	44	34
Yorkshire and North Humberside	157	9	52	51
East Midlands	82	5	52	32
West Midlands	161	9	50	45
Eastern Region	103	6	41	44
South East	238	14	44	48
Greater London	204	13	45	34
Southern	157	8	57	41
South West	166	10	51	42
Wales	79	5	58	61
Scotland	136	8	42	34*
TOTAL/AVERAGE	1,702	100%	49%	42%

*These groups are members of Scottish Pre-school Playgroups Association (SPPA).

membership survey 'Facts and Figures 1976' we learn that around 12 per cent of member playgroups also ran MTs (over 1,000).

1 Where is the meeting held?

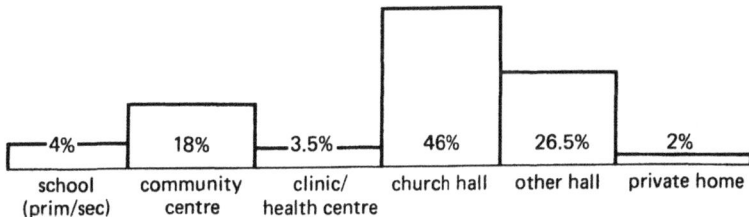

4%	18%	3.5%	46%	26.5%	2%
school (prim/sec)	community centre	clinic/ health centre	church hall	other hall	private home

While almost all groups met in shared community premises a number of interesting regional variations appear. More than double the average number of MTs meet in schools in East Midlands and Scotland. There were fewer community centre groups in South East – less than half the number in Northern region or Wales, for instance – which could be indicative of local authority and government grants for municipal development. West Midlands had a much higher percentage of groups meeting in clinics or health centres (9 per cent).

2   In what year did the group start?

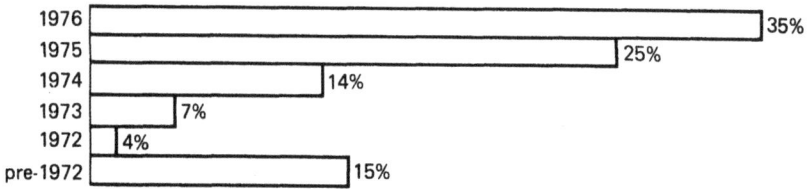

1976	35%
1975	25%
1974	14%
1973	7%
1972	4%
pre-1972	15%

The statistics reveal an astonishing growth in the number of new groups, which continues to escalate. Yorkshire and North Humberside had a higher percentage of older groups (17 per cent), followed closely by Northern and Greater London regions. East Midlands and Scotland had the highest proportion of newly opened groups – some 12 per cent more opening since January 1976 than in, say, Eastern region, South East (which seems to have had its boom in 1975/6) and Wales. Although an average 2 per cent of groups did not seem to know when they began, in London, where there was a good number of older groups, the figure was 5 per cent. A total of 18 per cent of groups either did not know or could not tell accurately when their group began.

3   At what time does the group usually start?
At what time does the group usually end?

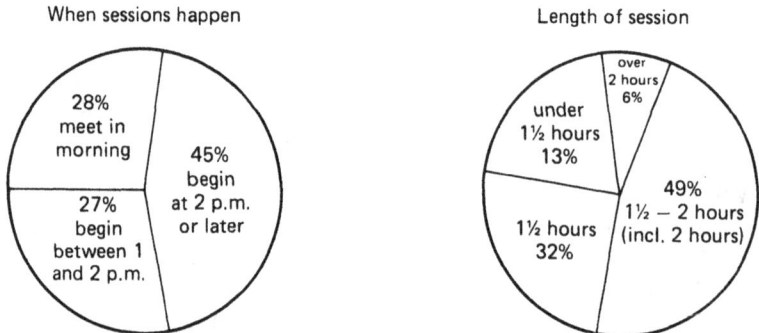

When sessions happen

- 28% meet in morning
- 27% begin between 1 and 2 p.m.
- 45% begin at 2 p.m. or later

Length of session

- over 2 hours 6%
- under 1½ hours 13%
- 1½ hours 32%
- 49% 1½ – 2 hours (incl. 2 hours)

4 How many sessions are held weekly?

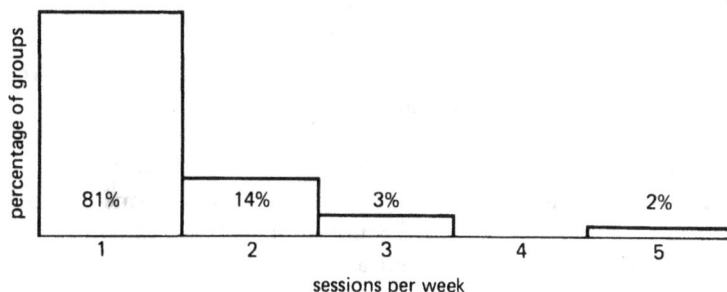

percentage of groups

81%	14%	3%		2%
1	2	3	4	5

sessions per week

Almost all groups running for five sessions are in London, presumably the one o'clock clubs which are completely funded by the local authority.

5 Are there evening meetings?

21 per cent of groups said they held evening meetings for parents but we did not ask how often these happened. More groups in Eastern region had evening meetings – just under one-third of all the groups there; London had fewest – about one group in six.

6 Does the group only meet in school term time?

27 per cent of groups continued to meet through school holidays. In Northern region only one group in six remained open throughout the year but in London two groups out of every five were open in school holiday time.

7 How many adults usually come?

27 per cent of groups had under twelve adults attending.
48 per cent had between twelve and twenty adults.
25 per cent had over twenty adults regularly at sessions.

8 How many children usually come?

The replies to this question were inconclusive.

9 What are the age groups of the children?

This question presented difficulties. We did not make our definition of age ranges clear enough. For example, in the ranges 0–1, 2–3, and 4–5: where does one place an 18-month-old? 60 per cent of the groups indicated that children of all ages up to five attended. 37 per cent of groups did not have over-threes attending and 4 per cent of groups were run for the pre-playgroup age (2–3 years) only.

10   How many families use the group at present?
This was as varied as the number of adults at sessions but our computer could tell us that 78 per cent of families connected with a group were represented at any one session.

11   How much does the family usually pay per meeting?

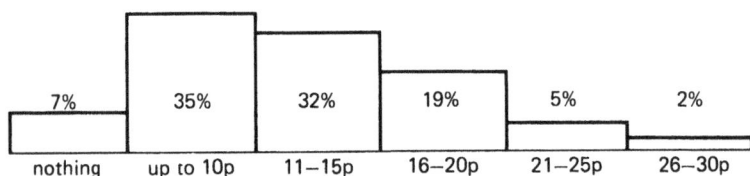

7%	35%	32%	19%	5%	2%
nothing	up to 10p	11–15p	16–20p	21–25p	26–30p

In all, 7 per cent of groups made no charge at all.

12   Does the group pay for rent and/or light/heating and cleaning?
If yes, how much per meeting?
Only 61 per cent of groups paid rent, 14 per cent of these groups did not give details so the amounts paid were based on replies from some 900 groups.

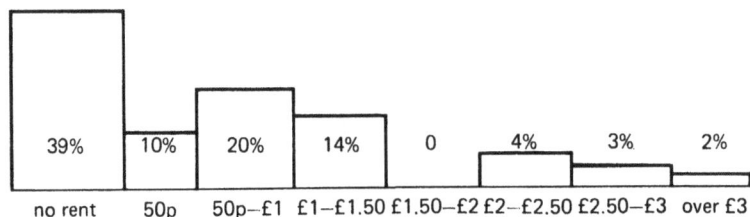

39%	10%	20%	14%	0	4%	3%	2%
no rent	50p	50p–£1	£1–£1.50	£1.50–£2	£2–£2.50	£2.50–£3	over £3

Thus 39 per cent paid no rent, a further 30 per cent paid £1 or less per session, but 8 per cent of groups needed to find £2 or more every session and there were 2 per cent who paid over £3 rent each time, which must have meant a struggle to make ends meet (1976 figures).

13   Does the group receive a grant or subsidy?

15 per cent of groups said they received a grant in that year, but we did not explore the size or source of the grant, nor whether it was simply a 'one-off' starter grant. In the London area 28 per cent of groups were grant-aided and in Scotland and Eastern region one group in five had received a grant. Areas least likely to have a grant were East Midlands and South East, where fewer than one group in twelve had received one.

14   Does the group raise its own funds?

79 per cent of groups raised funds, in the usual ways – bring and buy stalls, coffee morning/evening, raffles, 'as new' sales, etc.

15   How did the group obtain equipment?

Many groups built up equipment from more than one source and naturally returns record considerable overlap. Making equipment seemed least popular, with only 25 per cent of groups recording that they did so. Generous families and communities as well as other organisations made gifts to 63 per cent of groups and 63 per cent of the groups had bought some items. 4 per cent had equipment on loan – often from the linked playgroup, sometimes from local authorities or PPA branches.

16   What play materials were provided for the children?

With the wide range mentioned it was difficult to analyse replies in detail but it is worth noting that 60 per cent of groups mentioned an item of 'messy play' – sand, water, paint – in their list. Trying to draw conclusions from cold figures can be dangerous but two areas of the country are noticeable if we look at playgroup links, PPA membership and messy play together in regional figures. Wales recorded high percentage of playgroup links and PPA membership but low commitment to 'messy play' and in South East region there was a very high interest in sand/water and paint, with a low number of playgroup links but a proportionately higher membership of PPA.

17 and 18   What do the mothers do?
Which activity happens most often?

Activity happening most often	
Sit and talk	70%
Sit and knit (and talk)	1%
Play with the children	20%
Listen to a talk	3%
Mend/make toys	0·2%
Run the club	1·8%
Help the leaders	2%
Other activities	2%

In over half the clubs/groups mothers helped the leaders and in one third of groups they ran the club, but this was not seen as the important activity. 18 per cent of groups mentioned other activities – outings and swimming being two frequently mentioned but only 2 per cent regarded these as the main attraction. While 15 per cent of groups listened to a talk from time to time, only 3 per cent of groups regarded this as the main activity offered.

19   Do the children play in the room where most mothers sit?

In 93 per cent of groups – an overwhelming majority – mothers and children were together, so vital at this toddler stage where visual contact with mother is still an important need. Although nationally 6 per cent of groups said the children played in a different room, there was considerable regional variation here from East Midlands (2 per cent) and Wales (4 per cent) to Southern (11 per cent) and West Midlands (12 per cent).

20   Which best describes how the group is run?

This question was an attempt to find out about the structure of groups and their organisation. There was a good response and most groups saw themselves fitting into one of our five categories. Only in the London area did there seem to be a problem over identifying their own structure; or perhaps there is another pattern about which we do not know.

23 per cent had an organiser who takes responsibility for the group; 21 per cent had an organiser with a rota of mothers sharing various tasks; 44 per cent were run by an informal group or committee of mothers; 8 per cent had an organiser with a playleader to keep watch over the children's play; 4 per cent had an organiser and a playleader as well as a rota of mothers.

The distinctions as drawn by the questionnaire may not be as clearly cut as these statistics suggest for in some cases these categories may overlap. Groups run by an informal group or committee do frequently appoint an organiser.

21 **Who is mainly responsible for rent, purchasing toys, takings, money and fund raising?**

Organiser	37%
Treasurer	42%
Other	21%

While some 5 per cent of groups did not seem to know who handled their cash, the replies bore out an impression that many organisers have a great number of jobs to deal with, including money matters. Where there were committees someone was more likely to be deputed to be treasurer and look after the finances. The 'other' category varies greatly but sponsoring bodies and statutory authorities seem to need encouragement to help groups shoulder their own responsibilities.

22 **How was the organiser originally appointed?**

self-appointed	25%	
by a committee	20% }	39%
by an informal group of mothers	19% }	
local authority body (incl. health visitor)	7·5%	
church/charity/organisation	15·5%	
no organiser	13%	

This question helped us cross check others in the questionnaire and the working party feel that the figures gave an accurate picture of the state of organisation. Obviously groups run by committees and informal groups of mothers did choose organisers to help things run smoothly, but the 25 per cent of organisers who considered themselves self-appointed might feel rather vulnerable or unsupported in such valuable and necessary support work for the young families in their locality. Regional variations existed naturally and groups in Eastern and East Midlands regions were more likely to have self-appointed organisers. In London many more organisers were appointed by the local authority or other organisation and in South East and North West groups seemed to be supported by some other organisation who found the leader (church/charity or local organisation). Groups of mothers, either as a committee or informal group, chose the leaders in a high proportion of Welsh groups (62 per cent) and in just under half of Scottish groups and those in Southern region.

23   If there is an organiser, is she paid?

Only 24 per cent of groups had paid organisers. We did not ask how much and have good reason to believe it was often expenses, or token payment. Self-appointed organisers were least likely to be paid, for example, Scotland and Eastern region paid only about 16 per cent of organisers, whereas in the London area 40 per cent were paid. In the boroughs of Wandsworth, Hammersmith and Haringey nearly all MT organisers were paid, as were those who worked in all GLC one o'clock clubs and London Council of Social Service Family Groups. West Midlands also seemed 'to make rather more effort to offset organisers' expenses (30 per cent) but had a higher proportion of clinic-based groups.

24   Is the group visited by . . .?
Is help available from . . .?

Almost a quarter of groups seemed to be visited by no one and over one-third of groups (35 per cent) seemed to be unaware of where help would be forthcoming. Health visitors saw the highest proportion of groups – about one in three – and PPA personnel visited a comparable number of groups (32 per cent). 26 per cent of groups knew they could get help from a health visitor and 26 per cent knew PPA could help. 18 per cent were visited by social workers; local school personnel and community workers visited one group in ten but a smaller proportion than that knew them to be sources of help. Sponsoring bodies often sent visitors – vicar, area officers of voluntary organisations – and many groups listed playgroup advisers separately from social workers.

25 **What help would your group welcome?**

Finance	14%
Premises	6%
None whatsoever!	6%

Many groups wanted help with involving the mothers themselves more. Many comments were difficult to analyse.

Extra information
Altogether 46 per cent of respondents sent us comments on or longer histories of their groups (790).

Exploration of correlations could be endless but time and expense limited us to just a few.

We attempted to see if there was link between the way a group was run and the fact that it held evening meetings. There seemed to be. Over half the groups run by mothers (informal group or committee) did have evening meetings and a further 30% of groups where mothers helped on rotas had evening meetings.

We explored a number of activities of groups receiving a grant. Three-quarters of them also raised funds and 73 per cent of those groups did buy equipment, which is a higher than average figure. It was also more likely that a grant-aided group would pay its organiser/leader something (44 per cent), although this varied greatly regionally and did not seem to have any pattern. In both East Midlands (which has little grant aid) and the London area, groups placed a higher priority on payment for leaders (67 per cent) when they had grant aid.

We tried to see if there was a link between the structure and the appointment of an organiser. This confirmed that where there was no organiser there was an informal structure. Where the local authority made appointments there was more likely to be a playleader as well as an organiser.

Appointment of organiser	Self-appointed	Committee	Informal group	LA	Church/ Org.	No Organiser
organiser	38	29	10	23	30	0
organiser + rota	28	25	22	14	28	0
Informal group/ committee	25	33	63	20	23	99
Org. + playleader	6	8	3	33	13	0
Org. + playleader + rota	3	5	3	10	4	0

We wondered if there was a link between the type of premises used and the activities of mothers, particularly with those groups which listed listening to a talk as one of their activities. In all types of premises some groups listened to talks. More of those meeting in church halls seemed to have talks, sometimes with a religious slant. 26 per cent of groups in community centres also ran something for the mothers on many sessions. Groups in schools (6 per cent) and clinics (10 per cent) did have occasional talks but not to the extent that had been generally assumed.

The survey gives a useful 'average' picture of MT and its many facets. It may be of comfort to groups struggling against financial odds in the face of personal demands on leaders or organisers to find they have much in common with other groups and leaders. However, it is not regarded by the working party as a blueprint of good practice. It is evident of the desperate need for support on many fronts – financial, enabling skills, provision for play as well as sensitive professional help to back up an existing pool of mutual help and good will. Financial difficulties lead groups to maintain high membership which in turn erodes the benefit of the experience to both members and children. A general feeling that the support offered by groups to the young families in their area is unappreciated or unobserved by the community and its professionals seems to be a strand in many of the histories and comments. The fact that many areas do not yet have enough MTs to meet demands and that there is no positive encouragement to increase this type of preventive support in the young family field calls for action.

3

The Scene

The questionnaire had a blank page for additional useful information and nearly 800 clubs made use of this space to provide a wealth of information about how the groups worked in practice. In addition we made personal visits to more than sixty clubs and from this we were able to form a fairly clear picture of mother and toddler clubs nation-wide, their similarities and their differences, their strengths and their problems. We were able to see some clear trends and draw some interesting conclusions.

Aims

Common experience, in many cases, appears to have modified and reconciled the originally divergent aims with which different MTs were founded. Many report that they were begun with the needs of the children very much in mind: 'a chance to play with messy, basic materials' – 'somewhere they can run about without disturbing the neighbours', 'a very first social experience safely within sight and reach of mother' and go on to remark, 'But I now see that mothers need it more than – or get as much out of it as – the children. Not that they will say so for a long time. If you ask them why they come, they say, "He needs it", but you've only got to look at them talking to see the club fills a need for somewhere safe to bring the kids to meet other grown-ups.'

Visiting working party members heard many times that this was a much looked-forward-to weekly outing, or that the mother belonged to two or three such clubs – and pushed the pram some distance to get to them! – as some kind of lifeline out of the four walls of home into the accepting informality of a peer group. Mothers feel that their belief that 'He needs it' justifies them in spending a morning (or afternoon) sitting down and chatting, watching or playing with the children, the commonest way of occupying the sessions (see Survey, Activities of Mothers in Groups).

Clubs begun primarily for the children with the mothers in attendance report that they later realised that the mothers were making friends and using the MT as a meeting-place and opportunity to discuss matters of interest, ranging from their children to every kind of problem and pleasure.

Many who had set out to 'demonstrate the importance of good play materials' or to 'prepare mother and child for playgroup' described how they had come to see they were providing something for parent and child and modified both the sessions and the organisation to allow for this. Women who have since moved on to playgroup will openly admit. 'It was a high spot in the week; coming back home, nothing seemed so awful as it did when I went out', 'It was the only place to make friends.' Young family isolation, post-natal depression or many other experiences that undermine the enjoyment of the early years of motherhood are remembered by past MT members and 'It saved me from bashing her' is as classless as (from a senior education official) 'It saved our marriage.'

On the other hand, MT's begun with the needs of the mother uppermost in the minds of the initiators usually found that, without reasonable provision of equipment and some thought to making the afternoon worthwhile for the children, it was not a satisfactory afternoon for the mothers either, as noise and wild rushing about prevent the very relaxation and adult conversation the club was intended to supply.

Talks for the mothers are sometimes listed as an activity. The club is seen as an opportunity for health education, talks about child development or general interest topics, while others, aware of the lack of stimulation that many young mothers complain of, feel a session ought to include a talk, film or other adult attraction. However, the limited social skills of such young children and their inability to venture many feet from mother without checking that she will remain in one place are not always sufficiently taken into account by mothers or organisers, especially those with more recent experience of the playgroup/nursery age group. Problems arise whether the mothers and children are separated for 'the talk' or whether they remain together. If the children are left in the care of a helper or one or more of the mothers who take it in turn to 'look after' them, the sounds of distant cries and the coming and going of children in need of mother, or mothers going out to soothe their children, disrupt the talk; while anyone who has tried to speak to twenty or more mothers with an equal number of children present will know what a strain this puts on speaker and listener alike. While a minority of clubs see this element as a vital part of their programme, others report that they have abandoned it in favour of the play-and-chat type session, with or without occasional evening meetings which can supply that extra stimulus. 21 per cent of groups run evening meetings. However, evening meetings are not always possible in some areas, not only because of lack of cheap or suitable premises, transport, etc., but also because of husbands' attitudes or simply because father works late or mother does the twilight shift to increase the family income. In other areas local clubs, churches and societies offer suitable evening stimulus for housebound mothers.

Most groups aim to cater for both mothers and children although each group has its own emphasis.

Identification and Distribution of Adult Roles

The MT is almost always a locally based independent group, which may be entirely the responsibility of its own young mothers or may be supported by older women who are aware of the needs of young children and their parents.

A single individual may combine the roles of overall organiser, treasurer, playleader and hostess, or these roles may be filled separately. Who takes these roles, and how they are interpreted, reflects the aims and often the original history of the group.

Organiser

An individual opening or organising an MT is often the minister's or vicar's wife, or someone connected with the local playgroup. Few of these receive any payment for a very demanding job, although they may receive some help in the form of collecting dues, serving refreshments, setting out or putting away equipment. Probation officers, social workers, the NSPCC and organisations concerned with single-parent families have begun MT clubs, mainly to create meeting points for mothers with similar needs and give peer-group support. Health visitors tend to start mothers' clubs as a vehicle for health education but having done so many have observed the benefits to the mothers of mutual support and social contact. Some of the groups organised by professionals also involve voluntary helpers. Of these, some of the organisers working on behalf of voluntary organisations, and many of those mentioned above as running groups virtually single-handed, do so because they feel the mothers of this young age group need above all to relax and make friends. 'At this stage of their lives it's enough that they come,' said one; 'I remember how tired I always was when mine were young or when I was expecting; how can you ask them to do jobs?'

Statutory or voluntary workers start many groups with the intention of withdrawing at some future, unspecified time. In these clubs, the worker usually gathers an informal 'committee' together at an early stage, and finally works herself out of the job by attending for less than the whole session, but making herself available to discuss 'what went wrong' or 'how the MT is getting on' at other times. (It is perhaps debatable how far a founder or the person with the enabling roles can allow a club to deteriorate when she first withdraws. If the club met a genuine need, it should be possible for a fresh start to be suggested by an enabler with a sense of timing and the skills to gather a group without allowing it to be dependent on her.)

If the enabler is in touch with other MT clubs, she may act as a link or as the leader of an evening discussion group for active members of the clubs. Some PPA branches have a sub-group or section of MT members, who explore together the things they feel they need, have access to the local playgroup supplies scheme and are visited by a PPA volunteer who has made MT clubs her special interest.

Mothers may run the MT club entirely themselves. Such a club may be independent of any other body or associated with a playgroup or community or tenants' association, but responsible for its own affairs. It is usually started by an 'outsider' (community worker, social worker, PPA field-worker, etc.) or by a handful of mothers, sometimes with help – most frequently such help appears to be the health visitor – and surprisingly often entirely unaided because the mothers were unaware of any agency they might contact, or because they knew what they wanted and were determined to remain independent. Such groups are sometimes drawn into a local network at a later date. It is not uncommon for smaller groups to disband when the founder members' children reach playgroup age.

Clubs begun by a group of mothers may, like those begun in other ways, appoint one of their number or some outsider, perhaps an older mother with no pre-school children, with experience that seems to be relevant, such as nursery nursing, teaching or playgroup work. The variations on 'who is responsible for what' are similar to other groups, and the committee may be elected (see page 74) with a constitution or be a meeting of the leading lights, its composition changing frequently, reflecting the demands of young family life, including removals and the children's entry into the next stage of pre-school experience (nursery, playgroup, etc.).

A parent body, such as a church young wives club or a playgroup, itself run on committee lines, may appoint a hostess or playleader/organiser, who may or may not be paid. (The MT mothers may be represented on the committee of the parent body and take an active part in the working of the MT; the extent of their involvement seems to be dependent on the way the appointed leader interprets her own role.)

Some MT clubs are known to run as 'leaderless groups'. This style seems to suit the smaller (up to ten) clubs, particularly those that run in the homes of the members. One wonders how, in larger groups, newcomers are welcomed, and who is the 'listener to'. There are many pitfalls, unless the tasks of setting out, clearing away, paying for the room, etc., are clearly assigned.

Treasurer

Less than half the groups seemed to have a treasurer who handled the money, and in 37 per cent the organiser added this to her long list of tasks. But in others there seemed to be someone else who did it. An infant school head stated that he 'did that side of things' for the group which met in his school. Miraculously, groups do balance the books and struggle on, but the informality of the organisation in some groups could lead to financial problems.

The hostess will welcome each member, introduce newcomers, talk to small groups, listen to confidences, suggest sources of help or advice and generally make the club more than just a warm place with chairs. She may see herself as, and continue to be, a 'queen bee', or she may have highly developed skills of delegation regarding herself as the one who oils the wheels and lends a listening ear. The majority are probably somewhere in the middle, mother figures (slightly or considerably older than the majority of club members) or energetic, natural leaders – whether owing to their position as vicar's wife, say, or personality – who contrive to find sufficient helpers most of the time and are constantly on the look-out for new enthusiasts, perhaps even their own eventual replacement. Some find it difficult to 'get others to help', while others express surprise when they hear this mentioned as a problem elsewhere.

The playleader's interpretation of her role, determined by her own abilities and the aims of herself and the group, suggests the whole style of the session. Thus, clubs with a child focus tend to appoint a person with major responsibility for the children and their play, which may include involving the mothers directly or indirectly in the supervision of certain activities or in the play of their own children. Sometimes the playleader's role develops into something akin to informal tutoring as she shows how an activity – such as water play – not only is absorbing and enjoyable for the children but can be modified for home use.

Clubs with a mother focus may also have a playleader, but her role will be slanted to relieving the mothers from continuous involvement with their children, although in the majority of clubs the under-threes will be in the same room and gravitate at their own pace to the play attractions.

In all these roles, mature helpers, free of their own young children, might help to make the session more relaxed, enjoyable and profitable for mothers and children. Such regular helpers are free to nurse and play with a child whose mother is preoccupied without upsetting their own child. Because they are less likely to miss a session at short notice owing to a child's illness at home, they can be the most reliable members of a group of 'duty mothers' whose task it is to arrive early, unlock and set out the toys and chairs. Equally, at the end of the session they are more likely to be able to stay to put things away and tidy up, when mothers of young school-children need to be at the school gate, and those with babies and pre-school children are facing up to the demanding teatime/bedtime hours. Such helpers could prevent a leader/organiser carrying the whole burden, so relieving mothers whose children might be overtired at the end of that session. Where there is an appointed playleader, these other helpers provide more than one hostess figure to relate to, and can contribute much to the warmth and stability of a group.

The person who 'opens up, gets out, and puts away' is therefore sometimes the leader/organiser alone, sometimes a leader sharing the task with helpers and sometimes a small group of mothers taking it in turn with other members. If the club uses the same premises as a playgroup, such playgroup equipment as is used by the MT is sometimes left in readiness at the end of the playgroup session. If secondary school pupils are involved, they too may help. Some groups work on a rota basis, for example, a team of four may be 'on duty' together, having worked out that getting the room ready, registration and taking money, doing refreshments and putting away are four distinct areas of work. Each task may be organised by a leader or even broken down for a group of three or four to undertake.

Nature and Presentation of Provision for the Children

The range of activities for the children covers the whole spectrum from 'the lot, including finger painting' through to each mother bringing a plaything for her own child – though mothers usually learn that children invariably want what others have and will fill empty space with noisy play. Many groups seem to provide a scaled down version of the 3–5 playgroup, consistent with their aims of providing a pre-playgroup stage for two-year-olds and their mothers, but experience often modifies their choice and presentation of materials.

Most groups came by equipment in a number of ways – gifts of toys from members and the local community, loans from playgroups, other organisations or the local authority, home-made or toys made by local schools or workshops, and bought toys.

Those with younger children and babies do not always include enough of the simplest toys and equipment, whether bought or home-made, and the working party would like to emphasise the opportunity to use traditional and inexpensive items, such as boxes, pegs and cotton reels, alongside the well designed 'educational' toys, and to make toys which mothers can copy. Such items as large lightweight blocks, push-and-pull toys, attractive rag dolls, mobiles and a few early picture books extend the range without the management difficulties presented by, say, rocking-horses, toddler trikes and dressed dolls.

Over half the groups listed at least one item of 'messy' play (sand, water, paint, etc.): some groups have it occasionally, others avoid it. (This may be to leave these experiences for the playgroup stage or because the mothers have decided they do not want the trouble of them.) The ever popular flour-and-water dough, tinted with powder paint or food colouring, is often made up by mothers, who then make it for home use. Powder paint, brushes, etc., may be bought in bulk and sold for home use in small quantities. Some clubs set aside time for singing-games and nursery rhymes in which all the mothers and children take part.

Providing for babies and over-threes, while protecting the needs of the ones to threes (the traditional 'toddler'), calls for ingenuity, tact, energy and patience. While sympathising with those who have decided they cannot include over-threes or babies, the working party believes that if mothers of these age groups wish to come, particularly if they have children in more than one of these age groups, the introduction of such rules overlooks what the MT is giving the mothers themselves; mothers of three- or four-year olds, especially if these are the only or youngest in the family, may still need the friendship and social atmosphere of the club. Active membership of a community playgroup is not a substitute and mothers in areas where the playgroups do not involve parents or where there is part-time nursery education bring their over-threes to MTs 'because we want to meet'.

Children of all ages up to five were included in over half the groups. A small percentage ran their groups for children in just the 2–3 year age group (i.e. 'pre-playgroup') and over a third said they did not include children over three years of age. If there are over-threes in the group, they too need to be provided for, not only for their own sake but in order to prevent their more boisterous activities disturbing the mothers and little ones. One way of avoiding the over-threes' problem is to hold MT in the morning when playgroup or nursery school is in operation. This is dependent on availability of premises, but where these are available morning clubs are popular. Our survey showed that nearly a third of groups did meet in the morning.

In some rural areas, a three-to-five playgroup is not viable because of low numbers; under-threes are admitted if their mothers stay, and many mothers of older children also stay rather than travel long distances again, so that the playgroup session becomes a form of 'mothers and under-fives' or 'family club'.

The way the chairs and equipment are set out affects much of what takes place. If the room is prepared as for a playgroup session, but with chairs at one end for the mothers, this can inhibit or even prevent mothers from playing with their own children, and prevent some children from venturing to the more distant play areas. If the chairs are placed in a circle, with a baby area inside it, and activities for older children in corners of the room, movement may be restricted and a somewhat false 'big group' situation formed. A more successful layout seems to be groups of from three to five chairs placed in arcs near certain items of equipment, thus breaking down the adult membership into manageable groups for conversation, with the children's occupations close at hand and encouraging interaction.

Organisation and Administration

The number of adults at an MT session can vary from five or six to thirty or more. Many mothers have more than one child with them, so the total number of people in the room is often sixty or more. We regard this as far too many for the children to relate to, and too many for even the adults to relate to as a friendship group. Cliques inevitably form; there is less opportunity to feel needed and more likelihood of an inner group exercising a management function, all tending to a 'provider and consumer' situation remote from the mutual-help concept that encourages increased responsibility and personal growth. The shy newcomer may find herself isolated unless skilled helpers are on hand to help her integrate. (A working party member asked two mothers who seemed to be thus isolated why they continued to come to the group she was visiting. 'He needs it,' each replied, and concentrated on the child's play; other mothers were too absorbed in talk to move towards them and the organiser too busy with the children to notice them.) The club will be less of a group, more of a facility, in which the individual cannot enjoy the benefits of knowing and being known within fairly significant relation-ships which for many serve as a substitute for the lost extended family.

Overcrowding also means less suitable conditions for the children. Noise levels can be too high, it must surely be less hygienic, and restricted movement for the children may mean more clashes over toys.

Some groups are small and remain so of necessity, if they meet in members' homes. We feel that there should be much more encouragement towards the establishment of these smaller intimate groups, which are easier for both young mothers and especially their babies and under-threes to cope with. Many of course do not regard themselves as MT groups but they are of the same mutual-help nature and sometimes more effectively so than the large organised club. Sometimes small groups form themselves as an offshoot of a larger MT group, for example while pushing prams home in the same direction mothers found that they were neighbours, which sparked off a casual getting together over a morning cup of coffee. Sometimes leaders make a conscious effort to put mothers in touch with others in their vicinity.

The clamour for membership is one major cause for clubs being too large. Some clubs tell us they have waiting lists, but that the premises are not available for a second session, even if people are willing to act as leaders. Leaders say it distresses them to turn people away or institute waiting lists and if they open for a longer, say four-hour, session not only is it extremely hard for the leaders, but some people may simply stay on throughout the entire period.

Finance
The cost of keeping the group open is the other reason why large numbers are accepted by many clubs, and this relates to the rental. Variables like health and weather may cause very low attendance, but the rent has still to be paid. Even if everyone is present, an afternoon rental of £3 represents a contribution from each of twenty families of 15p before other costs can be taken into account. These could include refreshments, equipment (both capital and expendable), insurance, stationery, postage, phone, cleaning materials, helpers' expenses or token payment, rarely above 50p per session if paid at all. (The cost of travel to meetings with other MT people is often borne by individuals themselves when 'funds' are known to be low but are also a legitimate expense of the group.)

Rents for premises varies enormously but a third of the groups said that they met in rent-free premises, (varying regionally from a quarter of those in Eastern region to half of those in London). Of the groups paying rent, half paid £1 or less, which must have helped to keep dues low, but then with 7 per cent paying over £2·50 each time they met and more recent reports of rents up to £6 it is little wonder that groups are finding themselves risking pricing themselves out of the housekeeping purse.

What the mothers pays varies from nothing to over 30p per session but usually includes refreshments. Rates were very different over the county but in addition to the 7 per cent of groups which were free, one-third asked for 10p or less and almost another third charged between 11p and 15p. These figures apply mainly to late 1976 and costs have risen a great deal since then. It is difficult to imagine that it has been possible to maintain such low charges and meet the rising costs, such as rents.

Fund raising is necessarily undertaken by four-fifths of the groups. Events need to be simple as time and energy are precious to young mothers. Most popular are the regular raffle of groceries or toiletry and the 'good as new' or produce table with a percentage for the donor. Next comes the coffee morning or evening, with or without kitchenware, lingerie, children's clothes or cosmetics. If the MT is connected with another organisation (church, community centre or playgroup, etc.), it may be able to have a stall or other attraction at major fund-raising events of the larger body. Most clubs prefer to keep the dues as low as possible so that no one is excluded. Nevertheless, the constant money-raising tends to be a hidden expense which still hits the housekeeping purse when members make cakes to sell to each other.

Grant aid is reported by 15 per cent of the groups but from visits we know that many grants reported in the survey are small 'one-off' grants to help new groups get going, and there will be no ongoing financial support of any kind. The recent report of the select committee of MPs looking into family violence recommended local authorities to encourage the growth of MTs and to keep lists of suitable premises. Free or low-cost use of premises under the control of local authorities, some of which at present have a policy of charging the full economic rent, would be a great help, as would grants towards rental or equipment costs (see section 5 on recommendations). Membership of the local PPA branch may give access to cheap insurance and groups often buy copies of the quarterly magazine *Under-5* from PPA for resale at a slight profit.

One o'clock Clubs in London are an almost unique example of MTs funded entirely by the local authority. Mostly in parks, but sometimes on a housing estate, the buildings are always set in an enclosed area surrounded by a low fence. Clubs provide a wide range of outdoor play equipment and activities for the children, together with paid staff to provide and supervise these activities. The mothers must remain with their children and be responsible for them, but have great freedom to develop friendships while their children are occupied. In these groups, the mothers take no responsibility for management but may help with tea-making and are encouraged to play with the children if they want to. Groups are open to all comers every weekday afternoon; no registers are kept and no payments made except for refreshments.

Administration
Most groups keep a register of names and addresses of all families using the club – one group pointed out how essential this had been when it was necessary to inform all members of a case of German measles confirmed immediately after an MT meeting. An attendance register is kept for insurance purposes and a record of dues paid to ease the accounting. Other records may include a waiting list, birthdays, helpers' rota and monthly statement of funds for display at meetings.

Refreshments
These are an important feature of MTs and in the majority of groups the fee charged is regarded as one to cover the cost of serving a drink and biscuit for adult and children.

Some clubs have a mini 'family tea' with the children seated round a long table, or several tables with mothers supervising milk or juice and fruit or biscuits while they drink tea or coffee. In others adult drinks are available throughout (dispensed by rota mothers, helpers or schoolgirls) – children's drinks too, or mothers bring their own milk or juice for the children.

Transport
Most mothers walk, pram-pushing in all weathers and in some cases up to two miles. More often it was illness which

prevented attendance than the weather. Obviously some had cars available and attended groups which served a wider area but there were many groups which definitely felt themselves to serve a particular estate or district.

Sometimes those with cars helped out with transport, for bus fares (even if suitable services run) can be prohibitive for groups serving a wide area. One Welsh group reported members coming from as far away as ten miles. It has been commented upon that mothers coming individually tend to stay with the group; those coming in a group drift away.

Enabling and Supporting Agencies

Many groups want help and encouragement, but are simply unaware that there is anyone to give it. Communication seems to be sadly lacking and there is often little understanding of the wide range of people who are interested and supportive to such clubs.

Health visitors visited about a third of the groups and playgroup or PPA personnel visited almost as many, but there are many other sources of help which may not have been known to groups. Sometimes infant school staff, sometimes community workers, vicars or social workers visited, but support does seem patchy and spasmodic. However, a report based on the results of the Scottish groups which took part in our survey described them as 'alive and well and fiercely independent'. So perhaps it is from choice that about a quarter of the groups were visited by no one.

The needs of their own membership or special interest group may cause an organisation to set up an MT group. Gingerbread for one-parent families, the NSPCC hoping to reach families at risk, and playgroups who have very young children on their waiting lists are obvious examples.

Churches give a lot of support to some of the groups on church premises. The extent of church involvement in different groups ranges from 'as a vicar's wife I was asked to set it up' or 'the Young Wives' Club began it' through to members of the church serving refreshments and helping to clean up or to a lunch club followed by a short family service. One thriving club in a Methodist centre opens one whole day each week, the morning attracting mainly mothers and under-threes, the afternoons mothers with older children. A friendly leaflet explained the purposes and management of the club and invited mothers to take an active part. A coffee room was run at the same time for shoppers, especially the elderly. The minister made a point of dropping in and clearly knew every mother and child in the building. Although the project had not been started with a view to attracting church attenders it had certainly done so, and families in difficulties turned naturally to the minister for support.

Renting the parish hall or rooms (as nearly half the groups do) may be the group's only connection with the church. This impressive figure for the use of church facilities shows the extent to which the community at large relies for meeting-places on buildings owned and maintained by the minority of churchgoers. (Playgroup usage is similar.) Suitability for the purpose hardly enters into it; the church hall is so often the only building available in the area, or it is the only one with a management willing for mothers and young children to use it. The rent of church halls varies from nothing where the church leadership view setting up an MT or encouraging one to function as part of its extended pastoral role, to £5 per session where every organisation using the hall shares an equal part of the maintenance burden.

Some initiating bodies withdraw once a group is more or less in being, or they appoint a local worker or representative but appear to offer her little or no subsequent support or back-up, yet others pay a small 'retainer' and raise funds.

Organisations involved to greater or lesser extent in the MT movement are listed in Appendix B. Support workers mentioned most frequently are health visitors, PPA voluntary area organisers, playgroup advisers, social workers (including community workers, especially in inner cities or new towns), probation officers, nursery and infant head teachers.

The Health Visitor, so obviously a first line of support, is the most frequently mentioned visitor. Many health visitors make a point of calling in at MT, whether or not they were closely involved in starting it, and thus keep in touch with many more young families than they could possibly hope to visit regularly. From the geographical distribution of those few MTs based in health centres or clinics, it may be deduced that these numbers are dependent on area health authority policy and its enthusiasm or otherwise for formal health education, which may involve the separation of mothers and children for a talk or film.

PPA branches are increasingly appointed voluntary MT club visitors or including the visiting of MTs in the activities of existing voluntary fieldworkers; discussions for leaders and active mothers are held regularly in many branches which sometimes have a special local membership for MT clubs. New MTs are frequently brought into being by branch and/or playgroup personnel in consultation with the social services department or health visitor. Sometimes this is a first stage in developing a community playgroup.

Desiderata for Future Support

From the questionnaires and the follow-up visits we found that the help groups would most welcome was:

- Visitors – people to call occasionally, show an interest, advise and encourage.
- People to drop in regularly (especially professionals) and to be available to those with problems or help in the integration of those introduced to the group, for example, by social workers.
- Access to supportive agencies – especially health visitors and social workers.
- Introduction to and links with other groups, including discussion groups or seminars and visits.
- Grant aid – in the form of help with rent, payment to a leader or foundation grant to help group equip.
- Official encouragement – see below.

Before they started was the time when help would have been most useful; the problem is how and where to publicise sources of help. Enablers frequently mention coming across groups that have existed for years unknown to them, a sign both of healthy independence and the complexities of communicating in an impersonal society.

The plea for 'official encouragement' seems to stem partly from the need for funds, but also from a sense of 'being used' without recognition or expressed appreciation: 'If they send us five problem families, the least they could do is to come down themselves and help us with their difficult kids so that the other mothers don't stop coming.'

Lack of interest and support by the local community is a frequently mentioned disappointment. Too high a rent and therefore too little equipment causes discouragement, as does apathy from mothers assuming it is 'part of the welfare' – presumably an extension of the infant welfare clinic, where this is still held in a village or church hall. MTs and those who support them must be free from any hint of 'do-gooding'. Not for nothing may an official club operate with minimal attendance in a modern clinic while a self-help group thrives down the road in a run-down mission hall. 'This is *our* club,' say the mothers firmly, in much the same tone as one assumes in the unknown respondent to one of our questionnaires who penned in capitals in reply to 'What help would the group most welcome?': NONE WHATSOEVER'. One supposes that help to her was synonymous with 'interference' and the working party has noted and finds it necessary to record the great anxiety among MT enthusiasts that official help (grant aid or access to advice) might necessarily go hand in hand with rules and regulations. If grant aid were dependent on registration with the local authority under some powers similar to the Nurseries and Childminders Act, it is clear that many clubs would prefer to remain independent. (Simple notification of the club's name and meeting times, and of a person to contact, would, however, be acceptable.)

Because the mothers remain in charge of their own children, none of whom are 'received' in the sense of the Act, MT clubs do not come within the LA responsibility for oversight of sessional care and day care of children under five. They can therefore meet in buildings some of which would not be considered suitable for registration for playgroup purposes, and might be considered vulnerable to stricter controls.

The problems mentioned by workers or observed by visitors (apart from those caused by the nature of the premises or by shortage of money) were mostly to do with 'people skills'. What do you do:

- with the mother who 'switches off her kids for the afternoon', doesn't realise her two-year-old is causing havoc or is jealous of the baby, smokes in the loo if we put up a 'no smoking' notice in the hall, smacks her own child and upsets the other mothers, lets her three-year-old wreck the joint or grab everything or pull other children's hair?
- if you get a clique, or opposing factions?
- if they all go and leave you to clear up alone?
- if they all expect to be waited upon, asserting 'We've paid'?
- if you have arguments about different styles of upbringing?
- if they don't want paint?
- if the playgroup or caretaker or hall-owners are uncooperative?
- if someone takes to phoning or calling at all hours?

Who should we get on to? Who knows what to do?
And who prepares, briefs or supports the 'who' person? There is clearly a need for those involved as enablers and leaders to share insights and establish informal communication networks.

4

Reflections and Conclusions

Although our survey could not hope to cover every MT club in existence in the Winter of 1976–7, the figures on page 70 demonstrate the rapid growth in numbers over a period of five years and justify our reference to a 'mother and toddler movement'. Fifty-six per cent of the 1,702 questionnaires returned were from clubs started since January 1975 and of these over half had been running less than a year. Growth appears to continue unabated and PPA branches increasingly tell us of linked MT clubs in a proportion of one club to two playgroups.

Benefits to the children
Most mothers say that they go to MT for the sake of the child. What he or she gains in addition to experience of other children and adults in the safe company of a mother released from preoccupation with homemaking depends on the type of play materials offered and the extent to which the mothers and other helpers make themselves available to the children.

The opportunity to sit, watch and play with one's own child and the value attached by the club's leaders to children's play and the whole business of mothering is often commented on by mothers. 'They tell me I'm a VIP,' said one, glowing in new awareness of her status. Mothers who have since 'graduated' to playgroup recall adjusting expectations of themselves and their children as understanding of children's play needs increased, and many acknowledge that a more relaxed attitude resulted in a more easily 'managed' child.

Mutual help
The support of the others in the group is mentioned over and

again and the working party is impressed by the unselfconscious and indeed unconsciously therapeutic role of the group as well as the instinct to turn 'to those who have been there themselves'. Introductions at MT club often lead to firm friendships outside the group and frequently develop into a practical mutual support system, substituting realistically for the lost extended family. In some circumstances or where certain individuals are involved, clubs provide a focus for spearheading community development or neighbourhood revival. Baby-sitting schemes, help in an emergency such as the hospitalisation of either parent, reciprocal childminding, starting a new playgroup, evening meetings, outings, bulk purchasing syndicates and produce stalls are all familiar extensions of MT activity.

The all-embracing and outward-looking nature of much MT enterprise is shown by the ready inclusion of those in need. Clubs include a variety of parents in distress, from the recently deserted, battered or potentially battering mother (the group leader will probably simply know that she has problems) to a wide range of so-called normal but equally needful people, such as the newly moved-in, expectant or recently delivered mothers, fathers working shifts or unemployed, or more especially bringing up the family single-handed, and mothers who may be over-anxious, depressed or simply frustrated in their current state of being at home with young children. Grandparents and the retired, like childminders, are often sought out and invited to join the club.

An escape
Not all clubs become 'family' clubs, but it can and does happen. Even the least imaginative MT club is an opportunity to escape from the four walls of home, be it basement flat, high-rise, council house, terrace or commuter detached. Whether the club is more of an opportunity to relax and play with one's own child and others in a child oriented atmosphere or a chance to sit companionably near one's child while talking out the topics of the day depends, as we have stated earlier, on the intentions of the founders and thereafter on the pattern established.

Classless

The style and management of the session seems to be unrelated to class. MT is emphatically neither a middle-class nor a working-class phenomenon. It is apparently as needed and as popular whatever the family income or Registrar General's classification. One senior executive's wife hires a taxi and commutes eight miles weekly to a inner-city club with her one-year-old. 'The au pair's no company and too young; anyway she's not a mother!' 'The high spot of my week!' says the inner-city mum from round the corner.

Blossoms fade away

Despite the foregoing evidence, we feel it necessary to warn that we guard against an unduly solemn or portentous approach. MT clubs thrive with a judicious balance of outside interest and encouragement and wither with unwelcome 'interference', however well meant. It is essential to preserve their spontaneity, variety, ingenuity, freedom and flexibility. We must nurture the enjoyment, energy and incidental learning that imbue these clubs while ensuring that they lose none of the freshness and originality engendered by each group being an independent and unique growth. There are great dangers in clubs being taken up as 'the answer' for 'official' purposes, such as the promotion of positive mental health or parent or health education or the prevention of child abuse or family breakdown, however worthwhile. Like the proverbial crock of gold they may well disappear as the well intentioned researcher or adviser appears on the scene.

PPA help

Membership of clubs changes frequently for the prior calls of such young children on the time and energy of their parents mean that their degree of commitment is inevitably subject to abrupt change or sudden termination. 'Enablers' or visitors will need many community work skills, such as 'leading from the rear' and helping people work together and resolve their problems.

PPA members have helped many of these groups to form and they remain in a kind of elder-sisterly relationship. Many groups welcome the chance to 'belong' to a branch of PPA or a sub-group of it for MT clubs. The leaders and more experienced members are eager to meet others doing the same kind of thing and to pool ideas and problems. They enjoy speakers, slides and above all discussion groups and go back re-enthused to cope with 'Mrs Oddball', 'the town's most terrible two-year-old', the difficult caretaker or the antiquated heating system. They are somehow strengthened to discover that others have the same problems and worse, and are comforted to have discovered from one another's wisdom that in any group there are always those who give and those who take. With increasing understanding, the 'takers' are seen as those who most need to receive first and may need help in finding how to give.

Official help

If financial help were to be made available on a wide scale it would need to be administered with great sensitivity. Regulations appropriate to the sessional care of children in groups (i.e. playgroups or childminders) are irrelevant to these largely spontaneous groups of mothers gathering together for one or two hours a week with their own children. The requirements of safety – fire exits, insurance, etc. – and the exercise of common sense regarding hygiene and kitchens are acknowledged and call for friendly advice.

Professional help

As adult education is 'teaching among equals', so the visiting of these groups and the imparting of knowledge and expertise by the helping professions is most usefully and effectively accomplished in the sensitive awareness that the mother is the expert in relation to her own child. These mothers together are a greater support and influence than an outsider can ever be unless she is accepted by the group. The visiting professional sharing ideas and knowledge with a small chatting group of mothers over a cup of tea when they are ready to welcome her skills in slightly directed conversation will achieve far more than an official visit, however well motivated, by a representative of 'them' wearing the invisible hat of 'the expert'.

Care – mothers and children at play

We counsel caution, courtesy and care to any wishing to 'use' these clubs. We would ask them to be very wary of trying to take MT clubs faster along the road, or along a different road from that chosen by those for whom and by whom the club is run. To us, these clubs seem to have arisen as a 'natural' answer to many of the most pressing problems of today's young family, as the parents struggle, perhaps unconsciously, to find ways of including other known and trusted adults in the lives of the caretaking parent and the young child – a substitute for the old-style family.

The practical attraction and 'justification' for many who need reasons for joining and working with MT is that the clubs provide opportunities for young children to experience the existence of other children and to enjoy play materials which it may not be possible to use or supply in a home. The mothers gain in understanding of the art of child-rearing through exposure to others engaged in the same task. They learn from those of longer experience how wide the range of normal development and behaviour is and ways of coping. They come to terms with the state of parenthood, in which the needs of another small but ultra-demanding being, for the first time, take precedence over their own. This takes place against a background of the recognised difficulties of the early years of marriage, such as adjusting to one's partner, parting from parents and/or companions at work, learning to manage on a reduced budget and the physically tiring and exacting side of caring for a baby, a partner and a home.

All this seems to the working party to explain the success of mother and toddler clubs and reason enough to channel help to them.

From the DHSS publication *The Family in Society – dimensions of parenthood* (1974) following a seminar, we quote the remarks of Miss Joan D. Cooper, then Director of Social Work Services DHSS, Chairman:

'. . . the most effective policy to assist the family would lie less in precise educative work . . . than in community develop-ment aimed at engendering relationships between households within a local area in order to provide opportunities for people to act together to solve their problems rather than to meet them in isolation and to become over-dependent on specialised agencies.'

Perhaps the MT phenomenon should be seen historically and prophetically as a swing away from the limitations of the nuclear family towards various forms of shared upbringing more suited to human needs and the circumstances of the twenty-first century.

5

Recommendations

To the Pre-school Playgroups Association
The working party recommends that PPA should be actively involved with and supporting Mother and Toddler Clubs for the following reasons:

(a) PPA exists to help parents understand and provide for the needs of their young children. It aims to promote community situations in which parents can with growing enjoyment and confidence make the best use of their own knowledge and resources in the development of their children and themselves.

(b) Many PPA members and branches are already deeply involved.

(c) Many other bodies turn to PPA as an appropriate voluntary agency.

We recommend that involvement by PPA should be at all levels in the Association. We suggest that each PPA national committee undertake support work for the full range of under-fives and their families in line with existing policy for support to playgroups for children in the 3–5 age range and their families, that is to say that it should extend its work to cover the additional demands of the mother and toddler movement.

We suggest that, for at least an interim period, a national sub-group be established to spread information and, if necessary, act as a voice and publicist. This group should, through Field Services Committee, provide a central resource, support and links to PPA branches, enablers and others.

Through the Special Interest Committee for Mother and Toddler Groups in Scotland, groups there are already experiencing the benefits of having representatives of various voluntary bodies and regional groupings coming together to actively support MT groups and to publicise their needs and the benefits they bring to individuals and the community. Scottish Pre-school Playgroups Association has provided a constitutional and administrative base.

Further recommendations
The working party recommends the close co-operation of all relevant local authority departments and area health authorities with all involved in mother and toddler club work.

We urge departments to support the growth and development of these clubs by:

- making available the expertise of community workers;
- making more readily available the services of health visitors and social workers;
- offering grant aid to peg costs to families, thereby facilitating the existence of small, easily accessible groups;
- permitting the good offices of officials in obtaining the use of premises and negotiating a reasonable rent.

In general we endorse the recommendations of the select committee of MPs (First report, *Violence to Children*, 1977, HMSO) in asking local authorities to encourage and otherwise support MT clubs and self-help groups of parents. We would emphasise the many benefits to all families far beyond the prevention of child abuse and affirm their especial value in support to families at risk. During the period when a mother is most vulnerable to depression the club offers her support and, through her, support to the father and children.

We call for action on the recent joint circular from the Department of Health and Social Security and the Department of Education and Science, 'Co-ordination of Services for Children under 5', January 1978. This refers – in the Annex, 'Examples of Co-ordination in Local Practice' – to support for mother and baby clubs by local authority departments, health services and schools. It reads: 'Mother and Toddler Clubs and similar groups complement playgroup and nursery provision.

Clubs have been set up in child health clinics and infant schools by a number of authorities. Many clubs are organised by voluntary agencies and the mothers themselves.' Our survey shows us what a small proportion of groups are able to take advantage of such co-ordination or provision of premises (3·9 per cent of groups met in schools, 3·5 per cent met in clinics or health centres). There is obviously scope for improvement.

The isolation of the young mother and her unpreparedness for it have lasting effects on individuals and their families and thereby on society at large. It can be alleviated by peer-group contact and informal access to professional advice when needed. Society can reap rich rewards from co-operative support which helps towards happy, relaxed families. Here is an investment not only in mother and child but in society and its future which the working party commends to policymakers and those who carry through the implementation of policies at various levels. It has inestimable value.

Part Three

**Patterns of Oversight and Support
for Playgroups**

Introduction

Relation of this study to the two preceding

This report treats a third element in the rapid development of playgroup work. It describes the background which has affected the development of both mother and toddler groups and parent participation in playgroups.

Playgroups provide a form of child care, and local authorities therefore have to accept legal responsibility, which involves an overseeing role. Because this form of child care had no precedent, the form of oversight had to be worked out in practice, by adaptation from procedures already in existence for rather different situations. Council officers, already fully occupied with other children's services, had to extend their responsibilities without special preparation and without sufficient allocation of time to cover new playgroup work. Hence the varied patterns which have emerged.

One thing which came to light during this inquiry was the increasing interest of local authority departments in a parent-based child-care service, and on the development of oversight arrangements far beyond their minimum legal responsibility. A number of local authorities stated that piecemeal development of their playgroup supervision was now in urgent need of review.

Playgroups, meanwhile, have continued to build up their own support system, through a national association and the guidelines brought together from experience all over the country and made effective through PPA's communications system. The Association's almost completely voluntary working membership provides elements of self-authorised oversight as well as support.

It is apparent, therefore, that a dual system of oversight and support has come into being, and that playgroups meet both aspects in their local setting. The relationship between the two must influence the background of the developing playgroup movement, and its potential for growth. Roles need to be sorted out, not once only through a report, but constantly in the local scene, so that parents and playgroups and the local community get positive overall benefit. The alternative is that the systems fail to understand each other and pull against each other, and playgroups suffer in the middle.

Another factor is that playgroups are not only a child care service. They belong equally in the field of mind-stretching and communication, although there is no local authority department responsibility for this. Playgroups rely on the support, if not the oversight, of those branches of education, whether in the LEA – or in adult education departments of universities or in the Open University or in the WEA – which recognise their dual function. Supporters in the education system have also had to work out a relationship between themselves in a friendly but not legally responsible role and the social services departments, who have to oversee as well as support.

A further factor is that playgroups are not the most recent development in day care for children, and that there has been great expansion in the child-minder service and also in mother and toddler groups. We needed to study at much greater length the relationship of playgroups to each of these, as well as the relationship of the social services departments to all three, and the division of one person's time between them.

We recognised a role, as oversight and support developed, for the professional organisations which have come into being in this field in both England and Scotland, and the importance of their early decisions on membership and practice.

In a field of great complexity, we have obviously made only a beginning. Discussion in a group of mixed origin has already had its value, and led to greater understanding.

Setting up the study
One third of the grant from Barclays made it possible to call together a group of people involved in different ways with oversight and support of playgroups. We set out to make a study of current practice in the field, including the revision of playgroups at the receiving end, and the activities of voluntary associations, and of local authorities fulfilling their legal obligations and extending their advisory services. It was

essential to include in the working group, set up in 1975, representatives of relevant local authority departments and of playgroup or under-fives advisers' associations, as well as PPA. There was also limited representation from other voluntary organisations.

It soon became evident that the study in England and Wales would gain from concurrent thinking and experience in Scotland, and representatives of Scottish Pre-school Playgroups Association (SPPA), social work departments and the professional association SAAUFF (Scottish Association of Advisers for Under-Fives and their Families) were invited to join. They met most often as a linked Scottish base group, but the working group had joint English and Scottish chairmen.

Throughout we have been grateful for the encouragement of the Association of Directors of Social Services, and latterly of individual directors, who talked with us in interviews (Section 9). We are also grateful to social services departments which produced information, sometimes even more fully than was asked for. Not the least interesting discovery was the variety of presentation of budgets and of under-five statistics by local authorities, which made comparison difficult but shed much light on statutory practice and structures.

We were also indebted to the New Towns' Development Corporations' Association, and to development boards which supplied information (Section 8).

Because we have been considering patterns of oversight and support in local situations, we have made constant reference to local authorities and their different forms of intervention. We should wish, however, to record that this is complementary to what PPA/SPPA receive in support, both advisory and financial, from the DHSS and DES, the Welsh Office and the Scottish Office.

Method of proceeding

After determining what lines of inquiry we wished to pursue, and eliminating all but the most central, we asked different members to take responsibility for working on blocks of information. They were very different people, and this report is a collection of very different contributions. We have not tried to make the sections similar in style. This lack of uniformity highlights the different constraints under which statutory and voluntary workers carry out their tasks, and the effort needed by each to understand the methods of others. Some sections will be more easily understood by the playgroup members, others by statutory personnel. Reasonable familiarity with survey procedures has been assumed. Statistics are interpreted differently, and there is a different emphasis on encouraging playgroups where they grow or securing fair coverage of an area. Expectations of the giving and receiving of grant aid differ. As a group we think the apparently different approaches made a positive contribution to the study, since each is a part of the background with which playgroups have to live. We have valued the efforts of group members to understand how different sections and different patterns of oversight arise.

Our main method of presentation of each topic has been to analyse the material collected and then give space to reactions from other parts of the network. The section has then been drawn together in a draft produced by one or perhaps two people. There has not been enough opportunity for each draft to be considered by the whole working group, and interpretative comment has therefore been kept to a minimum. There has also been a minimum of editing, with summaries added at the end of each section, together with questions arising which need further airing. It is hoped that occasions can be found locally for an interchange of views on these.

Where materials from Scotland could conveniently be discussed alongside the other material, it is all presented together. Where the framework is too different, or for any reason it appears valuable to treat it separately, a Scottish version follows the rest of the section material. One general success which SPPA has achieved is the correspondence since 1975 between SPPA and local authority units. In Scotland the SPPA Regions are constituted bodies negotiating with identical local authority Regions. Divisions, districts and areas have corresponding SPPA committees at division, district and area level, except where there are local variations reflecting ease of travel, number of playgroups, etc.

The comprehensive study of registration procedure (Section

2) drew heavily on material built up over a period of time by one of our members. Details of department structure and of the organisation and follow-up of grant aid, together with statistics on under-fives and statutory provisions (Sections 4, 5 and 6), were contributed by social services departments. The playgroup questionnaire which provided the basis of Section 3 depended on voluntary interviewers and the co-operation of playgroup leaders and committees in selected areas and on the analysis of returns by a specialist who made her skills available. Members of the working group co-operated with directors of social services in valuable discussions of stages of development in the playgroup movement, and its place in the provision of services for under-fives and families (Section 9). The Scottish base group worked out an introductory statement about playgroup aims and practice, and the kind of oversight and support which would be effective.

It would not be possible to acknowledge all the voluntary time and skill extended in putting together and revising the collected report, or the contribution of one regional office of PPA in the actual production of copies.

Acknowledged limitations of the study

It was a matter of great regret that we were not able, within our resources, to study by interview and questionnaire the contribution of local education authorities. We obtained an idea, from some branches and counties of PPA/SPPA, of the variety of their support, and in particular the difference made when there was one person available to draw attention to resources. We had some links with recreation and environment departments, and would have liked to extend the study to approach housing and planning departments.

We were aware of one important but missing section, that of liaison with area/regional health authorities and community health councils. A complete study could have been added, covering also the organisation of hospital play. We have added (Appendix C) a draft questionnaire which would have been implemented had extra money been available. This indicates the two-way support which we could see possible between health services and playgroups.

In Appendix D we give a summary of library support offered by one London borough, and are aware that library services in general, if asked, would have had much to contribute.

Although we hoped at the beginning to extend the study to patterns of oversight as experienced by other voluntary organisations, and the potential links between playgroups and these, we soon appreciated that this opened up an area of study to which we could not give sufficient time. We could not, either, without a supplementary study, record some of the connected work of VOLCUF (Voluntary Organisations' Liaison Committee for Under-Fives), though we were given an opportunity at an early stage to tell this group of our study. It seemed better to record the need for further work on the experience of other voluntary bodies.

We are very conscious, as a mixed working group, of the need for some wide forum with local as well as national presence, in which the questions presenting difficulties between parents, professionals and voluntary workers can be fully and sympathetically aired.

We have also had to exclude playgroup courses from detailed inquiry, although they provide a very important factor in support. The different patterns of courses would need an independent study, and they are mentioned here only as they come up under other headings (for example as part of a worker's job description).

The area of consultation between statutory and voluntary workers is one which we see as a growth-point for the future, and we have given a little space to the varying stages which this has reached in different parts of the country. We hope that the slowly developing practice of inter-agency consultation will find a way forward, and will build up confidence in playgroups as well as drawing on their experience. We know that the present stage of joint discussion has to move to a more difficult stage of jointly agreed spending, and that this can be very hard. But it is a stage of development which cannot be side-stepped if there is to be positive oversight and support. At present we have an exciting stage of dialogue, in which PPA/SPPA are ready to share.

Finally, we know that considerable development has taken

place since our material was collected. We hope that the report will be accepted for its coverage of patterns from 1970, when departments of social services were given legal responsibility, up to 1977–9 when the work was completed.

1

New Skills for New Work: The Oversight and Support of Playgroups

We asked the Scottish base group, with the help of a practitioner with long experience of playgroup work in all kinds of settings, to give us a current definition of playgroup work. As a group we discussed, endorsed and adopted this definition. We used it then as our reference point as we looked at the original aims of regulatory legislation, and whether they are still relevant, and at the wide range of thinking about playgroups both in the voluntary network and in the overseeing departments. This is what the Scottish base group produced.

What is the right timing and place for advice and assistance to those working in playgroups? This may seem a simple question; yet as with other seemingly straightforward questions, once asked, a host of other questions crop up as a way of getting near answers. Working with people is inevitably complex, with each situation unique in its setting of time, place and stage.

PPA is about seventeen years old, and at that stage of development when it is no longer a new and unknown organisation, and yet in many ways there is still a feeling of 'newness' around alongside the present consolidation. Particularly in the jobs, both voluntary and statutory, that have been created in support of playgroups there is still a questioning about what the aims of these jobs should be. What difference does it make if the people working with playgroups are responsible to a group of playgroups (the PPA/SPPA branch), or to a local authority department? Can confusion arise around the roles of those with seemingly similar jobs and different employing bodies?

Those appointed to work with playgroups have many different titles; they are employed by a variety of bodies, some statutory, some voluntary, and have correspondingly varied job descriptions. Some are fully paid, some receive only an honorarium, some PPA Area Organisers work 'for free'. Some local authority workers are classified as managers, some as visitors. (See Section 4). But all can be described as playgroup fieldworkers and all have a great deal of common ground.

Whatever the title of the persons and however varied their task, the same questions need to be faced relating to the skills of working with playgroups. The fact that this kind of work is relatively new encourages us to ask: 'What are we doing? How are we doing it? and why?' As playgroups themselves evolve and change, the question 'What is a playgroup?' needs to be uppermost in the minds of those who work with them.

A playgroup in being

There are so many variations on the theme: the playgroup in a house, in a hall, or school classroom, or playbus. There are playgroups run by one or two people, or by the Church, SCF, YM/WCA, or other agency, or by parents who band together for this purpose. All have elements in common: the children and their needs, the provision for play, the parents, the social and fund-raising aspects and the need for responsibilities to be carried. Each playgroup has a different balance of these elements and, while aims for the children's play should be similar, the opportunities for the parents' growth and learning alongside their children will vary very considerably depending on how the group is set up.

In the playgroups where parents together take responsibility for the running of the group, and where decision making lies with them, there is an extra dimension of learning opportunity that affects adults and children alike. In these community playgroups the day-to-day meeting of the group is in many ways just the tip of the iceberg in terms of learning. Because the parents are involved in the play (along with the playleaders they have chosen), and aware of the materials the children are using (they will have selected and bought them), the learning about children and their play is very likely to be carried back into the home and family. These playgroups offer mothers the tools for extending the opportunities for play and interaction with their own children at home.

For any playgroup to be healthy, all aspects of the group need to be going reasonably well. This includes the play, the participation or interest of parents, and the parents' needs in relation to their children. These should in diverse ways be met, resulting in mutual satisfaction, growth and enjoyment. Inevitably, all playgroups have their ups and downs, as is true of any human endeavour. How can playgroups best maintain themselves? What kinds of encouragement, advice and assistance from fieldworkers are most likely to be of help?

Openness to change and passing on of responsibility

We remind ourselves that few playgroups are static. Most have a dynamic life in which change is possible. Descriptions such as 'good', 'bad', 'difficult' and 'friendly' may become labels that stick, whereas in fact the potential for change lies within every group. This is particularly true of community playgroups, where the gradual movement of parents through the group and the passing on of responsibilities and leadership in a democratic fashion offer many chances for growth and for renewal of ideas. Hence the importance of one generation of parents encouraging the next generation to participate, and to take over responsibility from one year to the next.

Change for itself is not necessarily always for good, or always for bad, but it can create conditions for growth and development, particularly within a reasonably stable framework. It seems that isolation and lack of contacts with the outside world can contribute to a playgroup's gradual closing in upon itself and its traditions, with an increasingly institutionalised approach to all that happens within it, and very little change taking place.

For playgroups to thrive and to meet changing circumstances within the community, there needs to be a continual flow between the energies within the group and those of the outside world. There needs to be a give and take, with visits received and other visits made, with help accepted within the group and help given to other groups; with some members attending courses, meetings to go to, and communal participation in co-operative bulk-buying schemes. All these help those within a playgroup to look at and question what they are doing.

Nothing contributes more to the process of learning than the need to explain what is learnt to others. One of the most beneficial settings for positive change can be during a playgroup course where the exchange of views between students and tutors is on the basis of equality and sharing.

The most lasting positive changes in practice in a playgroup over the whole spectrum of the children, the parents and the community are those which are undertaken willingly through the wishes of the playgroup members themselves, and not those which are seen to be imposed by 'authority' of one kind or another.

Oversight, encouragement and independence

From these observations it may be possible to begin to define some basic principles in an approach to the oversight of playgroups.

1 Playgroups are capable of self-help and improvement. They have a life, a dynamism of their own which fieldworkers should recognise and respect.

2 Within almost all playgroups there is the corporate wish to go forward, to improve. On the whole those working within a playgroup are doing their best, while many would like to learn more in order to do better. It is never easy to relinquish long-held ideas and habits in the face of new possibilities.

3 Playgroups can help and learn from each other. SPPA/PPA branches have a great potential for offering opportunities for learning, changing, and for sheer enjoyment of the job being done.

4 Playgroups, especially those where parents are responsible, are expressions of the community in which they have grown; communities have different cultures and values about which fieldworkers need to learn.

5 Playgroups can become institutionalised, with far less growth and change, and an overdependence on tradition. Sometimes the sheer size of a playgroup in terms of total membership makes change and development of any kind almost impossible.

6 Intervention with playgroups should be with the aim of developing independence, and interdependence between groups, but not dependence on the fieldworker.

7 All fieldworkers have their own 'inner vision' about play, parent involvement and other elements of the total playgroup. These ideas, which are the sum total of learning experience held at any one time, are constantly changing and being challenged in the face of new experiences. Ways have to be found of exchanging views and perspectives with others at different stages of experience – between those in statutory and voluntary employment, between those employing and those employed.

8 It could be something of a trap to assume that all playgroups need help and improving, almost to justify the existence of fieldworkers. Do we sufficiently respect the independent life of each playgroup and see it as a group of people with whom there can be two-way contacts? Giving as well as taking? Offering responsibility as well as being overseen?

The role of playgroup fieldworkers, whatever their title, is many-sided: for some there are statutory responsibilities, for others there are responsibilities conferred by PPA or other employing body. No one has a black-and-white role which is clearly defined for all time. Each person's role needs constant redefinition; each job will shift and change in relation to the growth of playgroups, courses, PPA/SPPA branches. The presence of other fieldworkers in any one area will vary in relation to the stages of experience of each group and person. Yet, however different the various jobs of playgroup oversight may be, *central to them all are the skills which facilitate growth and change, both in others and in self.*

Summary

People working with playgroups have very varied titles, remits and conditions of work, and may be employed by voluntary or statutory bodies; nonetheless the work has much in common. Playgroups are rarely static: the new skills seen to be neded in the new (seventeen-year-old) job of overseeing and supporting playgroups are those of facilitating growth and development within the context of change. If playgroup fieldworkers are to enable playgroup members to learn, to make changes and to take responsibility for them, the time they will need is much greater than if they are simply to 'impose' positive changes on the group. Fieldworkers need time to become familiar with the playgroups in their care, to work with the SPPA/PPA branch and on training courses; and those in advisory capacities need also to understand and work more extensively in the department or organisation within which they are employed and in related areas.

Questions

1 With how many playgroups can a fieldworker maintain the relationships involved in 'new skills?'
2 What previous experience and in-service courses are needed to develop the skills?
3 Are the 'new skills' compatible with under-five policy in local authority departments? If not, what opportunities are there for discussion? And what alternative definition would the authority offer for the fieldworker's roles?
4 Where more than one fieldworker is involved in visiting and advising, how and by whom can their roles be clarified?
5 How long can he or she stay in this kind of job and remain effective?

2
Registration Procedures: The Practice of Registering

The purpose of registration

Social services departments can approach the registration of playgroups from two angles. Some directors still limit their interest to the legal responsibility – 'We've got to do it'. Others see it as a first step in active promotion of a service. Host departments now see playgroups (and childminders and mother and toddler groups and the work of other agencies, for example the National Children's Home, but we are concerned here with playgroups) as a valuable resource in their work with the community, both children and adults. They are of value both for the service they provide, and also, as the Wolfenden Report on the future of voluntary organisations indicates, just by being there, an expression of community thinking and drive. Departments are therefore concerned to see more of them and to encourage high standards of care and involvement. They have a problem in that spontaneous voluntary activity does not spring up evenly, and they may find themselves therefore in an active development role which goes far beyond a legal duty.

The legislation which confers responsibility is designed to protect children in a vulnerable position from abuse by a small minority of individuals, rather than provide a positive structure for encouragement and growth. It can actually deter people rather than encourage them to start. The legislation is in addition ambiguous. A distinction is made in the first clause of the Nurseries and Child Minders Act of 1948 between registration of premises and registration of persons in their homes, but the requirements for each category take no note of different circumstances. Interpretation by different local authorities differs widely. Some departments insist on registering in the name of an individual when the playgroup is now a group activity. It seems obvious, then, although the department must satisfy itself as to the suitability of people looking after the children, that it is the premises which should be registered. Some register both premises and persons in charge. Sometimes it is the person in charge of daily sessions who must be registered, though she is appointed and paid by the committee, a legally constituted charitable body. On the whole, playgroups cope with these idiosyncrasies, but they do create unnecessary confusion and tend to discourage involvement of parents in community effort.

Some departments make a distinction between playgroups and childminders in applying the legislation. In the Act itself there is no distinction (except for the two categories of registration), and in practice there are some instances where it is blurred. However, some departments keep separate lists on a subjective basis, and there appears to be a case for creating at least two categories with different requirements. This could be based on the ages of the children taken, the length of daily sessions, the number of sessions per week, and the number of adults caring for the children. Some parts of Scotland already recognise a distinction between part-time and full-time care for young children in the private sector, with more stringent regulations covering the latter. The safety and health of the children and the quality of care they are receiving is of prime importance for everyone. The requirements for registration of a childminder, alone in her home all day, caring for a group of children of all ages under five, must be stringent. She may have little support or supervision apart from periodic visits from the social worker. In a playgroup there must be at least two and possibly several involved people who can support each other. The possibility of abuse of the children is negligible, although oversight is very necessary to see that standards are maintained. Ample equipment of the right kind and a lot of space are needed for vigorous 3–5-year-olds, which might be inappropriate in a house with smaller children.

It is probably true that legislation cannot encourage the

positive aspects of playgroups, but only ensure that the dangerous and inadequate are controlled. Even here social changes could mean legislative changes in children's interests, for example the acknowledgement that smoking constitutes a 'risk'. There could, however, be clarification of registration procedures and a distinction between childminders, playgroups and day nurseries. In practice, most departments not only comply with the statutory requirements but also seek to integrate playgroups into the general caring provision of the department. Where there is an increasingly interested department, and an active voluntary branch, each with fieldworkers serving in the playgroups, it becomes necessary to agree on their roles and secure that what they are advising in the same groups is compatible.

Different backgrounds of people starting playgroups

Some of those who consider starting a playgroup are familiar with legislation and by-laws, and the fact that they have to apply for registration and conform to requirements. Even today, it comes to others as a surprise, perhaps at quite a late stage of preparation, perhaps after starting. (We noted in some job descriptions, 'Keep the public aware of the need for registration.')

They have become interested in a variety of ways, perhaps from magazine articles, each with a different approach. Some of these, but not all, paint a realistic picture of the rewards and responsibilities of starting a playgroup. TV programmes or short Open University courses lead to local inquiries. Increasingly, young parents assume there will be a local playgroup. But existing ones may be too far away, or not provide what the parent wants. A health visitor may encourage a likely group of parents to take the initiative. Some welcome a chance to exercise old training and skills while their children are small, others join in because they are enjoying their children and feel confident in joining with other people's.

The idea begins to take shape, and in chatting round parents find they have to register. Or a local PPA/SPPA branch makes contact and puts them on the trail. But there is a blurred line between children coming round to play – or playing as a church activity – and a playgroup, and it may take time before groups become involved in registration procedures. There may be some dismay when they find themselves faced with forms.

We had the variety of people and background in mind when we started to study registration procedures. At every stage we were struck by the immense difference between a person bringing information and discussing forms and the receipt of a bundle of these through the post. 'A system is as good as the people working in it.' And, we could add, 'Having time to work in it'.

Response to inquiries registration documents

The working group received sample registration documents from fifty-three social services departments in England and Wales. Of these, ten were London boroughs, sixteen were metropolitan districts, and twenty-seven were shire counties. We also received returns from eight out of nine regions and two out of three islands in Scotland. A lot of the material arising, whether in England, Wales or Scotland, is similar, and we have highlighted only the points of difference. We noted that no Scottish circular followed the Health Service and Public Health Act of 1968, and most authorities used at their discretion the Ministry of Health Circular with its guidelines.

Of the registration documents mentioned and listed here, which can be subdivided into 'information' and 'forms', no authority sent out all, the greatest number sent out being ten, and the average four or five. They included: letter in response to application; information booklet and/or information leaflet, often combined, concerning regulations; list of equipment required, and of suppliers; details of infectious diseases, incubation, etc.; requirements for first aid box; details of PPA/SPPA representatives (local AOs and branch personnel); information on grants available. Forms to be completed included: initial application form; health declaration; declaration of fitness to care for children (in Scotland 'the statement', now also included in one area as part of a leaflet on 'The Playleader'); X-ray form (to be presented to X-ray unit);

illness or accident report form; notice of change of playgroup staff; planning application; insurance application. At an advanced stage, a letter informing the applicant that registration would be approved subject to certain conditions was finally followed by a registration certificate.

Information
1 *Booklets*
These tended to replace earlier and more easily lost *leaflets*, and to contain attractively presented information on toys and equipment, playgroup activities, first aid, health and safety, advice on group responsibility, as well as the local authority department's requirements for space, toilets, washing facilities, heating and general suitability of premises, outside play-space, and fire regulations. The language in the best of these books was clear and everyday, the visual impact from illustrations good. We welcome this trend, away from a listed 'legal requirements and minimum standards for the reception of children covered', given to intending playgroups as the *only* written information. Although it is essential that these requirements are got across, the total impression in this form is negative – all rules and prohibitions, and not very helpful in building up a forward-looking well organised playgroup. Scotland's recommended series of five documents, put together by Scottish Association of Pre-school Advisers, in consultation with SPPA and the Social Work Services Group, has two information booklets, with an accent on concise material.

We gave considerable thought to the need for personal introduction and discussion of information documents and forms, remembering that after registration there will be changes among those running a playgroup and the booklets can be a useful form of reference. Descriptive material should therefore be encouraging and comprehensive, even when personally introduced. When not personally introduced, still more depends on clarity and interesting presentation.

2 *Lists of equipment and suppliers*
(Either as part of a booklet, or as separate sheets)
The most helpful lists were separate, and some were very
good, with equipment grouped and recognition of financial
limitations. Some offered alternatives, and recommended
improvisation. Useful advice was given on activities and
ways of using equipment.

3 *Information on infectious diseases, and first-aid box*
Useful lists, including incubation and exclusion periods,
were given, usually standard. Some recommended a
booklet on first aid. It would be helpful if more suggested
the keeping of an accident book. Standard lists of contents
stressed that first-aid boxes should be kept in a conspicuous
position, and contents replenished as used.

Forms

1 *Initial application form*
As with information booklets or leaflets, forms depend on
the method of presentation, and the assistance available to
persons not used to form filling. If personally introduced,
the form can obtain and give a lot of information at the
same time, and can be both extensive and practically
geared. If sent by post, it needs to be simple, clear and well
designed. There needs to be a limit on the information to be
expected, given that the inquirer may not be sure herself
what she can do. In this case, there should be only the
questions necessary to elicit basic details – name, address,
whether the applicant thinks of starting a playgroup or of
becoming a childminder, whether she has premises in
mind, whether she proposes to employ staff, how many
children she proposes to take. There should be some
indication that if she cannot answer the questions she can
discuss matters with a named person.

This type of simple form can lead to a visit for
clarification or for inspection of premises. Some authorities
use a commercially produced form which asks for name,
address, marital status, qualifications, proposed number of

children, proposed employees, and registration of persons resident at the premises. The back page of the form is a declaration of fitness for signature by the applicant. Other forms are extremely complicated, asking for nationality, registered offices of the company, description of situation, construction and accommodation of premises, etc. It may be a multipurpose form, but to anyone not used to form filling it can be extremely baffling. We did not receive enough details of procedures to know whether such forms are only completed with the help of the playgroup adviser. (We do know of instances where, with inside knowledge of what interests the authority, she has sat with a group and helped them to erase and amplify, and returned to the office to receive the completed form in an official capacity.)

2   *Health Declarations*
In England and Wales these tended to be standard in content, although varied in design, and in amount of detail required. They included:

(a)   Are you in good health at present?
(b)   Are you at present attending the doctor for any reason?
(c)   Do you have any treatment regularly prescribed by the doctor?
(d)   Have you suffered from a nervous or similar illness, and, if so, what age were you when this occurred?
(e)   Have you ever suffered from tuberculosis, epilepsy or fits?
(f)   When did you last have an X-ray (chest) and what was the result?
(g)   Is everyone in your household (including lodgers) as far as you know in good health?
(h)   Statement. I agree that the Director of Social Services (sometimes the Medical Officer) by whatever title may make any inquiries of my own doctor which he considers necessary. Address of doctor:

These forms have aroused more antagonism than any other part of the registration procedures. They ask for confidential information about which some individuals are extremely sensitive, without saying that it will be treated as confidential, and without always ensuring that it is returned in sealed envelopes only to the medical authorities. It is not unknown for such forms to be handed to the playgroup adviser or the playleader.

There has been great disquiet about questions (d) and (e). Mothers may suffer from post-natal depression which requires treatment, or indeed suffer depression due to the stress of bringing up a family, and may recover completely. No indication is given on the form as to the reaction to a 'yes' answer to these questions. It should surely be possible to provide a more reassuring approach on the lines of 'If you have ever suffered from . . . please attach a note giving the circumstances, and include permission for the Medical Officer to approach your doctor in confidence.' We have received one letter from a very concerned playleader called for a medical examination at the local clinic and given no indication as to its purpose or result. She deduced from the questions that this was a result of completing the form and giving details of post-natal depression many years earlier.

The statement in (h) also causes concern, for a number of reasons. If a medical inspection is called for by the local authority and a charge is made, who pays? In some authorities it is routine to make inquiries of the doctors of all applicants, and not only if forms show a further inquiry to be necessary. It is quite possible that a doctor may have little first-hand knowledge of a patient registered but not under treatment, so how useful are these reports? The form does not make clear to whom one's own doctor's report will be made available. Some mention the Director of Social Services, one authorised a medical history to be made available to the local council. Again the shortcomings of a postal form are evident, in relation to an offer of personal community service. It is difficult to see what information could be gained from this which could not be acquired from personal contact with the applicant, or, in any case of doubt, by asking an individual to give permission for her doctor to be approached.

Apart from the use of this form in registering, we have

received evidence of resistance to question (h) from playleaders or helpers expected to sign a health declaration on taking up work in a playgroup later. Sometimes they have crossed out the question, stating that they are willing to answer any further questions as required. There is strong feeling that blanket permission to obtain confidential information from a doctor is an infringement of privacy which could be allowed only in exceptional circumstances. Some individuals have been lost to playgroup work because they would not sign such a permission. Possibly social services departments should consider what has been gained as a result of making these inquiries which could not have been obtained in any other way, and weigh that against the resentment which has been caused.

In Scotland, the procedure is different. Three authorities write to the applicant's GP, asking him to return a slip stating whether the applicant is or is not suitable to look after children. One authority gives the applicant a slip to take to her GP, asking the same question. Another writes to the GP, and asks for a reference 'with regard to the applicant's medical fitness for this work'. Of the others who replied there is no evidence to show that they do ask for any kind of GP reference, although in two cases the name and address is asked for on the form. Only one division and one region ask about mental illness. In no case does anyone give permission for her GP to divulge confidential information.

3 *Declaration of fitness*
This is the only document expressly required by the Nurseries and Child Minders Act of 1948, as amended in 1968. Some authorities produce a simple statement as follows:

'Section 60(7) of the Health Services and Public Health Act requires a statement regarding each person employed and all over 16 normally resident or employed at the premises whether or not there has been against him any order removing a child from his care, or cancelling registration under the Nurseries and Child Minders regulations: and whether he/she has been convicted of any offence specified under the first schedule of the 1933 and 1937 Children's and Young Persons' Acts (i.e. various offences against the person, cruelty, indecency, assault).'

This is followed by a declaration: 'No order or conviction of the above nature has been made in respect of me, or of any person over the age of 16 normally resident in these premises or employed here and I agree to any inquiries being made.' This is signed by the childminder or playleader. Apart from its not in any way involving the group behind the employee, this would appear to be sufficient, both to satisfy the terms of the Act and from a practical point of view to be understood by anyone signing it. Some departments, however, publish all the references to the various Acts, leaving confusion in the mind of the applicant as to what precisely she is signing, and little chance of finding out. Others publish in detail and at length the relevant sections of the Acts, a catalogue of crime and cruelty which can leave people either bewildered or angry. Here again, local authorities might perhaps consider what they are trying to achieve, and the effect on applicants of the build-up and framing of the form. Can the requirements of the Act not be satisfied by the simpler and less off-putting version?

4   *X-ray forms*
Requirements for X-ray examinations – though, as SAPA points out, most people are quite happy to have one – have been a problem for years, because the facilities for taking X-rays are in some parts of the country few and far between.

Most authorities have made things as easy as possible, only expecting regular playleaders and assistants to be checked, and producing a form to be handed in at the X-ray unit. Nevertheless, some people have to make very long, expensive and time-consuming journeys to comply. In some rural areas of Scotland, the cost could be prohibitive.

5   *Milk application forms*
These have to be signed by the Director of Social Services on registration and it is obviously sensible for the playgroup adviser to provide the form, and take it to her department on completion for signature and send-off. It encourages the playgroup to provide milk for the children when it might otherwise be daunted at the prospect of yet more form filling.

6   *Illness or accident forms*
Some area health authorities expect playgroups to inform them of infectious illness in the playgroup. (It takes some research to find out to whom to send this information which is often only available after the child returns). If it is really useful, a stock of forms on which to send the report should be provided.

7   *Notification of change of staff*
With many other preoccupations, playgroups sometimes overlook the necessity of informing the social services departments of proposed appointments or departure of staff. A stock of forms on which the department should be notified might help to keep records up to date. (Many advisers have referred to the proportion of their time which has to be spent trying to keep records reliable.)

8   *Planning applications*
This tends to be a variable and unsatisfactory area of registration, and playgroup advisers can be very helpful in advising what is expected in their areas. The forms sent out by planning departments can be extremely complicated. Nevertheless, it is not necessarily a good thing for the adviser to deal with all formalities, and this is one area where applicants can, with some help, get a sense of achievement. It is also one in which fathers can make a contribution and feel knowledgeably involved. A playgroup adviser may also be useful behind the scenes, helping to expedite the passage of a planning application through a normal contact in the department. Scotland does not require planning permission for a playgroup in a public

hall, on the grounds that cars are allowed to stop outside, some noise is allowed, and the hall will be used by the public. Therefore use by a playgroup does not involve change of use.

Mastering all these documents and coming to grips with all requirements can bring a group down to earth. These weeks can also be a period of great learning, and there is a big area for co-operation between the statutory and voluntary support systems as is shown in the next Section 3. A note on the front of the Scottish documents expresses this: 'The preparation time before a group is ready to begin can vary from 2 to 6 months approximately, but taking time at this pre-registration period is valuable as it is the time when the people involved learn to work together finding premises, and dealing with finance, staffing, equipment and the introduction of children and their mothers.' Some inquirers will have decided to go no further. For those who proceed, *the initial application form* completed is now returned to the department, whose job of processing and checking then begins. In many areas, good personal contact has already been established, and the adviser has become familiar with applicants and premises.

Checking of applicants and conditions of acceptance

It is clear from material sent by local authorities that some have highly developed checking systems for registration, while others rely more on personal contact with applicants and recommendations from advisers. The choice relates to the work-load of an adviser, the extent of her other responsibilities and the number of her assistants. It relates also to the size of population. Some London boroughs have most elaborate written records.

Some systems of checking

On receipt of a completed application form, even though requested repairs to premises will take time, the playgroup adviser opens a file. The following is a detailed pattern of procedure which some, but by no means all, departments follow through. A check-list, detailing various steps, is attached to the front of the file, and ticked and dated as the various papers are sent out and received back. (This can cover two sides of A4 paper). A reprint of relevant parts of the 1968 Act and other legislation is placed on the file together with the department's own additional requirements. The application form, completed by the applicant or by the adviser on her initial visit, is placed on the file. The adviser completes an initial assessment form, possibly lengthy, and including details of the building, size, toilets, washing facilities, state of decoration and cleanliness, heating and lighting, safety or exits, etc., as well as impressions of general suitability of premises, need in the area, and of staff and equipment available. Standard letters are sent out asking for information as to the suitability of people or premises to: fire officer, medical officer, or doctor, referees given by applicant, library, planning department, police, central records department, day care department. If these are favourable, he/she prepares a recommendation to whoever issued the certificate (social services/work committee, Director of Social Services, the authority's legal department, etc.)

It is obvious that most local authorities have given much time and thought to devising efficient systems. The process of checking needs as much care as the provision of information and forms. Further thought needs to be given to the balance which is kept between ensuring that registration is done efficiently and allowing people to take responsibility for things within their capacity, such as applications to fire officers, library, planning, etc. References may need to be taken up, but by no means all departments ask for them, and there are different kinds of referee. The point was made by SPPA that taking up references would be more meaningful if guidelines were provided for comment. Some may be inexperienced in this field, and not know where to start. One authority has raised recently the query whether under Schedule 1, Chapter 42, of the Local Authorities Social Services Act of 1970 they should have the function of taking up references relating exclusively to persons employed in playgroups, which is incompatible with recognising the responsibilities of a playgroup committee as employer. Not all of the working party were aware that in some areas routine inquiries concerning all applicants were made to the police. In Scotland, the practice was declining, only two regions now making police checks. If all applicants were aware, it might cause considerable disquiet. At least one police force has declined to deal with such inquiries on the grounds that it takes more exceptional circumstances than the appointment of a playleader for them to divulge information. It would be helpful to know which inquiries are merely part of routine, and whether any assessment of their value has been made. Although it is open to an adviser to make extensive inquiries about an applicant about whom she has reservations, routines can become ends in themselves. Why, also, does there seem to be no place for talk with the playgroup committee, as one of the checks to be made?

Most playgroup advisers like to have an adequate system to guide them through all stages leading to registration, provided that they do not have to spend more time writing reports than dealing with the people involved. Although some systems described were extremely detailed, it would appear that the majority served their purpose. At the opposite extreme we record the correspondent who contributed: 'Never in any area did I find anything remotely to be classified as a system.' It is noteworthy that during the extensive checking formalities the department's representative can be building up relationships with the playgroup, and with the area organiser working with it, which will last beyond the issue of a registration certificate.

Issue of Registration

1 **Letter outlining the conditions for registration**
   Some but not all social services departments send out a letter under Section 6 of the Act, informing the applicant of their intent to impose conditions for registration, giving 14 days to appeal, if not satisfied. If not warned of the significance of such a letter, applicants may be totally mystified. Most authorities provide the playgroup with a list of the conditions for compliance – usually a standard form issued to all their playgroups and concerning the number of children to be taken, provision of food, safety

arrangements; etc. In a number of areas there is now increasing consultation between department and PPA before these conditions are finalised and changing conditions will thereafter mean periodic, sometimes frequent adjustment. It is likely that the branch or county organisation will be able to agree on guidelines rather than on a definitive statement, thus preserving the flexibility distinctive of voluntary organisations. Nevertheless, it is extremely valuable for this consultation to have taken place when the department formulates its 'conditions'.

2 **Registration certificate**
The registration certificate, sometimes elaborate, sometimes just a duplicated sheet, is issued in compliance with Section 3 of the Act. It marks the end of a process which can take anything from a few weeks to many months.

Ongoing oversight

The department responsible continues its oversight by visiting, which is considered partly in Section 3, based on a questionnaire to playgroups, and partly in Section 5, based on job descriptions; by grant aid, which is discussed in Section 6, based on facts and figures from departments, and in Section 9, based on interviews with directors of social services departments; and by review, the aims and practice of which are still in a formative stage. It is of interest that of the set of documents devised for use in Scotland, No. 5, 'Review of Registration', has been the least taken up. Nevertheless, in planning this form, the Scottish Association of Playgroup Advisers (now SAAUFF) was endorsing the view that a periodic review is a necessary part of the overall care of playgroups.

Ongoing oversight cannot be considered apart from the elements of care, encouragement and support which have been built by many authorities into their basic legal role. These extended functions cannot be considered apart from the voluntary system of support; their interaction has already been introduced in the study of registering procedures.

When PPA centrally receives inquiries from individuals wishing to start playgroups, it follows a procedure which has changed radically within the last two or three years. A standard letter used to be sent from London, together with a list of publications available, a leaflet explaining briefly what playgroups do, a membership application form and the name and address of the nearest local area organiser. With the development of regional offices, it has become possible to make a much more personally geared response. The central inquiry is now referred to the appropriate office, and thence followed by a personal letter and full information about the supporting network which the inquirer could join.

Many social services departments refer applications at an early stage to the local branch and its area organiser, and in at least one region of Scotland membership of SPPA, with all its benefits of experience, is a condition of registration. As was said earlier, it is sometimes the PPA/SPPA branch which makes an inquirer aware that it must seek out the social services/work department. The new playgroup is thus likely to be aware very early that there is a local statutory network and a national voluntary network which will both be interested, and which will both have information and support to offer. The amount of help that anyone can get from PPA/SPPA will depend on the strength of the voluntary organisation in that area, and some local authority advisers rate highly among their duties the encouragement and strengthening of the branch. The amount of help forthcoming from the authority will depend on the time allocation for people to spend on this work, and the support for them within the department.

Playgroups and procedures

A small survey was done of playgroup reactions to their experiences when starting. These came from playgroups which opened within the past two years (1975–7), mainly in areas surveyed in detail by the working group. The total number was thirty five. They were asked to describe their experiences in their own words, but were also specifically asked who helped them, and what they thought of the registration forms and procedures. The main preoccupation was, as might be expected, the practical difficulties encountered – finding premises, fund raising, arranging storage space and other facilities, relationships with landlords, etc. The help they received varied tremendously but the majority did eventually get help from one source or another. We can never know how many playgroups never got off the mark because they did not receive enough help.

Not all the playgroups commented on registration procedures. Of those who did, some were brief: 'The premises were inspected by Social Services and passed' or 'The premises were inspected by Social Services who required certain work to be done.' From these it can be inferred that the departments in those areas either saw their role purely as inspecting and registering or arranged for other agencies (for example PPA/SPPA) to give the necessary help and support. At the other end of the scale was the comment that the social services department 'guided us through, couldn't have been more helpful', were 'the main source of help'. These are in a majority. A number found that the department referred them to PPA for literature or contact with the AO for additional help. One playgroup adviser was credited with telling a group 'all the numerous snags', whereas in another case the applicants felt they should have been warned about these. One person felt there was little expertise in her part of the country and could find no one who knew about registering playgroups! It appears that she and a friendly social worker learnt about it together. In another case, the only person who knew anything was off sick, causing a lot of difficulties!

One problem mentioned several times was that of delays. It can be most frustrating for an enthusiastic group to be held up by unexplained delays. In one case it took three weeks for initial information to come through. In two cases the fire inspection did not take place for weeks after the approach. Another experienced delay in hearing from PPA.

Comments on registration forms were equally divided between those who accepted them as necessary and creating no problems, and those who saw them as 'tedious, unnecessary, off-putting and irrelevant'. It has not been possible within our resources to correlate these reactions with the local described pattern of procedure, but what little evidence we have suggests that it may not be the actual forms which cause trouble so much as lack of help with them, especially if the person concerned was not accustomed to form filling. (Although one may wonder why an applicant had to state her husband's occupation.) Some playgroups were undoubtedly helped to complete the forms, though not all mentioned this. Some who were not so helped speak of 'piles of forms a mile high', or 'forms in quadruplicate'. Several did complain of the unnecessary complexity of scale drawings of the building.

It is clear that most playgroups have to overcome what they see as considerable hurdles before they can start. One which apparently had to deal with most of its problems with little help felt that 'a lot of determination was required'; another said 'we nearly became disenchanted.' It may be no bad thing to have to show determination, since that will continue to be needed. It did seem that underlying the complaints was a real sense of achievement in having overcome the problems, and great enthusiasm for making the playgroup a success.

Summary

The legislation concerned with registration is ambiguous and interpreted differently by different authorities. It was not designed to meet the needs of playgroup registration, and may occasionally be inappropriately deterrent; further, the fact that it centres on an individual rather than a group runs counter to the ethos of group-controlled playgroups. The legislation controls provision (and this is needed) but does not positively promote good practice. The only satisfactory way of coping with the variety of playgroup provision is through personal contact, which gives flexibility.

Local authorities generally send out four or five documents from a variety of seventeen or more types, and some may be very complicated. Again respondents stressed the need for personal contact, though written material is also useful, especially as it serves as a more permanent help for rapidly changing playgroup personnel. Most concern was expressed about the health forms, which were often seen as an infringement of privacy; the situation seems to be better in Scotland. References are differently taken up by different local authorities – in some cases (it would seem) without the applicant's knowledge – and the usefulness of many of these inquiries is questionable.

It is important for local authority staff to use the time taken over registration to build up a good relationship with the playgroup and to judge the nice balance between doing things fast and efficiently and enabling the playgroup members to do things for themselves and grow in achievement. Attention must also be paid to the interacting support systems, statutory and voluntary, to make the most of both.

There are big differences across Britain – between simple and complicated forms, between departments with elaborate systems and those with none, and between playgroups receiving much help and others receiving little or none. The difficulties involved in achieving registration are real, but may help playgroup members to be realistic.

Questions

1 Is there a case for greater consultation between statutory and voluntary bodies on local guidelines for interpreting legislation?

2 Is there a case for greater co-operation between statutory and voluntary bodies in the production and issue of informative literature?

3 Does personal introduction of registration procedures help to foster better links between voluntary and professional bodies?

4 Should the current practice in taking up references be given careful reconsideration?

5 Should the group responsibility of the playgroup committee (where there is one) be clearly recognised in all registration procedures?

6 What amendments are needed to the Nursery and Child Minders Act in order to take account of the different forms of day care now covered by its provisions?

7   How can legislation be made sufficiently flexible to allow for future changes and developments in thinking about the under-fives and their families?

3

Impact of Oversight and Support as Recorded in Playgroups: Response to the Playgroup Questionnaire

Central to our investigation into patterns of oversight and support is the playgroup itself. In order to try to obtain some assessment of what playgroups experience on the receiving end of the statutory and voluntary support network, a questionnaire was drawn up, designed to be administered by interviewers, who would complete it during a dialogue with members of each playgroup selected. The interview method was chosen because we were aware that the response to postal questionnaires can be both low in quantity and poor in content.

The method

Our interviewers all worked on a voluntary basis. They were recruited by the following criteria: they must be familiar with playgroups, but must not, on the other hand, be known to any of the groups they interviewed, or be seen by those groups as having some formal role (whether in statutory or voluntary services) which could affect the way in which playgroups answered the questions.

Because we were going to have to sort the results manually, we were restricted to an upper limit of about 200 questionnaires, and therefore had to adopt a process of selective sampling. After considerable thought about what was practicable, our final choice fell on the geographical area covered by PPA's Southern Region, with six local authorities (Buckinghamshire, Berkshire, Hampshire, Gloucestershire, Dorset and Oxfordshire), and Merseyside, with five local authorities, to ensure that we covered an urban population density. In Scotland, the same pattern was followed, with Tayside Region and the Lanark Division of Strathclyde as chosen areas.

If we had used a simple distribution of questionnaire per number of registered playgroups, this would have left us with too low an overall number in both Merseyside and Scotland and we were in any case principally concerned with differences between authorities. We therefore decided to allocate 120 to the Southern Region and 40 each to Merseyside and Scotland. Allocation of questionnaires within the Southern Region was made proportional to the number of playgroups in each county, and the same principle was applied to the metropolitan districts in Merseyside, the divisions within Strathclyde and the districts within Tayside. The results gave us a sample of approximately 1 in 15 groups in the Southern Region, and 1 in 10 in Merseyside and Scotland.

Of our possible total of 200 questionnaires, the returns were as follows:

Southern Region	109
Merseyside	34
Scottish areas	40
total	183

The discrepancy of 17 between the theoretical maximum and actual returns is explained partly by the application of random number selection and partly by occasional failure to complete the maximum number of interviews possible.

We used seventeen interviewers in the Southern Region, five in Merseyside and five in Scotland. The interviewers did some trial runs on neighbouring playgroups before coming together for briefing meetings. Any problems were then talked out with designated members of the working group, and agreement on strategy reached. Selection of actual playgroups was made from the complete list of registered playgroups as supplied by social services (social work) departments. A group of less than eight children, however listed, was not considered to be a playgroup for the purpose of this study. Using random number tables, each interviewer selected the appropriate number of playgroups from within her designated local authority, county, district or division, and then made arrangements with the playgroup when to visit. We endeavoured wherever possible to include both playgroup staff and members of the playgroup committee at the interview.

The questionnaire

The questionnaire focused on two aspects of the support network; first the visits made to the playgroup from statutory and voluntary agencies and also from other members of the community, often with specialist knowledge to offer; and second the places outside the playgroup where help and support were obtained. While this included open meetings of all kinds, attended by playgroup members, it excluded playgroup courses, whether held in playgroups, and drawing largely on internal resources, or jointly planned with other agencies (see the Introduction). Any groups which had opened within the last two years were asked to describe their own experience of registration procedures (see Section 1).

Background of the playgroups involved

Playgroups were asked to assess from what kind of area their children were drawn (they were allowed to indicate more than one category).

From suburban areas (this includes both private and council housing)	48%
From rural areas	33%
From small towns	20%
From new towns	11%
From inner cities	8%

The largest playgroup interviewed had 40 children per session, the smallest had 8. 70 per cent of all groups were held in some kind of communal hall; 3 per cent had purpose-built premises and 7 per cent were in private houses. The remainder were in a number of 'other' premises.

Of all groups 37 per cent were 'privately' controlled, 45 per cent were controlled by an elected committee, and 11 per cent by some other organisation which provided the group. The proportion of 'private' groups was higher in England than in Scotland, and so also was the number of 'provided' groups.

Responsibility for replying to the questionnaire
Since playgroups are most accessible during the actual session, it is not surprising that in 61 per cent of the groups the questions were answered by the playleader and helpers. These were joined in 27 per cent of the groups by members of the committee, and in 2 per cent members of the committee answered alone. (There seems to be no record of a joint response by all the parents involved.)

The findings

In presenting these, the findings from all three areas have been considered. Dependent upon the picture resulting, we have either given separate findings or expressed them in composite form. Interesting variations between the three areas, or in some cases between local authorities within the areas, have been pointed out.

Question 1   In the last twelve months, who has visited the playgroup and how often?
Visitors fell broadly into two groups: first, those who might be considered to visit primarily as part of an advisory, supervisory or supportive role; and, second, those who visited through the playgroup's links with the community in general. Some visitors in the second category would in fact also offer advice and support, but as a 'spin-off' rather than from primary intent to do so.

In the *first category* were social services work advisers; social workers; health visitors; PPA/SPPA advisers, area organisers or branch visitors, and training and development officers (these were not distinguished in our questions); and local education authority advisers. In the *second category* were included nursery and infant teachers, staff from secondary schools, representatives of the landlord, and a host of 'other' visitors specified by the playgroups.

In the Southern Region and Scotland Areas we found that the most frequent visitors in the *first category* were PPA/SPPA (advisers, AOs, etc.), followed by social services/work advisers, with health visitors in the third place. On Merseyside we found that the social services advisers visited most frequently, followed by the health visitor, with the social worker in third place.

The number of visits received by any one playgroup over the past twelve months was much the same for all three areas, averaging at seven for Merseyside and the Southern Region and six for the Scottish areas.

The identity of the most frequent visitor varied considerably between authorities. In five it was the social services/work adviser; in another five it was PPA; in three the health visitor; in one the local education authority adviser, and in one the community education organiser. In one authority the Save the Children Fund visited frequently, as did community development officers.

When visitors in the *second category* were added in we found that playgroups in the Southern Region were visited on average seventeen times a year, although one playgroup recorded no visits at all. Playgroups in the Scottish areas and on Merseyside received an average of eleven visits a year, but within one Merseyside authority there were an additional fourteen visits a year, making an average of twenty-five per playgroup. In practice there is considerable variation in the number of visits received between one playgroup and another.

It is worth noting that on Merseyside secondary-school staff visited a total of thirty-seven times, these visits being related to the large number of secondary-school placements on community projects.

The range of other visitors specified by the playgroups is of interest as it shows quite a high level of interaction between the community and the playgroups. Highest on the list from all three areas were teenagers on community projects. Students from related courses such as National Nurseries Examination Board, child care and pre-nursing, were high on the list in both

English areas. Playgroup-course students were also frequent visitors in the Southern Region. Old-age pensioners were involved with a number of Merseyside playgroups and police, road safety officers, Tufty Club organisers, representatives of local churches, and community workers of different kinds, in all three. On Merseyside people participating in Manpower Services Commission schemes were also mentioned. Some twenty-five other categories of occasional visitors were referred to.

The diversity of possible visitors on Merseyside was much greater than in the other two areas, and the amount of PPA activity was (perhaps consequently) lower.

Playgroups were asked whether they felt they were visited enough, too much or too little. Just over 50 per cent felt they were visited enough, about 40 per cent though they were not visited enough, and 3 per cent said they were visited too much. It appeared that the Scottish playgroups were visited less than the English ones, although 62 per cent said they were visited enough. It can be seen that these subjective assessments do not relate to the actual number of visits received. A frequent comment from all areas was that they were not visited enough by the 'right' people, or that they would have preferred more visits from one specified person, often named as the health visitor or other statutory adviser.

The many thousands of playgroup parents who visit the playgroups are not of course included in any of the above discussion. Many of them will have made important contributions to the running of the playgroup, and many will have received help from it, over and above the benefit to their children. However, the parents are conceived as being part and parcel of the playgroup and cannot be viewed as 'external' visitors. The parents *are* the playgroup.

Question 2   What help have you received from these visits, either at the time or as a consequence of the visit, and from whom?
Playgroups were asked to indicate what each visitor had achieved, whether positively or negatively, and following a standard list, with results set out in Table 1.

In order to arrive at an answer to the question, the interviewers were briefed to select those visitors who in discussion with the playgroup emerged as having made an impact, whether positively or negatively, and to complete a 'Question 2 sheet' for each of them.

In all, 488 such visitors were selected, an average of three per playgroup. 22 per cent of these were social service/work advisers, 18 per cent PPA/SPPA visitors, 14 per cent health visitors, 9 per cent social workers, 4 per cent were LEA advisers and 2 per cent 'other' advisers. The remaining 31 per cent were spread across the range of visitors referred to above (Question 1).

This follows closely the total number of visits made by each category of visitor (see Question 1). However, it would be an oversimplification to conclude from this that the most frequent visitor was necessarily always the most helpful in the playgroup's eyes. There were in any case variations from the overall pattern between one area and another, health visitors in the Southern Region visiting proportionately more often. On Merseyside, social services advisers predominated, although in both Scotland and the Southern Region, PPA and social services/work appeared to share the visiting equally.

Table 1 **The kinds of help visitors offered (or failed to offer) and received.**

Looking at the kinds of help which were offered by different categories of visitor, we found that in the Southern Region and Scottish areas it was the PPA/SPPA visitors, and on Merseyside the social services visitors who appeared to bring most material help and information, to make helpful suggestions about the running of the playgroup session, and to give general encouragement.

In the Southern Region and on Merseyside, the social services playgroup adviser caused the most extra problems, or in the playgroup's estimation neither gave nor received help. In the Scottish areas studied, no visitors appear to cause problems, but social workers were most often mentioned as neither giving nor receiving help. It is probable that these

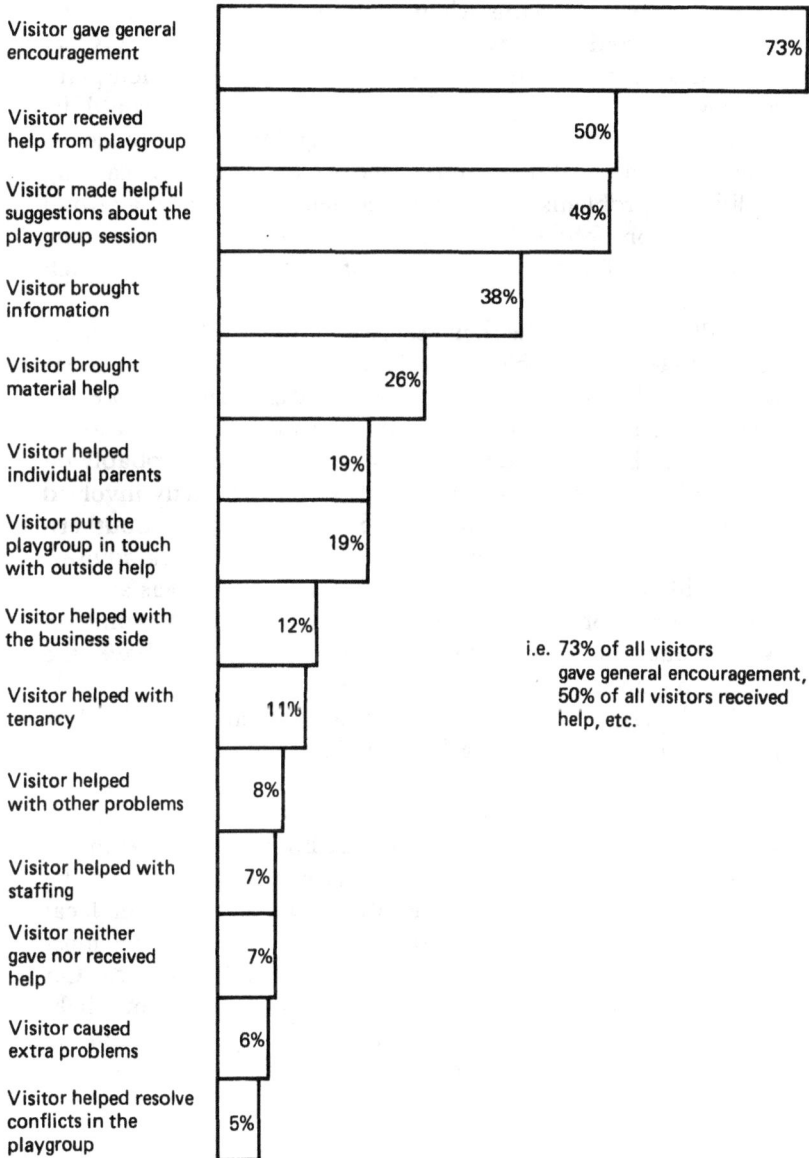

Visitor gave general encouragement	73%
Visitor received help from playgroup	50%
Visitor made helpful suggestions about the playgroup session	49%
Visitor brought information	38%
Visitor brought material help	26%
Visitor helped individual parents	19%
Visitor put the playgroup in touch with outside help	19%
Visitor helped with the business side	12%
Visitor helped with tenancy	11%
Visitor helped with other problems	8%
Visitor helped with staffing	7%
Visitor neither gave nor received help	7%
Visitor caused extra problems	6%
Visitor helped resolve conflicts in the playgroup	5%

i.e. 73% of all visitors gave general encouragement, 50% of all visitors received help, etc.

answers reflect occasions when a routine inspection was being carried out, and the playgroup was either unaware of this fact or regarded it as something to be tolerated but, from their point of view, having no particular value. 'Problems' could be caused by having to comply with regulations. Both social workers and health visitors were mentioned as causing additional problems and receiving help from the playgroup when they brought a child in need of a place. There was some indication of failure on the part of both to follow up such placements.

In all three areas, the social services/work advisers gave most help with tenancy problems; and landlords in the Scottish areas were helpful, though much less so on Merseyside. However, landlords on Merseyside were quoted as giving quite a lot of help on the business side of the playgroup. It can probably be assumed that this refers to landlords who are directly involved on the playgroup committee. In Scotland and the Southern Region, this help came from the social services/work adviser. Help with staffing was mainly given, in Scottish areas and the Southern Region, by social services/work and PPA, while on Merseyside the only help recorded was by the Save the Children Fund to their own playgroups.

Health visitors gave a great deal of help to individual parents, particularly in the Southern Region.

When it came to putting the playgroup in touch with outside help, SPPA seemed most active in the Scottish areas, and the social services adviser in both parts of England, backed in the Southern Region by the LEA adviser. One county in the Southern Region differed noticeably from all the other local authorities covered, in that the LEA adviser was the most frequent, and generally the most helpful, visitor. On Merseyside, social workers gave proportionately more help than in the other areas. PPA contributed less there than in the other two areas, but nevertheless accounted for the majority of visits in one district.

Questions 3 and 5   The contribution of meetings

Turning to the encouragement which playgroup members

sought outside the playgroup, we asked about the value of meetings.

Table 2   **Who organised meetings attended by adults from the playgroup?**

2% 5%   8%   12% 15%   58%

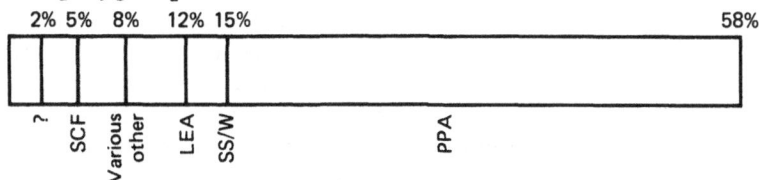

In the Southern Region, more meetings were run by PPA and the LEA, but fewer by social workers. On Merseyside more were run by a mixture of social services and other agencies, including 5 per cent by SCF, but fewer by PPA or LEA. In the Scottish areas more were run by SPPA and social work departments, but fewer by LEAs and other agencies. In all three areas, however, PPA/SPPA was the largest single organiser of meetings.

Attendance at these meetings was quite high. Only 7 per cent of all playgroups interviewed said they did not attend any meetings.

What did playgroups get out of meetings?
Playgroups in all three areas gave the same order of priority for what they got out of meetings:

Friendship; ideas for working with children; material help; help on business matters; and varied other help. Only 3 per cent said they got nothing out of the meetings they attended.

Question 4   Sources of information
We wanted to know how the playgroup got to hear about meetings and outside sources of help such as playgroup courses not organised in the playgroup, toy libraries, bulk-buying facilities, etc. We found that the main source of information was via PPA/SPPA newsletters, local and national (*Contact Magazine*), and secondly by word of mouth. Other sources of information included visitors to the playgroup, posters and the press.

Question 6   Looking for help

This question was complementary to Question 1, detailing where playgroups would look for outside help if needed. We found that in matters referring to home, child and family problems, the health visitor would be consulted, with the social services/work adviser as next choice. On matters to do with playgroup premises or tenancy they would turn to the social services/work adviser, with the PPA/SPPA as second choice. For help with other business matters they would turn first to PPA/SPPA and second to the social services/work adviser. On staffing problems this would be reversed.

Questions 7 and 8   To what extent is a playgroup conscious of needing support and does it feel it gets what it needs?

How much help does a playgroup, functioning normally, require? 96 per cent said they could cope with their own problems, 1 per cent said they were not coping, 1 per cent qualified their answer in some way (2 per cent did not answer). We did not get information about groups which had not managed and therefore ceased to exist, and responses thus indicated that a playgroup which is running successfully finds ways of dealing with problems which arise. Several said they would have liked more help at the early stages of their existence. 67 per cent said they were getting the help they needed, 16 per cent that they were not, and 16 per cent qualified their answer in some way.

General comments from those analysing the results

Taking together the actual number of visits to playgroups, the number of meetings and the communication network organised by PPA, there emerges a picture of a voluntary network which overall makes the biggest recorded impact upon playgroups. Since it is the playgroups themselves who bring this network into being, and produce the individuals willing to work within it, this is scarcely surprising. However, playgroups may not necessarily always be aware of the hidden help frequently given by both social services/work and education departments in supporting this voluntary network.

We have already referred to our reasons for excluding courses from our questionnaire. Playgroup courses are run in England by a variety of agencies, including PPA (roughly half of all courses), but in Scotland SPPA is the main and often the only agency offering these. It is not always a straightforward matter to distinguish courses from meetings, where the former are informal, and held in a variety of premises, including the playgroup. An increasing number of courses for parents and playgroup helpers are run in the playgroup itself. We noted that tutors from playgroup courses made a total of 84 visits, 37 of which were in one county. We cannot tell whether this included occasions on which the tutor actually ran a course in the playgroup itself, or whether it refers only to visits made by tutors from courses run in colleges and elsewhere who were following up students working in the playgroup.

It would seem from the comments made by playgroups that many would like more visits from people who in their eyes can offer 'specialist' help. The social services/work adviser and the health visitor were mentioned. Playgroups did not ask for more visits from PPA personnel, possibly because these are taken for granted, but clearly found PPA meetings a major source of encouragement, not usually paralleled elsewhere.

We noted that there was very little mention of contact between playgroups and other sources of professional advice, for example, speech therapy or child guidance which must be a cause for concern.

Very few groups thought themselves over-visited, and most had a positive attitude towards being visited, and enjoyed visits even where they did not need help. A few said that they preferred to ask for help when they wanted it.

Finally it must be stated that, while the picture which emerges is on the whole one of playgroups coping adequately in their own terms, it should not necessarily be interpreted as meaning that they would not welcome or do not need any increased input from both statutory and voluntary support services.

Comments from the PPA/SPPA network

Questions to branch/county/district officers and committees

filled out some of the findings in the playgroup questionnaire.

There seemed to be some difference of view. Even though PPA/SPPA visitors were active (the most active of all in Southern Region and the parts of Scotland surveyed), branches/counties/districts of PPA/SPPA felt the level to be inadequate, even though it was agreed that some of the work of AOs would not be recorded in playgroup visits – a lot was in relation to the committee side of playgroups (Section 5 showed that much support was needed about the process of applying for and using grant aid), and a lot was given in telephone calls. 'Visitors', for a few playgroups, were used to ease the load locally, and contact was kept by these or similar 'links' who delivered magazines and news. They might or might not become the experienced area organisers. The branch/ county/district officers did not reckon as a rule to visit, except in unusual crises, but they would on occasion back up an AO, and they would talk with playgroup leaders when they met in the range of courses and meetings. In Scotland, they appeared to do more actual playgroup visits, a committee member sometimes being responsible for two playgroups. The number of people available and the number of visits they could make depended largely on distances to be covered, notably in isolated rural areas in Scotland, and the question of finance is again involved. An interesting comment comes from the Scottish network – that if the structure including region, division, districts and branches is to be meaningful, playgroups need visits from people working at regional and divisional level, which at present does not happen.

It was not possible to get to know people purely by going to meetings. The network was two-way. At branch level, contact and help became more personal and included chairing playgroup AGMs, helping start new playgroups, helping with introductory courses. Another comment is that, where there is interest in the work of AOs, there are usually job descriptions for them. Where there are not job descriptions 'it would appear that little thought has been given to their work. We wonder whether the lack of thought is the reason for the lack of AOs.' One branch quotes each AO working twelve sessions a month, of which nine are playgroup visits (a session is usually defined as a morning, an afternoon or an evening). Nevertheless, there seems the impression that much more visiting could be done if more people were available.

These retuns from the network substantiate the findings from the playgroup questionnaire, that there is a lively programme of meetings and 'happenings' which people share in with interest – some providing a service, such as bulk-buying, or loan of equipment; some training for AOs, or committee members or visitors; others expressing common interest, and providing link-up points, and channels for extending skills and enlarging experience. This can be the value of attending in many cases, rather than specific need for help. (Gaps are quoted. In one area, 'County visitors visit playgroups in their sessions. Experienced county officers would surely have considerable expertise to offer playgroup committees, but little is offered, and this would appear a missed opportunity.')

The web of meetings at every level is wide, and makes it reasonably possible for people to attend. At district level, in Scotland for example, 'Support meetings include AOs' meetings, play leaders' meetings, meetings to help newly formed/forming branches, training and fund-raising meetings, apart from their average of ten committee meetings a year.' This, however, needs to be tied up with the findings of the playgroup questionnaire that individuals involved at playgroup level go to fewer meetings in Scotland than in England.

There are a number of comments to the effect that certain authorities make specific appointments of 'project leaders' under across-agency schemes, or of fieldworkers to what the Wolfenden Report would count 'specialist intermediary groups'. These are able to supplement the amount of visiting in playgroups, though they stand in a different relationship to normal PPA branch structures. PPA/SPPA at regional level is also able to contribute short-term fieldworkers on special assignments. But the AO or visitor coming from a confident, interested branch seems to be the main answer to the need for more playgroup visiting.

The comment was made, again from Scotland, that a local communications officer appointment had been given high priority, in the belief that this would develop the branch and from the branch would stem more AOs and visitors. This linked two forms of support, visiting and training, in a programme of branch meetings, instead of making them 'either/or'. Meetings strengthened the branch and made more AOs and visitors likely.

Summary

Playgroup visitors fall into two broad categories: those who visit primarily in a supervisory or supportive role and those (for example landlords, local teachers) who do not. The average number of visits by the first category was 7 (England) or 6 (Scotland). PPA/SPPA were the most frequent visitors in Southern England and Scotland; in Merseyside social services departments visited most often; but the role of the actual person who visited varied greatly from place to place. The frequency of visits by those in the second category ranged from 25 per year in one authority (Merseyside) to one playgroup that claimed to have had no visitors at all. Over thirty different categories of visitors were named, 'teenagers' being the most common. Just over half of the English playgroups thought they were visited 'enough', and 62 per cent Scottish (even though the latter were visited less often). Most visitors were received as helpful, but 13 per cent were said to have had no impact or to have caused extra problems. (Possibly many in this category were routine inspections or the placement of a needy child.)

Outside sources of help

Meetings for the adult playgroup members were mainly (58 per cent) organised by PPA/SPPA and were a major source of encouragement: all but 7 per cent of playgroups interviewed said they went (a lower proportion in Scotland). The main gain from meetings was friendship, followed by ideas for play sessions and material help. They heard of meetings and other sources of help mainly through PPA/SPPA newsletters. Playgroup members differentiated between possible sources of help according to the particular problem with which they were dealing; nevertheless 96 per cent of playgroups thought they could cope on their own. (Of course, those playgroups that needed help and didn't get it may have closed and therefore have not been included in the survey.) Many playgroups would have liked more visits from specialist sources of help, and there was a worryingly low incidence of contact with, for example, speech therapists and child guidance.

Branch/district/regional committees felt that visiting by their members was inadequate, even when the additional help given by phone was taken into consideration; and that this lack was because not enough visitors were available. The other important factor affecting the numbers of AOs and visitors was the amount of interest shown by the supporting branch. Besides visits, help was given with AGMs, courses, etc., but few visits are made to playgroup committees *per se*. There is a wide variety of meetings on offer. Each source of support seems to strengthen and support each other.

Questions

1   How effective is visiting as a form of: (a) legal oversight? (b) support?
2   Are playgroups aware of the statutory responsibility to visit them?
3   How can a proper balance be maintained between the needs of children and parents during the playgroup session and the value of visitors, even if they cause distractions?
4   How can contacts be increased with speech therapy, child guidance and other forms of specialist help?
5   How can we help both PPA/SPPA and local authorities to see that visits to playgroup committees are visits to an integral part of playgroups?

4

Persons in Support of Playgroups
(based on facts and figures from fifty three local authority departments, with some comments on workloads and communication from groups of advisers in post)

Local authority departments are interested in the number of playgroup places needed compared with those available, and in the number of persons necessary to oversee and support these. Fifty three deprtments sent us relevant facts and figures. In this section, material from England and Wales (44 departments) is presented separately from that received from Scotland (9).

Playgroup places and playgroups in England and Wales

Although we had asked for the total number of children under five in each local authority, answers were given from such a range of sources and over such a wide period that it was decided to use a common source for all, this being the Registrar-General's 1976 estimates.

In order to achieve a baseline from which to work, while at the same time avoiding as far as possible the production of a league table effect, local authorities in England and Wales were first listed according to their total number of children under *five* and the resulting list, in descending order of size, numbered 1–44 (Table 3).

The numbers 1–44 given to the local authorities in this table have been retained throughout Sections 4 and 6. In each subsequent table, the first column of figures gives the reference numbers for the local authorities described above.

This study being of the oversight and support given to

Table 3 Population aged under 5 in 44 local authorities

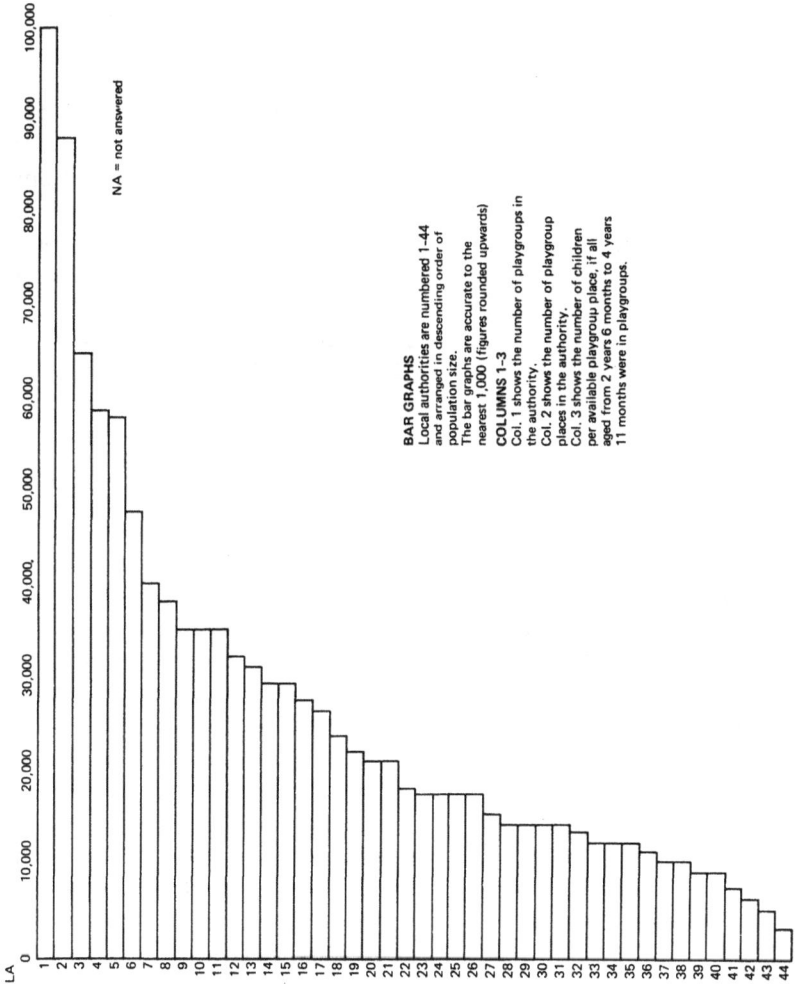

NA = not answered

BAR GRAPHS
Local authorities are numbered 1–44
and arranged in descending order of
population size.
The bar graphs are accurate to the
nearest 1,000 (figures rounded upwards)

COLUMNS 1–3
Col. 1 shows the number of playgroups in
the authority.
Col. 2 shows the number of playgroup
places in the authority.
Col. 3 shows the number of children
per available playgroup place, if all
aged from 2 years 6 months to 4 years
11 months were in playgroups.

LA	COL. 1	COL. 2	COL. 3
1	NA	13,066	3·8
2	308	7,720	5·7
3	287	6,000	5·4
4	262	6,246	4·7
5	261	5,974	4·8
6	207	6,026	4·0
7	285	10,236	2·3
8	299	6,062	3·4
9	241	5,562	3·5
10	190	4,934	3·9
11	221	5,976	3·1
12	297	5,525	3·2
13	204	4,304	3·9
14	371	6,266	2·6
15	94	2,589	6·2
16	102	2,235	6·7
17	73	1,739	11·2
18	154	3,225	4·1
19	121	2,931	4·3
20	43	1,173	10·3
21	92	2,403	5·0
22	63	1,564	6·8
23	55	1,349	7·6
24	38	914	11·0
25	89	1,966	5·1
26	68	1,700	5·8
27	122	4,290	2·1
28	82	1,858	4·7
29	93	1,960	4·4
30	46	1,210	7·0
31	57	1,450	5·7
32	40	1,103	7·1
33	41	1,173	6·6
34	66	1,823	4·0
35	28	1,092	NA
36	75	2,452	2·8
37	60	1,499	4·3
38	70	1,781	3·6
39	82	2,225	2·8
40	47	1,094	5·6
41	29	555	8·9
42	39	1,030	4·6
43	40	874	4·6
44	39	792	3·9

playgroups, we looked first at the number of playgroups and places as reported by each of these local authorities. The first column shows the number of playgroups in the authority. The second the number of playgroup places.

(It should be noted here that local authorities differed considerably in their interpretation of the questions asked in this section, some giving just precisely what they were asked for, others giving much fuller information. Several authorities sent copies of their most recent DHSS returns, whilst yet others presented us with difficulties in trying to sort data, as when one figure only was given for all registered premises, the terms 'playgroup' and 'day nursery' being discounted for the purposes of registration. Seven local authorities also quoted the numbers of sessional places available with registered persons and we have assumed these to be 'home playgroups', since places with childminders are not classed as sessional. Local authority 1 gave all premises as one figure, 602, and all persons as one figure, 1304, but 1515 of the sessional places are quoted as being with registered persons. Authorities 7, 9, 12, 14 and 40 included respectively 72, 229, 103, 858 and 17 places with registered persons (i.e. sessional places). Authorities 21, 30 and 33 include places in 2 social services department playgroups in each case. Authority 38 includes 396 places in social services department playgroups, and authority 40 includes 222 places in total in 5 of these and 5 area health authority groups. It is possible that local authority 7 has quoted the number of children known, or estimated, to be using each place, since it is otherwise an unusually high number of places per group. To discuss the full relevance of the variations in the figures in the columns would require study in great depth into other factors and their comparative effects on playgroup provision – for instance, the type and extent of the geographical area of each authority, the percentage of the total population which is formed by the under-fives, social and labour traditions and mobility, provision by LEAs, etc. Since the working group is not concerned to look into the reasons why playgroups are there, but rather to examine the support given to them, we have not attempted interpretive comment.)

We felt it would be useful to look at the number of playgroup places in relation to the number of possible candidates for those places and to arrive at a children:place ratio. We felt that it would however be misleading to use the total numbers of children under five for this purpose since it is unrealistic to suppose a situation where all children under five need or require a playgroup place.

On the other hand, figures can be equally misleading if one begins to try to take account of numbers of children who do not need or require a playgroup place, for whatever reason, since these factors bring in qualitative judgements. As a very simple measure we decided to halve the numbers of children under five in each Local Authority and to assume that this would give an idea of the number of children aged from approximately 2 years 6 months to 5 years 0 months, from which range the majority of playgroup candidates can (currently at any rate) be expected to come. In column 3 the figure indicates the greatest number of children in that authority who would need to share a playgroup place if all children of this age requested attendance at a playgroup.

The important point to bear in mind here is that none of the 44 local authorities in England would have a worse ratio than is shown here, since all have other forms of provision, although this may not be sessional provision. It can be seen that in 14 of the 44 authorities, the ratio is of fewer than 4 children to each playgroup place. When other provision is taken into account, plus the fact that playgroups do allocate more than one child to each playgroup place attending on different days, it is possible that in these 14 authorities most or even all of the children aged from 2½ to 4 can obtain a playgroup place if they require one, though we have no way of knowing if a place would be geographically within family reach. At the other end of the scale, there are 11 authorities where between 6 and 12 children would have to share each of the available playgroup places if such places were required. *This must be a matter of concern to the social services department which invests both staff time and financial support in an organisation, hoping for a spread of playgroups to meet community needs.* We know, however, that early admission to first schools caters for a large number of four-year-olds and there are other related factors. Still, the ratios are interesting and it would be useful to have the opportunity to follow up facts and relate them to influencing factors and unmet community needs.

Forms of support: personal, financial, and in kind

Having tabulated the statistical side of information given to us, we next looked at the actual support given to playgroups. This is in three forms: personal, by salaried local authority staff and/or through grant-aided volunteers; financial, through grants and subsidised fees, and 'other' assistance; and support in 'kind', such as access to local authority purchasing schemes, rent-free accommodation, and the like (Section 7). In this section we deal only with support by persons. Financial support and support in kind are covered in Sections 6 and 7.

Tables 4 and 5 show the extent of stated support by persons. Table 4 is arranged by order of the children:place ratio referred to above and shows the number of persons in each agency. For comparative purposes certain assumptions have been necessary. Where a post is stated as 'part-time' this has been taken to mean half-time; a post of, for instance, 'principal officer, day care' has been regarded as a managerial or senior advisory post and has been counted as one whole post for day care; a post of, say, 'principal assistant, children and families' has again been regarded as at managerial level, but having only part day care involvement.

For these tables, more precise job titles and specifications are not important. We are concerned only with the number of people giving support and whether this seems to affect provision. Table 4 shows persons as either those for whom visits to playgroups are a major feature of their work or those who have some managerial or advisory function, probably in day care or community development, at a senior level. We have not shown those staff who work in local authority day nurseries, centres or playgroups, nor staff who have a clerical function. These are also 'managers' with a day-care or community function apart from staff supervision (although supervision of staff might be included in their duties). In some cases it has been difficult to tabulate an answer; where, for instance an authority has stated that 'social workers carry out statutory duties as part of their case load', we have used the 'part of a social worker' symbol since there is no means of estimating how many people are involved, nor what proportion of time they are able to spend. The people symbols in the PPA column show the numbers of people who are grant-aided (salary or expenses) by the authority. (The number of registered area organisers has been added as a separate column, to complete the picture.)

From Table 4 we can see that the greatest number of specialist posts in any social services department is eight (full-time equivalent) and that three authorities have this number (a strong staff presence to service a new form of provision). Twenty nine of the authorities have specially appointed people and, of these, nine grant-aid PPA appointments. There are also PPA appointments in two local authorities with no specialist staff, and in three where playgroup support is part of a social work case load. There does not seem to be any pattern immediately obvious of allowing PPA appointments so that playgroups receive a planned amount of personal support.

It is difficult to codify on Tables 4 and 5 the local authority which grant-aids a co-ordinator and an office administrator (more than clerical) and seven fieldworkers to a voluntary pre-school committee, which is somewhat in the nature of a Wolfenden 'specialist intermediary organisation'. The link with the department is therefore for registering and advice, part of a senior day-care post.

Table 5 shows the average number of playgroups supported by each person specially allocated by social services departments. Because of the difficulty of measuring the extent of involvement of team social work staff who cover the work and because of the relatively small number of PPA, LEA and 'other' appointments, these have not been included in Table 5. It is useful anyway to look at those staff whose work is purely (as far as we know) in advice/support/registration for children's day care. The differences between the numbers of playgroups per member of staff is enormous. Each division represents twenty playgroups, and it can be seen that the work-load varies

Table 4

KINDS OF VISITORS

LA Ref. No.	Child: Place Ratio	SSD	PPA 'PAID POSTS'	OTHERS
27	2·1	✶		
7	2·3	✶ ✶ ✶ ✶ ✶		
14	2·6	✶ ✶ ✶ ✶ ✶ ✶ ✶ ✶ ✶	✶	
36	2·8	✶ ✶ ✶		
39	2·8	N.A.		
11	3·1	✶ ✶ ✶ ✶		
12	3·2	✶ ✶ ✶ ✶ ✶ ✶ ✶ ✶		
8	3·4	N.A.		
9	3·5	✶ ✶ ✶ ✶ ✶ ✶ ✶ ✶		
38	3·6	✶ ✶ ✶ ✶	✶·	
1	3·8	✶ ✶ ✶ ✶ ✶		
10	3·9	✶ ✶ ✶ ✶ ✶	✶	
13	3·9	✶ ✶ ✶ ✶ ✶ ✶		
44	3·9	✶	*Note*: excludes regional appointments	
6	4·0	✶		
34	4·0	✶		
18	4·1	✶ ✶ ✶ ✶ ✶ ✶		
19	4·3			
37	4·3	✶ᵁ		
29	4·4	✶ ✶ ✶ ✶ ✶		
42	4·6	✶ ✶		
43	4·6	✶		
4	4·7	✶ ✶ ✶ ✶ ✶ ✶		✶ ✶ⱽ
28	4·7	✶ ✶ ✶ ✶ ✶ ✶	✶ ✶ ✶ ✶	✶ᴿ
5	4·8	✶ ✶ ✶		
21	5·0	✶ ✶ ✶ ✶ ✶		
25	5·1	✶ ✶		
3	5·4	✶ ✶ ✶ ✶ ✶ ✶ ✶ ✶	✶ ✶ ✶ ✶ ✶ ✶ ✶	
40	5·6	✶	✶	
2	5·7	N.A.		
31	5·7	✶ ✶		
26	5·8		✶	
15	6·2	N.A.		
33	6·6	✶ ✶ ✶ ✶	✶ ✶ ✶ ✶	
16	6·7	✶ ✶		
22	6·8		✶ ✶ ✶ ✶ ✶ ✶ ✶	
30	7·0	✶		
32	7·1	✶		(Job creation)
23	7·6	✶ ✶	✶ ✶	✶ ✶ ✶ ✶
41	8·9	✶	✶	
20	10·3			
24	11·0	✶ ✶	✶	Recreation
17	11·2	✶ ✶		✶dept 'Beehive'
35	NA	✶ ✶ ✶		organiser

KINDS OF VISITORS (continued)

MANAGERS

	LEA	PPA Voluntary Workers	SSD	LEA

Row numbers along left: 27, 7, 14, 36, 39, 11, 12, 8, 9, 38, 1, 10, 13, 44, 6, 34, 18, 19, 37, 29, 42, 43, 4, 28, 5, 21, 25, 3, 40, 2, 31, 26, 15, 33, 16, 22, 30, 32, 23, 41, 20, 24, 17, 35

Note: excludes regionally appointed field workers

KEY

- 🯅 1 full-time person
- ∫ 1 part-time person
- ❘ part of a senior post
- ⵜ part of a social worker or assistant
- Λ voluntary worker (with expenses)

Notes

U = Urban-Aided SSD Post
N.A. = not answered

V = specialised staff employed in vol. liaison work.
R = 'recreation dept' officer for 'tiny tots'

- ● funded by LEA
- ⧯ funded jointly by LEA & SSD

  otherwise funded by SSD

specially created liaison post for vol. org. concerned with pre-school

4 'others' a one-off project

Urban-Aided PPA Adviser

between 16 and 17 playgroups each, in one authority, and over 100 playgroups each in four authorities. This raises questions regarding the nature and quality of support (see Section 1) and whether there is an optimum number of playgroups for any one person. The optimum will depend on what a playgroup wishes to gain from being visited as well as what a local authority thinks it should be offering, and on what relationship exists with voluntary support. We should also mention here that, although we have shown playgroups separately, most, if not all of these staff will probably also be supporting childminders and independent day nurseries. For this reason, the figures for childminders and day nurseries on the right of Table 5 are extremely important.

These tables suggest that the number of staff required in proportion to the number of playgroups and places is viewed very differently by different local authorities. It is affected by the extent of resources and by judgement within the departments. Each may appoint staff in the proportion thought fit, but not in the same proportion as others. It becomes important to consider the personal support available from the other network, the national associations, PPA and SPPA, and the effect of internetwork relationships.

Facts and figures from Scottish social work departments

Unlike England, it was felt important in Scotland to include only children over the age of three in the figures as the practice of playgroups accepting children under three was not usual. The fact that children use more than one form of pre-school provision was a relevant factor; regrettably it was not possible to find out to what extent this happens without comparable figures on nursery school places. Nevertheless, it was clear that where more than one form of provision was available fewer playgroup places were to be found.

Information was received giving numbers of day nurseries and day-nursery places in each region and some comparisons can be made from these figures. In an area with no day nurseries, there were 3,142 playgroup places. In an area with ten day nurseries and four times the population, only 7,915 places.

Playgroups far exceeded all other forms of provision in every region, taking one-tenth of the under-five population (that is about one-fifth of the 2½–5-year-old population) in larger regions, and from about one-third to half in smaller regions. It should not be forgotten that a playgroup may be taking twice as many children as would appear from the number of its registered places, by having different children attend on different days.

Appointments and other support to voluntary organisations
Five regions appointed staff specially to advise playgroups. In the central belt, there was a clear parallel between the number of appointments in local authority departments and the size of the under-five population. In one rural area with good relations between all agencies, it was thought that general encouragement to SPPA would be more productive than an appointment within the department. Elsewhere regions without specific appointments did not make complementary support to the voluntary organisation.

Most appointments were at district or divisional level, two being regional posts and one a divisional responsibility, heading a team of part-time advisers.

People appointed to undertake registering and visits included principal social worker, assistant director, deputy director, playgroup adviser, social worker, area social worker. In addition, five regions appointed advisers specifically for playgroups. The region with the highest total grant allocation also had the highest proportion of advisers to under-five population, while the sum given to the voluntary organisation was comparatively low. A region with the highest number of under-fives had a large number of part-time advisers, but also gave a special grant to different levels of SPPA. Patterns varied considerably between regions.

Advisers' comments on posts

We were able to look at these facts and figures a little from the experience of two groups of advisers in post – first a group who answered questions during a conference of the steering

Table 5 Number of playgroups supported by each specially designated SSD officer (and number of childminders and independent day nurseries in each authority)

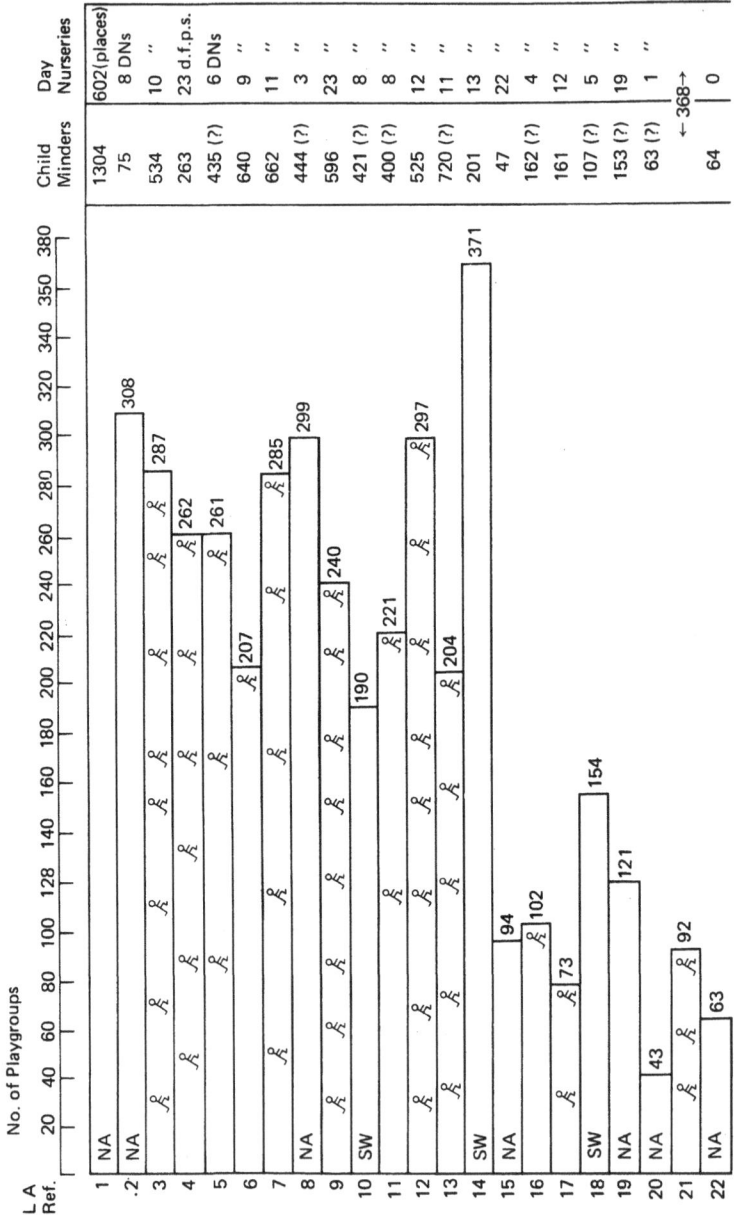

No. of Playgroups

L.A. Ref.	No. of Playgroups	Child Minders	Day Nurseries
1	NA	1304	602 (places) 8 DNs
2	NA — 308	75	8 DNs
3	(bar)	534	10 "
4	287 / 262	263	23 d.f.p.s.
5	261	435 (?)	6 DNs
6	207	640	9 "
7	NA — 285	662	11 "
8	299	444 (?)	3 "
9	240	596	23 "
10	SW 190	421 (?)	8 "
11	221	400 (?)	8 "
12	297	525	12 "
13	204	720 (?)	11 "
14	SW 371	201	13 "
15	NA 94	47	22 "
16	102	162 (?)	4 "
17	73	161	12 "
18	SW 154	107 (?)	5 "
19	NA 121	153 (?)	19 "
20	NA 43	63 (?)	1 "
21	92	← 368 →	
22	NA 63	64	0

Scale (No. of Playgroups): 20 40 60 80 100 128 140 160 180 200 220 240 260 280 300 320 340 350 380

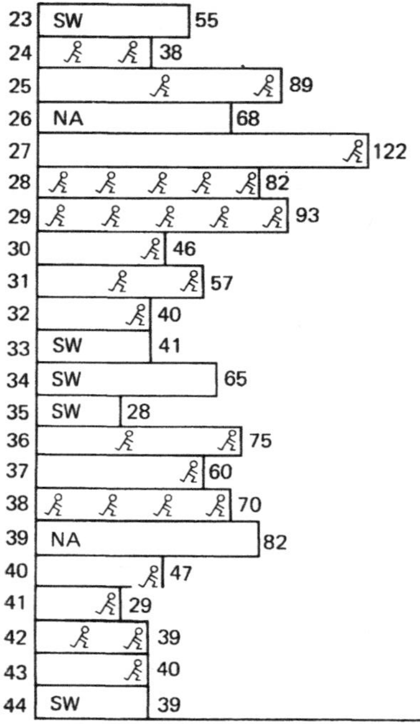

	3 DNs
154 (?)	3 DNs
167 (?)	4 "
117 (?)	8 "
385	8 "
348	14 "
467	14 "
96	8 "
138	7 "
280	3 "
228	4 "
263 (?)	14 "
172 (?)	9 "
36	8 "
155 (?)	2 "
?	1 "
290	3 "
252	2 "
318	7 "
217	3 "
221 (?)	6 "
225 (?)	8 "
35 (?)	? "

NA = not answered
SW = social worker

Bar chart (rows 23–44):

Row	Values
23	SW, 55
24	38
25	89
26	NA, 68
27	122
28	82
29	93
30	46
31	57
32	40
33	SW, 41
34	SW, 65
35	SW, 28
36	75
37	60
38	70
39	NA, 82
40	47
41	29
42	39
43	40
44	SW, 39

group for their professional association in England, and second a more representative Scottish group of advisers, circulated by post.

From an English group of advisers
We know that one was employed by an education department, one by a recreation department (interesting: appointed to support and advise playgroups in a department not the registering department), five by PPA, and thirty two by social services departments, nineteen worked full-time, and nineteen between 15 and 30 hours per week. Twenty three were specialists working in the area team, and two generic social workers, having to work with playgroups as part of their job, the others (fourteen) working centrally as advisers or community workers. As would be expected from this, seventeen were responsible to the principal social worker in the area team and four to a community services organiser; and others to a senior adviser or assistant director (the numbers however add up to more than thirty nine).

Asked about qualifications, twenty nine quoted playgroup experience and qualifications, eleven had educational qualifications, notably NNEB, and eight had administrative or community or voluntary organisation experience/qualifications. Evidently a number had a blend of the qualifications counted acceptable.

Nearly all referred to the support of working in a team, which could be the area team, or the local group of specialists in the team, or a central group of advisers.

The number of playgroups for which they were responsible varied very much: eleven between 30 and 50; thirteen between 50 and 100; while three covered between 100 and 200, and eight between 300 and 600. This needs to be related to the wide range of duties seen to be part of a job description (Section 5), especially as nineteen were also responsible for childminders, eleven for mother and toddler clubs, one for community development and six for a miscellaneous range, including play schemes, a children's home and an old people's home. Six(?) were able to spend only 25 per cent or less of their time on playgroups, twelve between 25 per cent and 50 per cent and only six between 50 per cent and 75 per cent. Thirty three had clerical help, six did not. Twenty three found a lot of time taken with registration, thirty three with support, thirteen with development, twenty three with liaison, twenty with attending meetings and courses, and three with teenagers. Eleven found that the job differed considerably from their job description, and nine commented on its rapid development. Nine found it what they expected, and three slightly different.

From a Scottish group of twenty nine advisers

Responses followed similar patterns: twenty one were employed by social work departments, seven by SPPA and one by the Church of Scotland Home Board. Seventeen worked full-time, twelve between 10 and 25 hours.

They were responsible to a senior member of the local team (five) or a community development officer (four), or at Divisional level to senior members, social work department (eight), supportive services officers (five), or divisional senior advisers (five), or the the General Secretary SPPA, or to the Home Board Playgroup Committee, Church of Scotland.

A large amount of space was given to their training commitments, including the dominance of the term 'sharing in', rather than 'setting up' (cf. Section 5, 'Job Descriptions').

Advisers' emphasis on liaison, including co-ordinating committees, is included in Section 7, but the big difference, compared with English replies, is in relation to the number of playgroups served. Eighteen out of twenty nine worked with less than 50; three with 10–20; nine with 20–30; five with 30–40; one with 40–50. Three served between 50 and 70; one with 50–60; two with 60–70. Only four served more than 100. One did not work directly with individual playgroups.

Pattern of personal support within the PPA/SPPA voluntary network

Voluntary workers and employed or commissioned staff

We originally tried to describe PPA/SPPA's full-time and part-time staff force in terms of manager and visitor, and parts of shared-responsibility person symbols, and to allocate numbers of playgroups served by each, in order to match the facts and figures tables earlier in this section. What was most interesting in this exercise was to work·out why it could not be followed through, except in a limited way, by indicating in Table 4 the number of parallel PPA local appointments.

This seemed to be for two main reasons:

1 Each appointed person works in relation to a voluntary group, and therefore represents many more persons in support.
2 The member of the voluntary organisation, in its different 'layers', are all part of, and indeed produce, the support system. If they not active in doing so, the whole system collapses. Playgroups jointly make up branches and county organisations, and regions and national PPA/SPPA, which are enabled to appoint TDOs and advisers and fieldworkers and area/county organisers, who support counties and branches and playgroups. Where this two-way process fails to function, the structure has got out of balance, and there is constant vigilance in the national network to restore this.

Within each layer of PPA/SPPA ther are various focal points for work: Conferences, special Days for different groups, publications, mailings: courses: fact-finding and action research: bulk buying and budgeting and book-keeping: all dependent on member participation and mutual support. *These pass out to playgroups the pooled experience of a national network, and bring in members' thinking through the collecting points of appropriate groups, committees and commissioned workers.*

The two diagrams on page 174 show the voluntary support network at every level, in PPA and SPPA respectively.

Interaction of voluntary and statutory support systems

This two-way PPA/SPPA system is based on initiative and authority from within the Association, and is therefore different in character from the best of support systems based directly on local authority and indirectly on public responsibility. At long distance, they derive from the same sanction, the will of the community to provide patterns of service, but in such different ways that each has to work hard to recognise the link.

At local and practical level, both systems of support interact through figures, personalised, allotted to the same playgroups within the framework of the voluntary branch/district/county and of the local authority. With the large number of playgroups involved, it is common sense that each support network should plan to complement the other. It is most useful that with different strengths and constraints one set of workers can do, in agreement, what the other finds impossible.

The first meeting-point for the two differently geared systems, and the place where their work has both to be and also to appear to be rational and complementary, is the playgroup.

The second meeting-point is the group of playgroups, the branch, on which much of the constructive thinking of PPA/SPPA is at present concentrated. Although the more distant region is undoubtedly helping to educate branches in underdeveloped areas of work, such as the handling of major amounts of money, the branch must have enough field of action, or its experience is wasted. As a return from the Scottish network pointed out, neither the region nor the department must 'do everything' or in the interest of speed and efficiency 'overstep the autonomy of the branch'.

In reverse, and also from network replies, 'Is the personal support forthcoming from the county always sufficiently developed to take advantage of a local authority which takes PPA seriously?' Or is the voluntary support system working well when 'the new, perhaps inexperienced branch is asking for money when the county is involved in a delicate stage of negotiations'?

Development of professional associations for those working with under-fives

As the number of specialist playgroup appointments multi-

**DIAGRAM OF PERSONAL SUPPORT AVAILABLE TO
PLAYGROUPS WITHIN THE VOLUNTARY NETWORK,
ENGLAND and WALES**

From policymaking representatives   *From employed and commissioned persons*

National Executive Committee
and specialist subcommittees

General Secretary &
four National Advisers

Regional
Committee

13 Training &
Development
Officers, &
8 Development
Officers in Wales

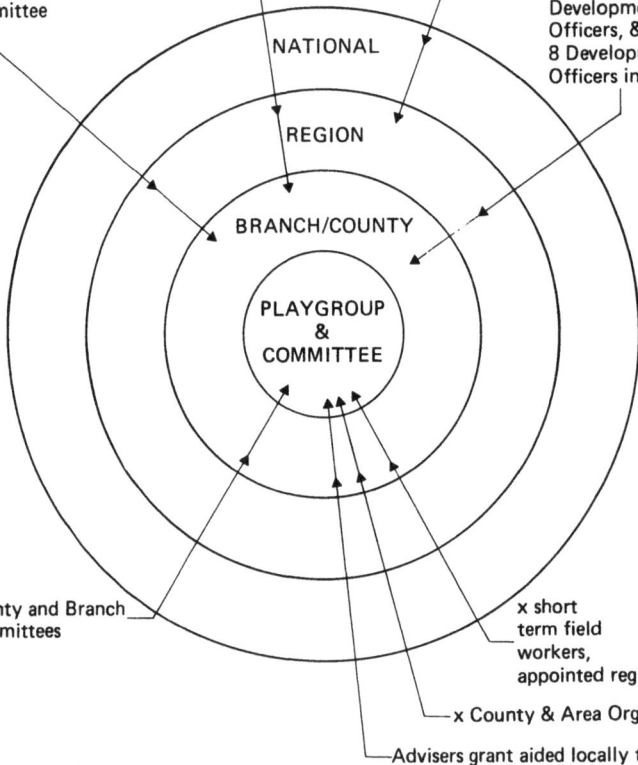

NATIONAL

REGION

BRANCH/COUNTY

PLAYGROUP
&
COMMITTEE

County and Branch
Committees

x short
term field
workers,
appointed regionally

x County & Area Organisers

Advisers grant aided locally to PPA

*All of these made up
from representatives
chosen through the
local playgroup field*

*Each responsible to the whole
organisation through its
representatives at different
levels*

**DIAGRAM OF PERSONAL SUPPORT AVAILABLE TO
PLAYGROUPS WITHIN THE VOLUNTARY NETWORK
SCOTLAND**

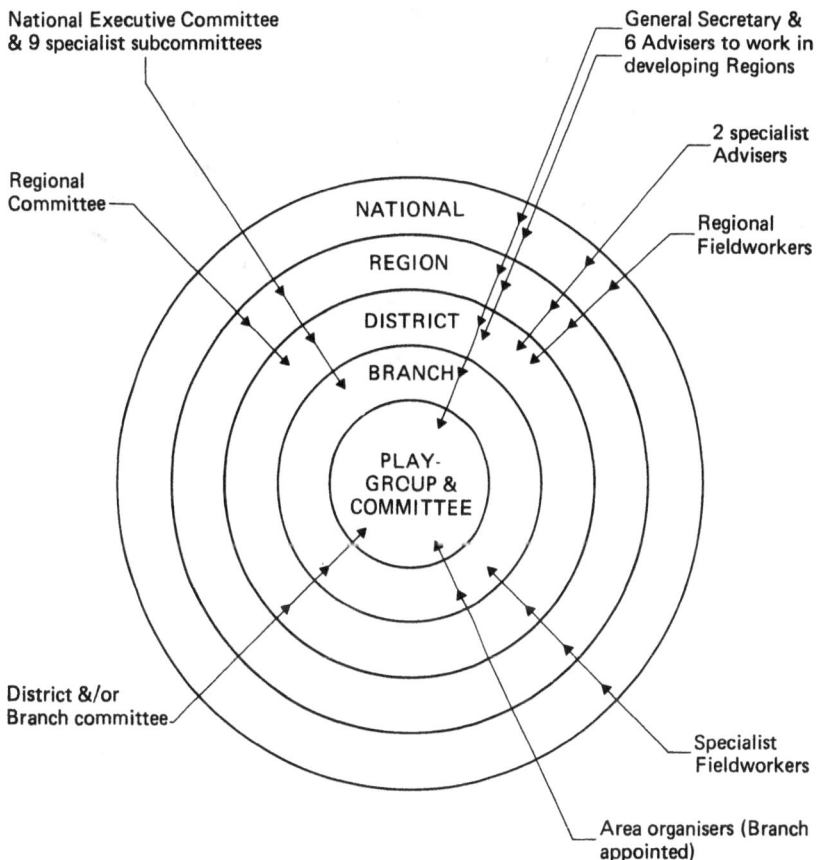

National Executive Committee
& 9 specialist subcommittees

General Secretary &
6 Advisers to work in
developing Regions

2 specialist
Advisers

Regional
Committee

Regional
Fieldworkers

NATIONAL

REGION

DISTRICT

BRANCH

PLAY-
GROUP &
COMMITTEE

District &/or
Branch committee

Specialist
Fieldworkers

Area organisers (Branch
appointed)

plied, it was natural to find movemement towards the pooling of statutory and voluntary experience and mutual support. We quote from the following account of developments in Scotland.

'Scottish Association of Advisers for the Under-Fives and their Families (SAAUFF) Formerly Scottish Association of Playgroup Advisers (SAPA).
To enable those working together in different areas of Scotland to communicate with their contemporaries in other areas, it was decided in 1971 to form a Scottish Association of Playgroup Advisers (SAPA). SAPA began with very few members, all of whom felt a need to meet together and discuss the contents, some good, some bad, and remits of their positions, whether with the statutory or voluntary body. It became increasingly obvious that many Advisers worked in isolation and SAPA became a great support to these people. As the number of Advisers increased in Scotland, so did the SAPA membership and the variations in members jobs remits were always very much under discussion.

'Some members were responsible for registration, others not; some were responsible for training, others not; but nevertheless the "coming together" of the association was proving very valuable. Small working parties began to be formed to look into mutual problems and possible solutions. This too brought playgroup advisers together in a very practical way. A working party did a great deal of research into application forms for registration used throughout the country and compiled a set of SAPA recommended forms and guidelines which are now very widely used. As the association grew, new members having new ideas were given themes for research and several valuable documents were prepared.

'In addition to working parties and sub-committees, SAPA held many open meetings and even two-day conferences on topics of interest, and attendance has always been good. At one conference, the future of SAPA came under discussion, and various developments were suggested.

On the basis of these, SAPA has not become SAAUFF (Scottish Association of Advisers for the Under Fives and Their Families). Advisers now believe that the pre-school child cannot be seen as a separate part of any family and that advising on the care of children must include others involved with him at home. . . .'

SAAUFF's new constitution includes:

'. . . that it is essential to promote opportunities for parents to become aware of the important roles they play in their children's development, especially during the pre-school years. These opportunities would add to parents' confidence in their own ability and give recognition to the important status of parenthood. The association believes that this developing awareness enables parents to seek their rightful place in planning and sharing decisions concerning services for pre-school children in their own community. Parents, by being involved in community life during the pre-school years of their children, will build a strong base for that community's involvement in its own growth and development.'

Similar, but not identical developments took place a little later in England and Wales.

Association of Pre-school Advisers
Since 1971, there has been a movement among playgroup advisers, later widened to include others working with pre-school children and their families, to form an association which would provide opportunities for discussion and research on matters of common interest, and a support group for those in post.

Appointments increased all over the country, some as administrative conveniences related to departmental responsibility, others reflecting growing interest in local authority departments in playgroups and childminders as one aspect of their caring policy. Some advisers held grant-aided posts in PPA or in SCF, and related in different ways to statutory departments and the developing voluntary structure.

The first two national meetings were sponsored by PPA at Imperial College, London, in 1971 and the University of Aston in 1975. Thereafter a more representative steering committee planned national meetings, and continued to study the formation of a national organisation. Between 1975 and 1978 regional groups held meetings to discuss matters of common interest, the first meeting convened by request by PPA's regional training and development officers, and then according to regional wishes.

Three more national meetings have been held, the most recent in Westminster Central Hall, under the chairmanship of the Director of Social Services, Warwickshire. On 12 May 1978, those present discussed whether to become part of the National Institute of Social Work, or to become an association with closed statutory membership, or one open to those appointed in statutory and voluntary organisations working with under-fives. It was decided not to become part of the National Institute, and to call the proposed association the Association of Advisers for Under-Fives, not incorporating the phrase 'and their families' as Scotland had done.

'At a meeting on 8 October 1978 a constitution was accepted, on a decision by a majority of 88 to 11 to include the wider membership. As there were still a lot in favour of extending the title to include 'families' it was decided that this should be a topic for discussion at the first AGM in May 1979. (See also Section 7, page 218).

Summary

Fifty three local authorities contributed facts and figures.

England and Wales

Authorities vary greatly in size, having under-fives populations of anything from 100,400 to 6,100. Even allowing for different interpretations shown in replies, it seems clear that the number of playgroups, and of playgroup places, is not closely related to this child population. A calculation was made to estimate the number of children in an authority who would have to share a playgroup place if all children aged 2½ –5 were to want one.

This showed that in 14 authorities, all or most children could obtain a place, but that in 11 authorities from 6 to 12 children would have to share each place. It is acknowledged that other factors (for example age of primary school admission) would affect this finding.

Tables 4 and 5 show the amount of personal (cf. financial) support available to playgroups. Though it was impossible to tabulate precisely all the very different replies received, it seems that 3 social service departments have as many as 8 (full-time equivalent) posts and 29 authorities have specially appointed personnel. In different authorities, one specialist staff member may be caring for anything from 16 to over 100 playgroups (as well, probably, as nurseries and childminders.) Clearly authorities do not necessarily appoint staff in proportion to the number of playgroups, and playgroups can flourish whether or not such staff are appointed.

Scotland

Playgroups exceeded all other forms of provision, taking from one-tenth to one-half of the available children in different regions, but the more other provision there was in any area the fewer playgroups were found. Five regions appointed staff specifically to advise playgroups and one other which made no appointment had decided instead to encourage SPPA. Six different grades of social worker were responsible for registration and visiting. Each region showed very different patterns of appointment and/or help to the voluntary association.

Advisers

About half the English respondents worked full-time, and nearly all were appointed by social services departments or the PPA. Only about a quarter had educational qualifications (mostly NNEB). They were responsible for from 30 to 600 playgroups each, within a wide range of other duties. Scottish advisers were also mainly appointed by social work departments, and about 6 in 10 worked full-time. A difference from England was that only 4 served more than 100 playgroups, and well over half worked with less than 30.

Scottish advisers put more stress on training as one of their commitments.

Diagrams are given of the personal support available to plagroups within the voluntary network. Appointments within PPA/SPPA are made by the members, and this two-way dependency marks the crucial difference between these and local authority appointments. Nevertheless, each set of support workers can and should complement the other. It is important to strike the right balance of helping without 'taking over'. Scottish advisers developed a professional association in 1971 now called SAAUFF. The English and Welsh association (AAUF) accepted its constitution in 1978.

Questions

1 Is it the generally accepted aim to provide a pre-school place for all children under-five?
2 With a number of different agencies in the field, it would appear that parents have a choice of pre-school facilities. Is this choice intentional or the result of haphazard growth and where a family lives?
3 Do playgroups need a planned amount of personal support? If so, where should this come from?
4 What is it hoped that the Associations of Advisers will achieve?

5

Job Descriptions

We thought we might get some interesting sidelights if a few job descriptions were available. Instead, we collected a considerable number of job descriptions of different vintages, and observations on them would provide a book on the development of playgroups.

Historical development: some signposts

The first playgroup adviser post of which we have a record was for Inner London, 1964, from an LEA grant. PPA published a guide in 1968, both for the interest of authorities considering such appointments and for the playgroup leaders who would like to know what help they would get from such advisers. An adviser appointed in Scotland in 1968 was followed in quick succession by others.

SAPA, the Scottish professional Association of Playgroup Advisers, was drawing up a draft job description in 1972, prior to a great increase in Scottish appointments which came in with local government reorganisation in 1975. Mary Bruce, then General Secretary, PPA, wrote in April 1973: 'The time I spend talking to LAs about the appointment of Playgroup Advisers is increasing. Local Authorities seem to want advice about terms and conditions of employment, salary scales, pension funds, as well as job-descriptions. They want to know what advantages there are in making a grant to a PPA Branch compared with the benefits of appointing someone to their own staff.'

We noted posts which changed with circumstances: part-time advisers appointed by education departments, taken over later by social services departments, till review in 1979, 'growing to a team covering development in poor areas, liaison with departments and organisations, and training'; many new posts created after the Local Authorities Services Act, transferring responsibility from health to social services departments; a further acceleration of appointments following local authority reorganisation, both in Scotland and in England, but with some posts lost in the process.

From two discussions about roles of local authority advisers and branches/AOs

1   An education adviser in the South-East, 1974: 'The Adviser is dependent on the AO's knowledge of an area: she is the back-up and not the initiator. The AO works; the AO and adviser talk; both need to visit playgroups together. Usually the AO visits regularly (termly, or more often) and the adviser when asked, or when in an area.' 'The adviser is responsible to her department for training . . . providing courses and tutors . . . putting in estimates . . . speaking about playgroups to her authority . . . liaising with the county committee, the TDO, AOs.' The adviser can back the AO, particularly with non-PPA groups. A main point of interest is that this adviser was appointed by an education department.

2   A meeting in the Social Work Department, Edinburgh, 1975: 'Communication could seem to break down between the LA people and the voluntary organisation, and this was potentially dangerous. The LA advisory services should not be seen as an alternative help system for playgroups, but complementary to the help given by SPPA. The enabling of the growth of people, which is part of playgroup philosophy, could be in danger of being lost if the bureaucratic machine took over completely.' 'Playgroup advisers are doing with groups what social workers are doing with individuals or families.' 'Another very important function is the educational role within the authority helping to increase the understanding of other members of staff about playgroups and parent partici-pation.'

Job descriptions for AOs were collated from experience in the early 1970s, partly because the current PPA thinking was towards an AO, with financial adjustment, attached to every area team. A number of authorities adapted this to appoint a specialist part-time post within each team, often drawing on experienced playgroup personnel to fit it. One department commented on a job description: 'The emphasis of the job description has changed as the department became more aware of what the job entailed and how it evolved.' Discussion continues on the need for local authorities to grant-aid voluntarily area organisers, and an interesting point comes from Scottish advisers:

> 'One of the foreseeable problems in an extension of the Voluntary Movements Area Organiser Scheme is that the advisers, while operating at one remove from individual playgroups (in Scotland work with individual playgroups forms the bulk of their commitment), might then find that too much time was being spent in training and support of area organisers. Initially it would be difficult to avoid this, as any scheme requiring use of local authority finance will require to be monitored and evaluated for a period of time. However, there are reasonable grounds for feeling that the voluntary movement should be able to deal competently with the ordinary problems of playgroups affiliated to SPPA.'

Today there is a network of local authority appointments, and another network of voluntary, or expenses-paid, or minimal-salary-paid PPA/SPPA AOs, and some PPA (but not SPPA) grant-aided branch or county advisers. In the job description for either, content is surprisingly similar, which must prompt joint discussion, but the reference point for work and the language of description are surprisingly different. Today's problem for playgroups is to distinguish between statutory and voluntary roles, when people visiting them have moved from one to another; to think why both are necessary; and to see how they make a job of working together – or to worry, if they don't. There is a growing concept of two sets of supporters working in partnership, with both in a position to initiate, and some patterns allowing scope for this.

When the first few appointments were made (usually under Urban Aid, from the time of its third issue, which was an exciting innovation) it was not a great concern of directors of local authority departments to think where those in post would end. Today, a director comments that those brought in to the teams with voluntary experience 'have made their jobs'. He thinks the system works admirably and suggests the working group probe further into team relationships. This is one of the many subjects which, within our resources, we have not been able to explore fully.

However, considerable thinking has recently been given to the relationships of posts within the voluntary field, relationships between administrative and field staff, and between staff and voluntary AOs and branch workers. SPPA has brought a study of secondment for further training to fruition, in the first secondment of a team-leader of advisers for CQSW training.

One of the conditions for the development of fieldwork posts, both statutory and voluntary, has been the explosion of playgroups, and the volume of work attached. In Scotland it would seem that a plateau has been reached. 'It seems unlikely that there will be any dramatic rise again in the emergence of new playgroups.' This will mean a change of balance in registering and advisory and supporting work for advisers. Another condition of development has been the changes in local authority organisation, and SPPA made a thoughtful adjustment here in ensuring, at the moment of change, that there would be SPPA units corresponding to the new regions, divisions, districts and areas. The correspondence in England and Wales, with implications for negotiations on grant aid, is not so close. Wales has shown initiative in accepting smaller units as most effective, for example in the appointment of part-time staff.

Areas of work included in fieldworker job descriptions

We took as our main basis for consideration those job descriptions supplied to the working group by local authorities, and then considered them in relation to the total support service for playgroups. We recognise that some of the wording and details included could come as a shock to branches and AOs if the jobs were implemented unilaterally. But we think that what branch personnel might assume to be authoritarian could be developed with great value if worked out in full co-operation with the voluntary supporting branch. Areas of responsibility quoted below are taken both from job descriptions for members of departmental advisory groups and from those of specialists working in area teams. Whereas in general the wider commitments belong to the adviser roles, there is great variation in pattern and a group of part-time, experienced playgroup workers, each within a local team, may be able to make a more general contribution than one central adviser sharing her time allocation between playgroups, childminders, day nurseries, mother and toddler groups and a variety of playbuses, children's homes, old persons' homes, and one o'clock clubs, with which different posts are linked.

The following list covers items from all the job descriptions sent in

1 *For some, sharing of time and organising of work-load* to cover shared reponsibility. In Scotland, the average spent on playgroups varies from 50 to 95 per cent of total time. In England, the average is much lower, and some in post give playgroups only 15 per cent.

2 *Registering.* Cover all the stages of registration as detailed in Section 2.

3 *Visiting*

   (a) To maintain standards. Visit once a term at least. Be knowledgeable about stages of child development, play equipment and activities. Advise where to buy; organise equipment pools and toy libraries. Advise on the use of indoor and outdoor space, and the layout of play. Advise on the daily management of the session. Examine records and finance of playgroups; document visits fully, with annual report on each registered playgroup. Keep registration under review; withdraw this if necessary.

   (b) To provide support and encouragement. Hold

monthly meetings for all playgroup staff and helpers; see that they are familiar with agencies to refer to.

4 *Development.* Give special support to new playgroups. Set up discussions with parents and staff; act as mediator between playgroups and other interested parties, 'landlords, cleaners, caretakers, clergy, youth leaders'. Deal with complaints from parents and public. Advise on problems arising from parental involvement. Give most attention to new groups in areas notable for lack of facilities.

Watch the overall coverage of the area, and see that each area gets comparable service. Co-ordinate activities of all agencies with this in view: WRVS, SCF, Job Creation Programme, community industry, community associations. Set up, staff, equip, watch over social service playgroups where they are needed. (It is possible to co-ordinate groups provided under single sponsorship, but not others except by agreement with their own supporting structure. And yet good sense indicates talk about some degree of co-ordination.)

5 *Encouraging local community action.* Innovate a wide range of services in which voluntary effort is used. See that they remain related to the community.

6 *Financial support and related procedures.* Supervise grant-application by the branch; process annual grant and budget; advise department on grant or refusal; advise branch on allocation; or allocate grant.

7 *Liaison.* (Early job-descriptions contain comparatively little on liaison, except with the local PPA Branch, though not in all cases.)

(a) Within the department. Liaise with area teams and social workers with special responsibility. Relate to Department Management Group. Attend to referrals by social workers, and administration and finance connected with these. See that social workers know all resources.

(b) With other departments. Consult complementary appointments under LEA, so far as time allows.

Liaise with transport on all transport needs of children, and on playbus. Liaise with libraries. Give advice to peripatetic teacher/playleaders on priorities. Liaise with area health authority, and especially with health visitors. Help playgroups in negotiation with planning.

(c) With other agencies, mainly PPA/SPPA. Attend branch/district meetings, and conferences if required. Advice on deployment of AOs. Provide joint meetings for LA staff and AOs. See that PPA/SPPA knows the range of pre-school provision and support available.

(d) Formal consultation. Be a member of, or convene, under-five standing committee.

8 *Public relations and communication.* Keep a two-way register of playgroups with places, and parents with children to place. Use surgeries, libraries clinics, etc., for posting useful information.

9 *Courses.* Encourage and set up training. Liaise on training budget. Contribute to courses by lecturing, taking sessions in schools and supervising pupils in playgroups. Set up courses on pre school children for social workers, PPA/SPPA and others. Assess training needs and develop appropriate courses.

10 *Latest trends in pre-school thinking.* Advise departments on under-five projects under consideration or in practice. Keep the department abreast of trends in pre-school thinking. Research and evaluate day-services for children.

11 *Advisers' Association.* Be a member of a wider than local group of playgroup advisers.

Playgroup advisers within the social services/work department structure

It would appear that the following patterns, with considerable variation in the title of the playgroup worker, are common. The titles of persons most commonly seen in the playgroups are printed in italic. It is also known that a principal social worker may actually appear regularly. Sometimes the registering process is carried through in the area team, and the adviser/support function given to the adviser and her assistants.

Pattern 1   Director
Deputy Director
Principal Social Worker
Area team leaders
Social worker, carrying out playgroup oversight as part of normal duties.

Pattern 2   Director
Deputy Director
Principal Social Worker
Area team leaders
Part-time specialist playgroup worker, attached to each area team
Perhaps on social worker, perhaps on ancillary scales. Sometimes with an adviser, out of the management line, co-ordinating. Sometimes with one area team leader as the co-ordinator. Increasingly recruited from experienced PPA network.

Pattern 3   Director
Deputy Director, with additional responsibility for playgroups
Principal Social Worker
Area team leaders
Social workers
Playgroup adviser; Perhaps *team of assistant advisers*
Responsibility of the adviser sometimes to a deputy director, day care. Sometimes to deputy director, community development. Will have to work out registration procedure, on local scene, in relationship with area team leader.

One particular example of the way things work

It seemed useful to consider a topic of general interest to playgroups and to explore how it would be dealt with among the different people responsible. We chose the referral of children in special need.

When referral to a playgroup seems of value, by what series of events would a child reach playgroup? The recommendation might come from local social workers, with knowledge of the area team leader, to the part-time specialist in the team, and thence to the voluntary AO for advice on the most appropriate placement. Or it might go from a generic social worker in the team to the leader for passing on to assistant or playgroup adviser, and thence to AO or playgroup. It is easy to see why the number of children referred is often so small. Often the social worker in a team is unaware of the playgroup as a resource. A principal social worker may call together team leaders to make sure they are aware, and the team leaders may pass on information to social workers, and yet no referral may result. The pressures of everyday work-loads may be too much. More is likely to happen in a team with a specialist used to playgroup work, and able to make introductions. If there is a team of assistant playgroup advisers, it is probable that one will be given special responsibility for referals. She is likely, after a child has been placed, to have to follow up the attendance and reasons for non-attendance and the mechanics of payment (in advance? In arrears? With what delay? For a playgroup struggling to pay its way?) with the finance section of the department or even the borough treasurer's department. There may be transport problems. The playleader may need to discuss the child's settling in and progress quite often. With whom? Placing a child in a playgroup can have value for the child and for relieving stress in a home, which may or may not result later in a mother participating in the playgroup. *But the whole process means care and time, and in the structure of many departments there is simply not the allocation of time to make referrals effective.*

Department and branch in the referral process

From the playgroup point of view, linkage through AO can prevent many difficulties, though again there may be no AO or she, like the statutory workers, may be overpressed with other priorities. At least one branch has one of a team of AOs responsible for referrals alone. (There is equal value in making an AO responsible for links with child-minders, and their introduction to playgroup and branch activities.) If the contact in the local team is a generic social worker with no experience in playgroup work there may be problems and misunderstandings. One director wanted to talk about in-service training to improve this link, and spoke of his difficulties in seconding a social worker even to an excellent locally available course.

Do local voluntary and statutory support systems duplicate each other?

Increasing interest and the number of statutory and voluntary appointments have indeed produced a situation which demands a closer look. One statutory adviser, formerly working in the voluntary organisation, said, 'I find great variation in the interpretation of job descriptions.' A director made one such interpretation which PPA could not accept. 'If staff appointments were only for playgroups, there would be no need for voluntary AOs.'

The working group was somewhat puzzled by the areas of duplication evident in job descriptions for advisers or assistant advisers and voluntary area organisers. On paper, these jobs could include going into playgroups and to talk and advise on exactly the same things – for example the management of daily sessions, the use of outdoor space or the usefulness of courses (in which one or other was taking part) – and to spend time with peripatetic leaders. There were other aspects of role relationships to be considered. A tremendous control could be seen to be in the hands of advisers who helped to formulate grant applications, advised a department on acceptance, and then distributed grant money. Some directors felt that this was right. Playgroups advisers should be identifiable as the source of income. Speeds of work also presented problems. There were many cases where an AO had to confer with the branch, whose worker she was. In some of these cases, statutory fieldworkers, having consulted with AOs, would hope to take speedy action. It would be easy, for speed and convenience and without any real intent, to bypass the responsibility of a voluntary branch. Or it would be easy for two workers to give incompatible advice, again without realising this, and for the playgroup to stand confused in the middle. Yet we saw two sets of supporters, each trying to do a good job with an unmanageable number of playgroups.

We looked again at job descriptions, to see whether they really were in duplicate, and found that, although job descriptions were similar, different jobs were described in different language. However, this difference may be reduced by the increasing number of people entering local authority departments from the voluntary field.

Job descriptions in the voluntary network: the different language

Job descriptions for national adviser, general secretary, regional training and development officers (TDO), short-term fieldworkers within a region, and for voluntary area organisers are all based on the sharing of responsibility between individual and group. Because of this, the language of their job description is different. In place of the unilateral viewpoint – 'Set up courses', or 'Organise monthly meetings,' or 'Innovate a wide range of services,' – a PPA/SPPA worker is asked at any level to 'Be involved with the bulk-buy store', or to 'Encourage better standards tactfully, allowing groups to learn slowly from mistakes', or to 'Contribute to a course, either by leading a session, or as a link-tutor, if this is what the planning group wants'. They are asked generally to 'Keep before each generation of new parents that the playgroups are theirs, not the supervisors' ' and to 'Consult branch officers rather than take unilateral actions.' Time-consuming and slow in results, but at least one director envied the voluntary organisation the right to take time, without councillors pressing for a quick response. The PPA voluntary worker works, with national backing, by bringing facts to the attention of groups, and encouraging them to choose their action. SPPA, in rewriting its job descriptions, contributes: 'The General Secretary will function mainly as an enabler, allowing maximum possible independence of working to staff, within their individual terms of reference'. The advisers' jobs will be 'Helping with playgroup development, in particular regional development and training', and 'Being available for advice and consultation to the Fieldwork Course', 'Sharing in the planning and staffing of the Short Course Training programme' or 'Sharing in the linking with organisations'.

There are statutory appointments where the concept of support work for playgroups has moved parallel with that of PPA/SPPA, and where the language is enabling: 'It is hoped that the adviser will have worked closely with parents and be committed to helping them understand and enjoy their children', or 'Routine visits, to offer continuing encouragement, advice and support which will enable the childminder, the staff of a day nursery or a playgroup's staff, parents and committee to work purposefully together', or 'Helping to identify areas where facilities for the under-fives and their parents are specially needed, and working with individuals and organisations to promote appropriate facilities and attitudes'.

Planning ahead and establishing priorities

One significant current development in the voluntary structure is that of the regional forward planning session which takes place in each PPA region at least once a year. With every part of the region represented, it looks at developments, relation of staff and voluntary roles, priorities ahead, experiments in formal and informal consultation, and allocation of resources. This process could not be contained in any one person's job description, and the whole exercise is based on faith that grant aid of various kinds will continue, but it provides the element of forethought and planning which the Wolfenden Report sees lacking in much voluntary work. The mutually agreed co-ordinating exercise is an essential part of playgroup work and stimulation, and gives the parts of a region a real choice in allocating the time of its TDO.

Another significant development related to job descriptions is the strong support available to PPA's regional staff, the

TDOs, in residential group sessions, with also an increasing invited membership of volunteers. This pattern of conferring would seem to be developing in a different way from that of a professional advisers' association, and the value of both forms of support needs to be further considered. The same problem exists for nursery advisers and other groups who meet regionally as 'like meets like', and yet see the value of a wider forum.

Movement of personnel between statutory and voluntary posts

Those who have transferred from posts within PPA/SPPA to others in a local authority find there is much in common but that some expectations and ways of working are different. To be related to the power to register and the ability to provide grant aid confers one kind of lever. It gives an entry too to the kind of playgroup which resists any suggestion of ways which might work better with a defensive 'Are you from the social services?' To need things to happen more quickly, in order to satisfy a local authority committee, is on the other hand a form of constraint. Movement between statutory and voluntary posts should bring appreciation, from experience, of different ways of working for results. 'We couldn't do this, but *you* could. Your turn.'

Unfortunately mobility is at present virtually in one direction. Salaries and prospects in a voluntary organisation are not competitive, and secondment from education or social services departments has not generally been practical. One rare case of this, a two-year secondment of officers from two departments to work among playgroups, stepped up voluntary–statutory co-operation immediately. 'You don't know' said the woman in post, 'what motivates other people, how other people work, until you join them. You think you do, and you act on what you think, and that can be dangerous.'

Another attempt to give teachers and head teachers a real sense of playgroup activity came in the involvement of members of a nursery conversion course in local playgroup experience, both in playgroups sessions and in branch activity.

Those involved tried consciously to divest themselves of the head teacher's hat; playgroups tried consciously to divest their visitors of it. Some good relationships were developed, but the number of these experiments in the statutory–voluntary direction is negligible. Other experiments in working jointly are proceeding. In one part of the country local authority departments grant-aid voluntary workers not as AOs but as special workers in areas of special need. These leaders of projects work alongside purely voluntary AOs and district organisers in the social services department, with a co-ordinator working from the education office.

In another area, considerable money is used to support co-ordinated voluntary work with young children and families. It is interesting that the director there sees PPA as in some respects very authoritarian, with the use of such terms as 'area organiser' and insistence on procedures. One local authority recently sponsored a residential two-day meeting when statutory and voluntary fieldworkers, some of whom had very recently 'crossed over', began to talk through their roles. The working group is very aware, talking of mobility of personnel, that playgroup helpers often do not know 'who works for who', and relate to a person, in whatever role, once a good contact has been established.

Job descriptions and the job in practice

Facts and figures (Section 4) in conjunction with job descriptions reveal an impossible work-load in many departments, even on a minimal view of oversight. One playgroup said that it had never had a visit. Departments which have developed their concept of playgroup support far beyond what is mandatory can find reason for stepping up their playgroup staff. Many advisers feel very vulnerable because they have not the time, nor sometimes the sanction in practice, to carry out the job as they hoped and intended.

Both with statutory and with AO commitments, the balance between visiting playgroups and liaison on their behalf has changed over the last few years. Liaison has become potentially full-time work, and has resulted in new posts being introduced to concentrate on the original visiting functions (though in Scotland visiting is still the main job for local authority advisers). The voluntary visitor has emerged, concerned with only two or three playgroups, and there are visitor-type appointments in a large number of social services area teams. What comparison is possible between the 'playgroup job' in an 'authority with one appointment shared with childminding and another with twenty three part-time advisers? In some departments, also, the proportion of time to be spent on childminders has been stepped up, at the expense of playgroups, partly because playgroups are known to have a complementary support system.

Need for review of posts and prospects

A number of directors of social services expressed the view that playgroups had so developed, with a more clearly seen relationship to the rest of the work of the department, and the number of related part-time and full-time posts had so multiplied that the time was ripe for review. The effects of boundary changes could also now be assessed, with their impact on playgroup organisation and support. They queried whether any present qualification was relevant, and a look at the area of work included in job descriptions would confirm this. 'A high standard of communicating skills both written and spoken, methodical approach to covering the very large divisional area, warm and understanding personality, theoretical and practical knowledge of the under-fives, ability to understand the relevant complicated legislation and guidelines' summed up what one department was looking for. Others point out that the post involves not only statutory duties but also wider advisory training and development duties, and a capacity to work closely with voluntary organisations, while some social workers 'do not find it easy to work with volunteers'.

Although there was no specific qualification enabling its holder to produce a good playgroup by working with mothers rather than playleaders, nevertheless status in the department was affected by absence of thinking on qualifications for the job. 'This restricts progress through the department and causes frustration. Possibly needs a new course with modules on the lines of some health visitor training.' Another director commented: 'A playgroup adviser has at present no prospects, but she has a valuable job in itself.' And another: 'Growing concern about non-accidental injury would mean an element of study of this in any in-service training. My department would consider future thinking about CQSW for those in post.'

No one gave any indication how long they would expect someone experienced in work with young children and families to stay in this post, and where they would proceed to next.

The involvement of PPA/SPPA in such a review would highlight:

(a) the continuous range of experience for those who had worked for years in a voluntary, responsible capacity and at a later stage of life wished to use the experience in statutory employment;

(b) the problems of getting accepted to any professional employment and even of acceptance or allowance for experience as part of mature student training;

(c) the value to society of these people's potential contribution.

Arrangements for later employment are of great importance for an organisation which depends on opportunities for members to move on, in order for other voluntary workers to extend their repsonsibility. The working group believes that a review of prospects within departmental structure should be combined with a wider review of movement between statutory and voluntary employment within playgroup work. The statement from a playgroup adviser's job description in 1972 (Scotland), with allowance for the changed value of money since, is still relevant: 'We feel that a salary that will draw people from different backgrounds is essential, and that a salary that is comparable to that of a community worker, a nursery school head, a senior social worker, etc., is necessary. The starting salary should therefore be at least £2,000 with regular assessment and with regard to the size of an area, responsibility carried and so on.'

The second essential discussion which the working group could include in such a review is the relationship between the two emerging systems of support, and the need for the highly responsible job of AO to be made financially viable, if the voluntary and statutory support functions are to be linked more effectively. It is clear from the playgroup questionnaire (Section 3) and registering procedures (Section 2) that persons in support do encourage voluntary service, and that people in both support systems are in short supply. We hope that reviews will not be only of inherited practice in a system which remains unchanged, but of practice to bring a much more developed voluntary service into a new and agreeable relationship with statutory provision.

Summary

The first recorded appointment of a playgroup adviser was by the ILEA in 1964, and the first Scottish appointment was four years later. Many posts were created during local government reorganisation. From the early years there has been a continuous concern to differentiate between the roles of playgroup fieldworkers appointed by local authorities and by PPA/SPPA, with the contents of remits being close but the way the work is described strikingly different, the PPA/SPPA remits laying greater emphasis on encouraging self-help. The amount of time spent on playgroup work varies from 50 to 95 per cent in Scotland, much less in England. Eleven different areas of work could be distinguished in the remits sent in, covering registration and supervision, development and support (encouragement, training, finance), liaising and public relations, and keeping in touch with current thinking.

Local authority playgroup workers may be generic social workers in an area team, part-time specialists in a team, or playgroup advisers responsible to a deputy director. Even the simple referral of a child to a playgroup may involve three or four staff, and effective referral takes an amount of time and care for which many departments do not allow.

Job descriptions show areas of duplication. Ways of working, on the other hand, may be very different, with statutory workers seen to have power and voluntary workers progressing more slowly because of the necessity continually to consult playgroup and PPA/SPPA members. PPA/SPPA job descriptions all stress shared responsibility – enabling rather than providing. One example of this shared responsibility is seen in PPA's regional forward planning sessions, which provide the element of forethought the Wolfenden Report saw as lacking in much voluntary work.

Movement between voluntary and statutory posts is all one-way, largely because voluntary organisation salaries are not competitive. However, there are a few experimental attempts to help voluntary organisation and statutory workers to understand each others' viewpoints, strengths and constraints. Many local authority playgroup workers are grossly overworked, and in England emphasis is moving away from visiting because of the demands of liaison work. However, it is impossible to make valid generalisations about how the job is done when it is seen that one department makes one appointment, shared with childminders, and another appoints twenty three part-time advisers.

There has been so much playgroup development that several directors saw need for a review of relationships, staffing, staff prospects and possible qualifications. PPA/SPPA would stress the importance of experiential qualifications, and the importance of future employment prospects in an organisation which depends on opportunities for members to move on. It is also essential to review the financial position of AOs and their relationship to statutory workers, especially since it is clear that persons in support do encourage voluntary service.

Questions

1 What forums can be made available for establishing relationships and discussing complementary functions between LA playgroup advisers and voluntary AOs?

2 Have the liaison and research aspects of playgroup

fieldworker posts taken over at the expense of visiting? How can the two be reconciled?

3   As a specialist working with generic social workers, and not necessarily a qualified social worker, what is the status of a playgroup adviser in the social services/work department?

6

Grant Aid: Facts and Figures

As stated in Section 4, local authorities were given numbers from 1 to 44. These are used again in tables in this section.

On matters dealing with finance, we found it more convenient to deal separately with facts and figures, and comments, from two sources. A Scottish section follows that based on England and Wales.

We had asked departments for their total allocation for playgroup support and then for a breakdown under:

1 Grants to individual playgroups,
2 Grants to supporting voluntary organisations,
3 Grants for free or subsidised places for children in special need,
4 Other items, including support in kind.

Total budgets, England and Wales

Table 6 shows the total budget available for 'playgroup support' as defined by each local authority. Care should be taken when interpreting these figures since many of the headings under which information was requested could, and probably do, include the budget for other forms of day care. In some cases it could be that the authorities have included salaries, on-costs, administration, etc., but this is not always clear.

The first general point we considered was the possible link between salaries within departments and other forms of support to playgroups. Financial tables do not add greatly to the assumptions we made in the section on staffing (Section 4). Do authorities tend to compensate, or do they provide support

Table 6 Total budget available for playgroup support

Up to £5,000	£10,000	£15,000	£20,000	£25,000	£40,000	£60,000	£75,000	£100,000	N.A.
LA Nos	LA Nos	LA Nos	LA Nos	LA Nos	LA Nos	LA Nos	LA Nos	LA Nos	LA Nos
1 + S.1	3→	7	4	23	29 + S.1	17	28	40	2
6 + UA	8	11	5						15
9 + S.1	18	12 + S.1	10→						20
16	24 + UA	13	22						38
21 + S.1	27	14→	30						
25 + S.1	33	19	35						
31	39	26→							
32 + S.1		41							
34									
36									
37									
42 + S.1									
43									
44 + S.1									

KEY

S.1 = money available under Section 1 of the Childrens Act
UA = Urban Aid
→ = amount shown is minimum specified, but LA has indicated that other grants are also included in budget

in persons and financial aid in the same proportion? It is unfortunate that so many authorities have left blanks either in their staffing or in their financial details, thus making the number of comparisons smaller than we would have liked. It is still possible, however, to think that the variations in grant budgets are not related to variations in staffing patterns. Although individual authorities may well have policies relating to the ratio of finance to staff allocation, it is still possible that no two authorities have used the same yardstick. The largest authority studied has one of the smallest stated budgets and one of the best ratios of children to playgroup places; it looks as if there are five staff permanently involved in support and 'others' who do some work. Here, it might be said, is a pointer to number of staff being more important than size of budget in achieving a good number of places; but other authorities with as many or even more people involved in support do not achieve such a good ratio of children to places.

One of the smallest authorities to take part has what appears to be the largest budget and yet a figure of 5·6 children per sessional place, though this authority does achieve the second best day-care ratio of children to places, 8·8 per place. Whether to provide for full day care or for sessional care may be the most important decision in determining a local authority's policy. Again, we should have liked to explore this concept further, since it is so important in planning to meet future needs. We have only so far made the start shown in Table 7, which contrasts the availability of independent playgroup places with local authority provisions, within social service departments (LEA nursery schools are not included).

Break-down of grant aid

1   Grant aid to playgroups

Criteria for and purpose of grant aid to playgroups
Most authorities said that grants were given according to need, the size of the grant varying between £25 and £3,500 according to agreed policy. Some authorities distinguished between new and existing groups, six stating that they grant-

Table 7 Availability of independent playgroups against social services provision

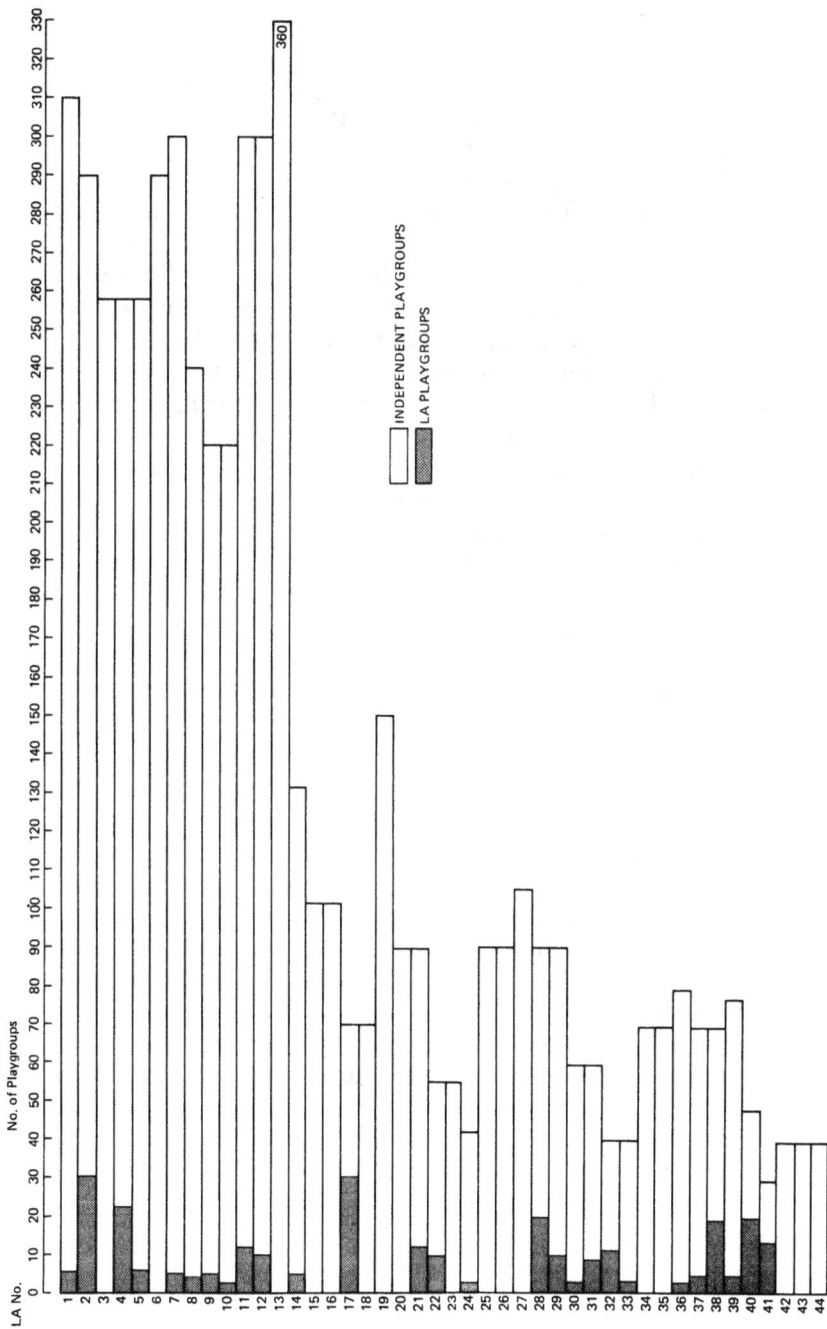

No. of Playgroups

INDEPENDENT PLAYGROUPS

LA PLAYGROUPS

LA No.

aided all new groups. One quoted 'saving threatened groups' and 'encouraging committee-run groups' as reasons for grant aid, but apart from this few went beyond the 'need' description, though this was sometimes qualified as the need of the community for a playgroup, as opposed to the need of the playgroup for money.

There were disappointingly few quoted criteria for assessing the amount of the grant, most authorities using the 'according to need' measure again, or quoting an agreed standard amount. One authority meets one-third of the rent up to a maximum of £250, and one meets 100 per cent of the net deficit (presumably of all groups) but expects all playgroups to charge at least 15p per session, so is not completely subsidising the groups.

In general, authorities seem to wish to encourage certain qualities in the groups, since they more often aid groups which are committee run, non-profit-making, in a disadvantaged area, and willing to accept referred children. Some also quote the need for a constitution, one requires a financial statement and a trained supervisor in charge, another requires that no more than twenty five children attend any session and that none of them shall be under 2½. One authority asks playgroups to account for the spending of the money and another states that it must be spent for the previously agreed purpose.

Only one authority mentioned day nurseries as qualifying for grant aid. It seems that grant aid can be used as a way of encouraging those aspects of good practice which cannot be imposed as requirements under the Nurseries and Child Minders Act. In two cases grants to playgroups were administered via the PPA branch.

Table 8 shows the amount available in each authority for grants to playgroups and the amount (in brackets) which each playgroup would receive if the total allocation for the purpose were to be divided equally between all playgroups.

2 Support to local branch of PPA or other voluntary agency

Twenty two of the social services departments appear to give grants to PPA and a further three to unspecified voluntary

Table 8 Grant aid to playgroups

LA No.	No. of Playgroups

Scale: 20 40 60 80 100 120 140 160 180 200 220 240 260 280 300

1 NS
2 NA
3)
4 £4,000 (£15·27)
5 £11,013 (£42·20)
6 £3,000 (£14·49) + UA
7)
8 £250 (84p)
9
10 NS
11 £2,815 (£12·74)
12
13 £6,000 (£29·41)
14 £1,450 (£3·91)
15 NA   380
16 NS
17)
18 £1,188 (£7·71) + UA
19)
20
21 £1,790 (£19·46)
22 £1,875 (£29·76)
23 £405 (£7·36)
24 £1,940 (£51·05)
25
26 £14,500 (£213·24)
27 £2,730 (£22·38) (UA)
28 £3,129 (£38·16)
29 £26,985 (£290·16)
30
31 £2,200 (£38·60)
32 £1,580 (£39·50)
33 £4,200 (£102·44)
34 £475 (£7·20)
35 £800 (£28·57)
36 £500 (£6·67)
37 NS
38)
39 £3,410 (£41·59)
40 £64,850 (£13·79)
41 via PPA £12,800 (£441·38)
42)
43
44 NS

KEY

NA   no figures available
     from the LA
)   exact amount not
     available, but some
     grants given
NS   Not specified
     whether amounts given

This table shows the amount
available to playgroups
and the amount (in brackets)
which each playgroup would
receive if the total allocation
for the purpose was divided
equally between all playgroups

bodies. Ten of the authorities giving grants did not state whether these were for any specific purpose. Expenses of AOs were mentioned four times, and among those mentioned once were administration, branches, county organiser, training, voluntary visitors, project leaders, adviser and toy library. The amount of the grants ranged from £100 for a toy library, to £12,344 (purpose not specified). Five were for £5,000 or more. Three LEAs gave grants to PPA, one amount being £5,000, the other two not specified.

We are well aware that the information presented, while complete in itself, is only the introduction to a much wider study. It has not been possible with the available resources to follow all the interesting sequences of thought which have occurred, nor to marry up all of the data so far collected. We have tried to present the facts as they have been given to us, rather than attempt cursory conclusions.

3   Sponsored places

Only nineteen of the authorities quoted a specific amount for 'sponsored' (free) places. Four said they did sponsor but did not state the amount; seven said they used separate funds under the Children's Act; one used an unspecified amount under the 1963 Act; one of those having a specific budget also used 1963 Act funds; one quoted '48 free places', and one said that free places were included in local authority playgroups. The nineteen authorities quoting a specified amount are listed in Table 9 opposite. Also shown is the number of places this would buy (assuming a place as £5 per week for 50 weeks of a year) and, in the fourth column, each child's chance of a free place (counting all children 0-4 in the authority). Under the Children's Act some local authorities register as playgroups some which operate for a full day or admit children below the age of three.

4   Other items, including support in kind

The remainder of the playgroup support budget included, oddly, such items as day fostering, assisted daily minding, play centre, special needs groups, and a family centre.

Table 9   **Sponsored places**

LA	Amount Available £	No. of places (approx.)	All 0–4 chance of a free place
1	4,400	18	1 in 5,705
7	6,000	24	1,967
8	5,070	21	2,022
10	14,000	56	679
11	9,900	40	947
13	4,164	17	2,029
14	6,689	27	1,200
18	554	2	11,847
19	10,245	41	617
22	850	3	6,294
23	702	3	7,260
24	210	1	23,929
27	4,600	18	962
28	2,440	10	1,783
33	1,210	5	3,182
35	2,310	9	1,569
36	4,000	16	869
39	3,840	15	801
43	775	3	2,581

Twenty-three authorities listed some form of support in kind:

Equipment loans was the service most often mentioned (15).
A purchasing scheme was mentioned by 6.
Low- or no-cost furniture by 5.
Premises for meetings or for playgroups by 4 and 3.
Office space by 3.
Training by 4.
Discussion groups by 3.
Literature by 2.
Assistance with administration by 1.

Seven authorities classed inter-departmental co-operation in this category. One or two specified advice (which could illustrate what a director described as 'special-approach' as distinct from normal-channel on going advice) but we have not included this, since so many authorities must have assumed that the facility would be taken as read. Authorities mentioning most features in this section are local authority 3 (6 types of help in kind), LA 9 (4 types), LAs 7, 8, 13, 16, 23, 27, and 43 (3 types each). Authorities 4, 6, 18, 19, 20, 24, 29, 30, 33, 35, 36, 41 and 42 all refer to some one contribution of support in kind. The three authorities standing out in Table 6 as having the largest stated budgets offer no kind of help in kind; the fourth largest budget-holder offers interdepartmental co-operation. Of the three authorities mentioning the most forms of help in kind, No. 9 has one of the smallest budgets; Nos 3 and 12 are in the main block of budget amounts, that is between £5,000 and £15,000.

Facts and figures on grant aid from Scottish social work departments

In looking at the Scottish financial allocation it has again to be remembered that the size of the social work grant may be decided in relation to other grant-aiding of playgroups, for example by education departments. In two cases, playgroups receive financial support from both education and social work departments, and in one of these a number of community education playgroups run by the education department receive grants for staffing, property and supplies. In general the reshaping of local authority departments at regionalisation (May 1975) resulted in social work departments becoming the main source of financial assistance to playgroups.

Grants to individual playgroups and to SPPA

Grants to individual playgroups took up the major part of total allocation, though four areas gave no grants to playgroups and the biggest region gave less than half the total. The major portion of grants to the organisation was given at different levels for payment of SPPA area organisers, for playleaders in urban areas, and for administration. Although the criteria for playgroups' grants were not always given, there were common elements, some detailed and specific: for example, grants may not be automatic annual payments, though playgroups may apply each year; applicant playgroups must be registered with the department and comply with requirements laid down by the Nurseries and Child Minders' Act; several regions required playgroups to have an elected committee, a constitution acceptable for charitable status and staff attending relevant training.

The grant itself varied: it could be a negotiated fixed amount, or up to a maximum for each playgroup, or arranged on a sliding scale based on average attendances. Two regions quoted separate amounts paid as initial grants to new playgroups. Only the region where individual playgroups received the biggest grants gave details of how grants to playgroups were to be used, namely for staff allowances, insurance, and towards rent and heating costs; this region also required fees to be held to 10p per session.

Support for SPPA under grants to voluntary organisations

Given as a total figure, this could mean money to support area organisers or branches or regional committee expenses, or for use to be decided by SPPA, possibly including several of these. Seven regions gave money to SPPA in this way, three gave no grant to voluntary organisations and two did not reply. In one area, the grant was agreed through consultation at regional level between social work department, SPPA and the education authority.

Special fees

Except in one case, no figures were given for grants to children in need, though a sum might be set aside in annual estimates or included in the amount allocated to individual playgroups, or it could be simply stated that the social work department met the fees of children with special needs.

Other items including support in kind

Under other heads, two regions gave amounts towards playgroup work training, one to playbus costs, and another a sum to committees with special needs. From the few indications of help in kind, secretarial assistance, loan of toys, free use of community centres and other premises were listed.

Indications of directors' thinking on grant aid

We had contributions on the subject of grant aid from two
other sources. The first represented views of directors of social
services departments, and the second comments from some
parts of the PPA/SPPA network.

Inevitably, in interviews, talk turned to the aims, conditions
and practice of grant aid. Problems highlighted were those of
producing playgroups or alternative provision in *even coverage of
the area, with special attention to those parts where need was most
obvious:* 'I wish, bearing in mind where playgroups were
needed, that PPA were more missionary minded', 'We would
probably give a bigger grant for projects in deprived areas'.
Did grant aid commit a branch to helping the department
service its whole area? 'I don't think I see it as a bargain, but
I'm sure my committee does.' In one area with a big dock and
services population, and unmet need for community activity,
the director rather depressingly did not see playgroup work,
specially supported or not, as relevant. Several would express
departmental support for playgroups as 'providing' social
services playgroups.

Should money be given as a general grant, or closely tied?
There was considerable appreciation of the social value of
letting PPA or a voluntary organisation choose how it spent its
money – 'Budgeting and choice of priorities being part of the
self-help and independence which we want to characterise PPA
in the future.' Others believed in a more rigid control over
public money. One said: 'No strings. Probably Education
would expect it to go on training, and social workers on
supporting groups in difficulties. I feel it is vital that the branch
is free to make its own decisions.' Another: 'The only strings to
our grants are that the objectives expressed by the grant-aided
organisation must be met.' At the opposite extreme: 'The
money was not used for educational purposes, so now it is
given in the form of equipment.' One director was firm that
grants should be spent for specific use only, but allowed the
largest possible range of categories: 'Grant aid must be used for
the purposes offered, and, in return for the interest and money,

they must use it well.' Flexibility could be allowed for in various ways, for example, 'a discretionary grant for AOs to use to help playgroups' or a sum reserved so that when a branch wanted to use its initiative in a way not foreseen it could be financed (but the grant would not necessarily be confirmed if the experiment did not prosper). One director gave guidance on the gearing of applications. 'The future for playgroups depends on how they see themselves. Anything which develops relationships between adults and children will always be supported. If it turns to ''educational techniques for children'' they would belong to Education.'

Mechanics of grant aid
There was again a wide range of practice, from the director who sat on a County committee, and was fully involved all through, or another who overlooked the application and informally advised a branch to go and check some playgroups' calculations, to those who referred everything to the statutory worker. On the processing of an application through estimates and pruning, it was clear that a lot depended on the personal interest both of the adviser, who did a preliminary pruning, and of the director, who took the application on. Several indicated that branches had no idea of the fight which had to be put up for their application when axing was on: 'Money for advisers or for bulk-buying is something the department has to fight for. Playgroups and branches need to do their part in the fight . . . good preparation, spade work with councillors, etc.' 'Playgroups should be doing more to lobby councillors when money is short.'

The tough fight to keep posts is not always won, and a branch may blame the department or director, and have no concept of the fight he has made. (This ties in with the lack of knowledge of grant allocation and its mechanics which is apparent in some replies from branches. It is a new area of involvement.) On the other hand, some directors admitted that their minds were made up about some items before a grant-aid application was made, which made nonsense of any consultative exercise. Some directors showed ingenuity in supplementing an official grant. They regretted that so much depended on Urban Aid, which made planning ahead difficult. They found expenses for AOs from casual car users' funds, and drew on Children's Act funds and other area team resources for needy children's fees.

No director took up in discussion the major financial issues of including playgroup fees in what was available automatically under supplementary benefit, or paying for playgroup as for nursery school places in order to give parents real choice. Nor did they expand on the confidentiality issue when a playgroup committee was asked to indicate when a child should have his fees paid.

Allocating grant aid

Although no one referred to the withdrawal of grant aid as a strategy or punitive exercise, there was a general agreement that 'it was necessary to show that public money given was productive, and that the department was watchful of what it gave'. The strain on a branch handling sizeable grant-aid for the first time was mentioned. Should playgroups get their grant aid through the branch? Should the adviser handle it? There did not seem to be common policy. We turned for possible further information on this to the last of our sources – questions asked of some counties and branches in the areas where the playgroups questionnaire had been used, knowing that a more extensive inquiry would be useful here.

PPA network response

Confusion was again possible here. 'Playgroups' could mean individual playgroups which received grant aid, or the work could be used generically to convey the local playgroup presence – probably a county, or branch, which was helped with administration, training or personnel.

In England, two counties say there are no grants to playgroups. One county says that grants are distributed by the county association. One county says it has some part in the social services, but not the education grant. Two counties have representatives on the grants committee, but do not say how effective these are. One county does not say what is the outcome of estimates it has put in.

One replying branch which is part of a joint voluntary set-up has a say in allocation of grants. Two branches make no comment, and one described consultation which took place recently for the first time, at the instigation of the social services department. There seems great variety in applying: to the director of social services, to the chief officer and then to the appropriate finance officer (usually social services). One branch applies also to education, result unknown, and one gets money from education without applying for it. Some apply through the social services adviser.

Two counties suggest that one needs 'experience' to know the right moment to apply, others that the adviser tells them to, and probably gives them a form. More experienced branches are fully primed, know the local authority year, are in consultation in between, and apply at the right time and without difficulty. In one county and branch there appear to be small, informal groups, (local authority and PPA) meeting to discuss grants. These meetings are followed by an application in writing. There are, however, difficulties. One branch says it applies annually and has been successful for the first time in 1977. Several worry about delays in actual payment, and the adviser and/or the AO has to mediate between finance sector and branch. Most PPA committees manage to plan but there is a widely held belief that the department prefers branches to reach the red and then be baled out. Considerable experience of making-do will help, but for many there does seem to be anxiety in the background of their work, and difficulty in tracing activity between different sections of the department.

Assisted by grant aid, counties and branches offer different services to playgroups. It may be duplicating facilities, loan of equipment, free literature, loan of books, bulk-buying schemes, usually on a branch basis. It may be small grants to new playgroups, payment of the first year's subscription to PPA, help from a contingency fund in an emergency. Most counties and branches are involved in training courses at grass-roots level, and either run training courses or give financial assistance to students.

SPPA network responses

Obviously in Scotland grant aid is in the main a regional function. Some divisions, districts and branches say they have no say in the allocation of grants, but those whose regional committees negotiate the grant do have their democratic right to ask their regional representative on the regional committee to make their opinions known. All those replying to the questionnaires get grants of some kind, nearly always from social work departments. Two or three exceptions are grants from education departments for training courses. The other concerns a region which appears to get a joint grant from social work and education departments. One region reports that the social work field services section funds the playgroups whilst the SPPA regional committee gets a grant as a voluntary organisation through the combined services division of the social work department and through the community education service. Despite the fact that negotiating for grants is largely left to to the regions, the method of informing them seems very haphazard. The region with a consultative committee is informed via its workings. The others 'sometimes get to know through the playgroup adviser' or 'get to know through advertisements in the local press' or have a grants working party 'that sometimes gets to know' (this region can also try through the voluntary organisations liaison officer or the 'grapevine').

Two regions are paid at the same time each year, in two instalments. One region comments that more effort has been made to keep the voluntary organisations informed since regionalisation. Once again one region has to rely on the local press. Two say that it is often touch and go whether they go into the red. There is general agreement that the method of making grants does not allow them to plan ahead.

There is considerable support for the regions from their divisions, districts and branches for their views on payment of the grant. Two districts say that there can be little forward planning. One quotes as an example that they are still waiting in January 1978 for the March 1977 grant. Two districts state that payments are made quickly and annually and they can plan ahead whereas their region thinks planning is difficult because payment is irregular. Branches indicate, as in England, that either the branch knows the system or it doesn't. Some just do not have the experience; some spell out the procedure step by step, including three payments a year and easy forward planning. In one region, branches seem confused. The region has clearly stated that it negotiates the grant, but all have different views of who tells them when it is available, how often they get the money, and whether they can plan ahead. Two say that the SPPA district tells them when money is available and that application forms are posted or handed out by the playgroup adviser. One branch says that payment is annual, they don't have to wait, they don't go into the red and they can plan ahead. The second says that payment is annual, that the grant is paid quickly but they do go into the red, and then adds that they can plan ahead. There are other variations, including one where the Branch AO's grant is paid quickly but the playgroup grant less so. We feel once more that some of the confusion is in the term 'playgroups'. Does this mean individual playgroups or is it a comprehensive term like 'schools'? A region may sound disenchanted, and yet its districts and branches think the system good, because the region does not have a regular payment but the playgroups do and districts and branches are answering for the playgroups.

It is worth noting that *nowhere* in these regions of Scotland at the moment *is there any adviser employed by SPPA on a grant* or seconded to SPPA and working at region/division/district/branch level. *SPPA Advisers*, overseeing two regions, are *employed by Executive Committee of SPPA on grant* from central government.

Summary

Grant aid
Information was sought about grants to PPA/SPPA under four headings: to playgroups; to the supporting organisation; to children in need (in the form of free playgroup places); and help in kind. Unfortunately the replies were confused, as some included costs for other forms of day care.

England and Wales
Budgets appear not to be related to staffing patterns nor to the numbers of playgroups in the area nor to the under-five population. The largest (in the middle-sized local authority) is approximately £75,000; and the sixth largest authority has one of the smallest budgets and staff allocations. Grant aid to playgroups is frequently used as a way of encouraging good practice, and varies between £25 and £3,500. Averaged between all playgroups in an area, grant allocation varies between 84p and £441 (the latter in a small authority, which gives out the money through PPA). About half the responding authorities grant-aid the organisation side of PPA, six giving £5,000 or more. Nineteen authorities quoted specific budgets for free places in playgroups; a further fourteen appear to finance free places through various sources. The chance of getting a free place is nowhere higher than 1 in 617, and one authority funds only one place for its 24,000 under-five population. Twenty three authorities list help in kind, the most frequent service being loans of equipment.

Scotland
Most aid comes from social work departments, though two areas get grants from community education. Most money goes to individual playgroups, in spite of the fact that four regions out of nine give no money to playgroups. The region giving the biggest grants detailed how they were to be used; other regions used various criteria as in England and Wales. Grants to SPPA organisation were mostly for payment of AOs, playleaders in urban areas and administration. Two regions gave set amounts for training and one for a playbus. No figures were given for 'free places' grants. Support in kind featured mostly secretarial help.

Directors would like grant aid to encourage the growth of playgroups in areas of need. Some were personally involved to a much greater degree than others, and there was a wide spectrum of opinion as to how closely controlled by the authorities PPA/SPPA spending should be.

English counties and branches vary widely in experience and expertise in the matter of applying for and handling grants, but for many finance is a continuous source of anxiety. Branches use some of their money to offer services to playgroups – secretarial, bulk-buying, etc. In Scotland, handling grants is in the main a regional function, but the authority keeps committees informed only in a very haphazard way. Here again, confusion and delays can make for considerable difficulty in planning ahead.

Questions

1 Could the branch participate more fully in the process of grant aid applications through the local authority department?
2 Are understanding and administering grant aid of real value to the development of responsibility in playgroup or branch?
3 Does the level of grant aid for personnel and for free places allow for effective handling of referrals, meeting of financial implications, and follow-up interaction between department and playgroup?
4 Has the grant aiding department a right to expect a playgroup or branch to co-operate in its general policy?

7

The Contribution of Education Departments: Moves Towards Inter-Departmental and Inter-Agency Consultation

We looked first at the local contribution of education departments, as noted in some parts of the PPA/SPPA networks.

Categories of assistance to playgroups

Posts with special responsibility

Eighteen out of sixty LEAs had posts with special responsibility for playgroups. Playgroups often came into the brief of the nursery/infant adviser; here, however, playgroups were usually felt to be of lesser importance. One county had an education adviser plus two advisory teachers, able to support and advise nursery schools and playgroups, in two out of three divisions. One had a liaison officer for pre-school education; of the 270 playgroups in the county, she had to concentrate on playgroups in schools. One city council sponsored a joint appointment with the social services department – a teacher-adviser working among playgroups. One county had a joint policy, with a team of project leaders and a supervising organiser. Another had a county organiser for under-fives, paid for by the education department and expected to represent, in the advisory team and the education service, the participation of the voluntary agency. A number in the south indicated no statutory appointment, but a grant for appointments in PPA. No Scottish region had an education department appointment with special playgroup responsibility.

It is interesting to note, among those present at the meeting to constitute an association for advisers of under-fives, these education department appointments: 'pre-school developer', 'primary inspector', 'adviser for the early years', 'infant/nursery adviser', 'county adviser, early childhood'.

Help offered by nursery advisers
Because they could not stray from their brief, a number felt the help they could give to be limited. They were too busy to offer help to individual playgroups, who were therefore often unaware of what was possible. Some nursery advisers were included on PPA county committees. Some advised, or ran playgroups courses, or took part in discussion preceding courses, but because of a personal relationship, not as part of their brief.

Three or four briefs included relationships between playgroups and secondary schools. In Scotland, half the nursery advisers said they helped playgroups, half said not, depending mainly on personal relationships built up. In Scotland, AOs and playgroup leaders have been invited by one nursery adviser to join a short course for nursery and pre-school teachers.

Help offered by other advisers and teachers
Experience was mixed: in some parts of the country, adult education advisers were available. Many teachers made themselves available, depending on personal contacts and relationships. A music teacher, for example, might become a well-known speaker at playgroup events.

Contacts other than advisory in LEA
A good number of replies indicated that there was a regular person to contact, but were not specific. It might be the education community organiser, or the NNEB tutor, or a number of people in the FE college. In Scotland the executive officer was mentioned, often at assistant director level. There was general agreement that when a good contact had been established this was the one to stick to.

Administration
There was more than one statement that playgroups dealt with the social services or PPA playgroup adviser, and thought of education administration as remote. The same seems to be true in Scotland, where an approach to the education administration would be rare, because the social work departments were available. A branch could ask for help for individual playgroups, but would be unlikely to. This was the case also in Scotland, where nine areas thought it possible, but not likely. It would seem that any approach to the LEA, particularly in the south, would be by branch or county, and help forthcoming would be likely to be to the branch, for the running of courses, or to playgroups, for help in kind. In Scotland, help would be for courses, to the branch, or for any use of premises.

Paper, duplicating facilities, etc.
It appears that many playgroups and branches are able to make their own arrangements and do not even know that facilities might be available from the education department. Half, however, did receive duplicating and secretarial help, but paid for the service. In Scotland, all regions had help with typing and duplicating but paid for the service. There is considerable use of educational supplies, with benefit to budgeting.

Assistance in communicating
Some branches seemed to use the LEA circular as a means of communicating with all schools and educational recipients. Other LEA services available include the use of LEA vans for transporting heavy equipment.

Use of premises
Some LEAs were willing for playgroups to use empty classrooms, but there is a mixed reaction nationally from the teaching profession. Head teachers were usually in favour because it helped later with home/school relationships, and they also felt themselves available to give advice and support to playgroups. Teachers, on the other hand, gave priority to the redundancy problem, and would prefer the empty classrooms

to be used by nursery classes. A statement was made in one area: 'Empty premises and surplus plant present important opportunities which must be grasped boldly and with imagination based on the universal view, and not on the fragmentary statutory service approach of the past. A starting-point is the assumption that variety of provision can operate from the same accommodation base.' Thirteen of seventeen Scottish regions/divisions have known empty classrooms used for playgroups, but report much more use of the youth and community wings in secondary schools (thirty seven in the Grampian Region). These playgroups would generally be registered by social work departments, in the usual way. Teachers' centres or adult education centres were available and used.

Surplus school furniture
This seemed to be generally available on request, rather than offered. Usually it was free, sometimes at a nominal charge. Less was likely to be available in future. The concession worked best when one person was responsible to supervise fair distribution. In Scotland, a request would generally be met, though less certainly since reorganisation and cut-backs.

Courses
The obvious link with the LEA, which all playgroups and branches expect to exist, though with a variety of relationships, is in training. It is of value briefly to note the change of balance in this field from a service asked for and established from 'nearest' resources, often with little discussion, to a jointly planned exercise based on local adult need. It is of interest also that in this new relationship the LEA has potentially a major and exciting role, bonding parents and professionals more closely and strengthening links between schools and home.

Teachers' centres were widely used, and accommodation of different kinds, for different purposes, in FE colleges. Forty two out of sixty responses quoted some help in kind, including loan of visual aids, films, projection equipment and books, which could also come from the education section of the public library. One branch held back from using all this, on the grounds that 'They do it all. No chance for playgroup courses and tutors.' A welcome practice in Scotland has been the payment of tutor and speakers drawn from the local voluntary association/branch.

Fees

Practice varies, not only from place to place, but yearly. Further education authorities will often support 8–12 week courses free, or with a subsidy for tutors. Sometimes a grant for these is given jointly with social services departments. (On occasion the WEA is able to put on a needed course much more locally and quickly, and is ready to use AOs and other experienced playgroup workers as tutors. In one area, two experimental appointments have been made, linking the work of PPA and WEA in relation to young parents.) For advanced courses, there can be joint finance from central funds.

Grants to playgroups or AOs

Over 50 per cent of AO's honoraria and/or expenses come from education grants, though there is some confusion about the source or these. They can come from LEAs or social services departments, or by joint grant, usually administered by social services.

Grants of £5,000–£6,000 for distribution to playgroups were quoted several times. In distribution, priority was given to new groups, these sometimes getting £25, sometimes £50, as a setting-up grant. One rural county gave aid in block sums, on a *per capita* basis. In many areas grants are small or non-existent. Rent, heating, light and equipment as well as course fees were frequent categories for grants, which could be given on joint PPA, social services, and LEA recommendation. But grants do not come to playgroups from education departments in all districts. In Scotland, the practice seems perhaps more variable. Bursaries, travelling expenses to courses, and course expenses are the most frequent, but ten quote no grants, or do not know of grants either to branch or to playgroups. Variations spread across different authorities include large amounts to playgroups and branches; £1,000 to the branch for training and equipment; £50 per playgroup per annum; £3,694 to playgroups, £2,250 to the branch (this indicates education as the main local source of finance); £632 for branch and AO expenses, £526 for playgroup rental; occasional help to needy playgroups; £500 for training. Finance of courses means most often payment of fees, but fees can be subsidised. £1,500 was given in one area in one year, but in another area no course fees were charged, and in another there was a movement towards payment. For fieldwork courses, travelling expenses were often paid, as well as bursaries.

Key to take-up of education department assistance

This rather variable and miscellaneous list of help available, directly and indirectly, needs to be read as the record of what a number of branches and county PPAs *think* is available to them. It could be that help under more of the categories would be available if they sought it, but that no one in their LEA has time allocated in which to *offer* help. Playgroups need to, and do, spring from very different backgrounds, and it is clear that in the take-up of educational resources, as in the application for social services grant aid, there are some who know the system and others who don't. Where an adviser or other person is appointed by the LEA with playgroup support as the whole or part of her brief, take-up can become much higher, because communication improves. The LEA–PPA/SPPA liaison then becomes much more positive. For example, in an área where communication is difficult for a branch an adviser can initiate the use of the LEA circular. A branch may not even know that it exists, and certainly may not be aware that they would be allowed to use it. Or, in the case of finding the most appropriate speaker for a branch meeting, the adviser may be able to make suggestions and introductions to the branch. At present, the adviser may only feel able to use what remains of her time when other priorities have been met – and who has a remainder of time? As was clear in the Section on registration (Section 2), *an interested person, with time, brings the formal and theoretical to life.*

Part of the hesitation in approaching the LEA administratively results from the fact that parents recognise

tension in the local authority. They know that the one department is responsible for them, and are not sure of their position
in approaching another. A strong line of encouragement is
needed. Their sense that there was often less than harmony
between departments came out in some responses to the
question 'Could Social Services Departments ask help from
Education for playgroups?' This was seen as an interdisciplinary relationship, and answers were vague. Some
commented that departments were unwilling to confer, 'to the
detriment of those in the community under statutory care'. In
the south, two-thirds of the replies thought this contact 'highly
unlikely'. One said. 'They would rather die first.' Seven
Scottish authorities said that the interchange.of views did take
place, and in at least one region registration involved referral to
the education department.

It is necessary from the consumer end, in order to encourage
playgroups and parents to take full advantage of all resources,
that *there should not only be, but be seen to be, full, interested co-
operation between all interested in their young children, and their own
development.*

Liaison and consultation

It is apparent from the analysis of job descriptions (Section 5)
that informal liaison between all working with the under-fives
is occupying an increasing part of advisers' time, whether they
work from a department or within a voluntary organisation.
We asked for the views of branch/county/district PPA workers
on this.

Liaison on teenagers
This growing liaison between playgroups and schools presents
an area for future thinking by PPA/SPPA and the DES, as well
as LEAs. Southern Region PPA has made available guidelines;
CSV and PPA have jointly produced a very full guidance kit,
'Teenagers in playgroups'; several regional days have been
held on the subject, bringing head teachers and teachers as well
as PPA personnel to think through the implications. One PPA
branch has an AO working solely on this link, and several LEA

advisers include teenage/school/playgroup/branch relationships in their brief, but without sufficient allocation of time. In
Scotland, the quality of liaison was said to vary according to
personalities and schools. Co-ordination varied, though SPPA
has lately issued guidelines, and is working to improve
relationships.

The different relationships, including familiarity between
the three backgrounds of the teenager's home, school and
playgroup, could be the topic for courses of the ATO/DES
type, with full representation from playgroups and branch
included. The beginning of this wider membership in
appropriate courses is welcomed in the isolated cases where
playgroup personnel, probably at national adviser or TDO
level, are invited to help staff such courses.

Liaison with other departments and health authorities
It seemed from PPA replies that all branches and PPA county
associations except for one branch have contacts with their
local authority: all with social services, but, in the case of one
county PPA and two branches, only with social services. Most
quote contacts with social services and education and health
authorities, but one branch and one county PPA not with the
health authority. One branch also quoted links with the local
CVS, but the general impression is that contacts could be more
extensive. County PPAs record more satisfaction than
branches. The words qualifying exchanges vary through
'reasonably effective', 'reasonably', 'usually' to 'not effective',
'not very'.

SPPA analyses contacts with social work departments, and
their effectiveness. Regions have contact with assistant
directors and advisers; SPPA districts and divisions with district
managers; and branches with the playgroup adviser. This
hierarchical division is thought to be satisfactory if the channels
of communication within both social work departments and
SPPA are good. There is some evidence that from the SPPA
point of view communication in the LA could be better, but
also that their own has room for improvement. Eight out of
eleven regions, divisions and districts quote good
communication with education departments, in one region

almost exclusively with community education, but it is interesting that no branch has this. In contrast, three branches have contact with health authorities (local health visitor) but the lack of other contact with health authorities at any level seems an obvious gap. Only four replies whose contacts were playgroup adviser or health visitor expressed real satisfaction, the others again ranging through 'so-so', 'not really', and 'sometimes'. There are three general comments: that contacts with social work departments are more effective than those with education departments; that the autonomy of branches and playgroups is sometimes overstepped by the LA playgroup adviser; and that in Scotland, the contact seems all one-way, SPPA giving information to the LA, and not the other way round.

Liaison between voluntary organisations

Relationships between PPA and other voluntary organisations working with young children and families seemed very variable. Considering the range of voluntary services represented at the recent Advisers' Association meeting – including, besides PPA and SPPA, the WRVS, SCF, NSPCC, and those who regularly meet under VOLCUF, adding among others the British Association for Early Childhood Education (BAECE), the Family Service Unit, Gingerbread, the National Association for the Welfare of Children in Hospital, the National Children's Bureau and the Child Minders' Association – there would seem to be an opportunity for more interchange of voluntary thinking at local level. Nevertheless, it is probably true that people now accept that care of the child should not be in the hands of single departments and organisations. *The stage of pleasant friendly talk between agencies has arrived. A further stage of more formal consultative groups received a fillip in England and Wales in January 1978, from the DES/DHSS circular recommending joint thinking and planning.*

Moves towards a more formally shared policy of provision

In areas where there has been inter-agency contact PPA/SPPA have been grateful for practical assistance and personal interest from education department staff but it may seem to the local branch/district that local authority policy remains unaffected. We therefore grouped together references from job descriptions, interviews with directors, and PPA/SPPA comments relating to the topic of liaison to see whether they added up to a significant indicator of any discernible effect on policy.

There seems to be growing awareness of the need for interdisciplinary groups to meet regularly to consider provision for under-fives, but not so often of the need to consider the adults related to the child. There is no unanimity on the inclusion of PPA/SPPA or other voluntary organisations. Scotland quotes general reluctance to involve playgroups on decision-making bodies, but in some areas groups are beginning to meet to discuss local situations – for example planning courses, grants committees, forums with local nursery teacher, primary teachers, etc. *The forum for interchange of information and the widening of its membership is probably a necessary intermediate stage until it becomes credible that there could be joint planning.*

Emergence of consultative groups

Of seven PPA county associations replying, two have no kind of joint consultative committee. Of five which do have groups, one is in the process of starting and one is an under-five panel. Of the six PPA branches replying only two have a consultative committee in their area, and one of these branches is a constituent of the joint voluntary committee for under-fives. This branch says that PPA is not included in the consultative committee, which is however largely made up of PPA people!

All the consultative groups include education and social services departments, but two do not include the health authority. Other people sometimes included are NUT, BAECE, councillors, Gingerbread, and child-minding groups. There is no indication that any of these consultative groups, except the joint voluntary committee, are formally constituted.

Of the five counties who have a joint group, the replies were not encouraging about the interests of playgroups. One county PPA said that their interests were generally (another said partially) served. One said, 'Yes, in some areas'; and one that it was not true consultation and that a lot of work was needed to make it so. The most recent group said that they were trying hard to make it useful.

Two county PPAs said that they have no consultative group, and it appeared that they had little liaison of any kind. In one there are termly meetings between AOs, teacher/advisers and the social services department, and in the same county the PPA county chariman has personal contact with the statutory bodies 'at any level' if required. In the second county, the contact seems to be only through one working representative on a working party inquiry into under-five provision. Anxiety is expressed in one county that their good, personal, informal links have now been replaced for some reason with a formal, constituted, consultative group.

The position in Scotland shows similarities. There seem to be few consultative groups developing within the Scottish regions. Only one has such a group, and it is made up of the assistant director of education, the education primary adviser, the divisional officer (Day Care) from the social work department and five SPPA representatives. This region considers that the committee does serve the needs and interests of the playgroup.

A second region makes two interesting comments:

(a) The regional department set up a working party on the needs of children under five years. They involved equal numbers of education and social work staff. After a time the SPPA regional chairman was invited to join and some months later the SPPA adviser for that region was also invited. The working party is soon to produce a report but in the meantime all initiative seems to be frozen.

(b) SPPA started in 1970 a committee for the under-fives. This group now consists mainly of LA personnel, but SPPA is still represented.

Two branches report that there are consultative meetings in their areas between branch personnel and the LA playgroup adviser in one case, and the community development officer in the other. Neither branch is over-enthusiastic about the long-term effects of these meetings. They are 'regular' rather than 'formal'.

Statements of joint policy

It is of interest that a number of authorities have made sufficient steps towards joint policy to find it useful to sum these up in statements of policy, perhaps with a wish to communicate this within and beyond their area. Among these are the following:

1 Booklet issued by a joint group, including social services and education departments, health authority and PPA. Chairmanship of this group rotates, but the secretariat remains with education.
2 Statement of policy issued by two departments (social services and education) establishing the machinery for joint action. (Local leaders and consultative groups work in areas of need, serviced by social services; co-ordinator and central consultative group are serviced by education. Social services district co-ordinators and PPA branch and AOs are closely involved.)
3 Preliminary statement in one city of joint policy for under-fives, including two experimental joint staff appointments.
4 In a number of areas, co-operation between social services and education departments, health authority and PPA in interpreting for local -guidelines the legislation covering playgroups, nurseries and childminders.

Consultation moving towards agreed spending

We found a variety of views about the degree of progress represented by consultative groups and even statements of joint interest or policy. It was said of the earlier phase – pleasant talk, leading towards more purposeful consultation – that it had no effect on unilateral policy. Meetings arranged by a social services department and bringing together a number of voluntary organisations including SPPA, Alcoholics Anonymous, WRVS, and others were said in one reply to cause frustration and serve few interests other than social ones. But the personal meeting and talking-shop may have a prolonged place in acclimatising people to joint thinking.

In the same way the more formal talking round a table, with an element of communicating plans already made unilaterally, may be a necessary stage in growing towards confidence in wider than unilateral action. Comment from a variety of bodies represented in the group may have its effect on the next round of decisions, though they may still be unilateral. There has to be a gradual stabilising of right to membership of these joint consultative groups. At present, membership varies substantially, as well as the initiative to convene such a group. Again there is frustration while the process is worked through, while the health authority in quite a number of areas is not included, while there is mixed reaction to voluntary representation. If the principle of voluntary representation is allowed, there are the difficult mechanics of representing such varied voluntary groups without swamping the total group. There are other difficult balances, which cannot be decided suddenly. How long can a voluntary organisation bind its changing membership to the same policy? How long can departments expect a voluntary organisation to continue its agreed policy? Who pays for rather early changes in arrangements? Or for the expression of changed policy in the form of new booklets? *It has to be realised that joint consultation has to be worked at, and that there will be crunch-points, notably when priorities on spending are involved, when the old tradition of unilateral action will be difficult to change.*

The two or three bold experiments in joint policy making will be precursors of many more, and it would seem that during the 'talking-shop' phase there has grown general recognition that unilateral provision for under-fives has produced over provision, unbalanced provision, and in some cases virtual competition for children. The next steps are taking time to work through, and one interesting feature of the process is that *informal, personal talk does not have to be superseded wholesale by more formal consultative committees, and then by policy making committees. They all need to go on concurrently.*

One authority is establishing the practice that all matters for discussion in this field have to be aired in the informal group before departments discuss them in their own policy making. One finds it easier to focus consultative group thinking on decisions about making money. Another finds joint thinking and action coming through at senior-officer rather than chief-executive and money-deciding levels. And there are areas when the impetus from the circular letter has not yet been felt and individual bodies are still trying to find forums where matters of joint interest can be aired.

PPA is represented in many areas on community health councils, and in others finds the problems of waiting in turn among a wide range of voluntary services. Priorities on the spending of money are not decided here, but can come under discussion from many different angles, and be expressed on behalf of the council.

Views of directors of local authority departments

It seems logical to refer in this section to directors' expressed views on the realities of consultation and informal consultation. They seem in general to recognise an increase of personal interaction, a considerable move to set up machinery for talk, and a perplexity about the next stage. What degree of agreed policy about funding different forms of under-five provision is realistic? Is there the likelihood of talk and unilateral policy going on side by side, and accusations of 'bad faith'?

'Consultation gives you the best you can get out of the resources you have,' said one director. 'The whole community holds responsibility for under-fives and young families, and voluntary and statutory contributions are complementary and part of an active partnership.' But some were wary of consultative committees, preferring to consult at personal level, or through their deputies. Some are holding tentative initial meetings, usually with health or education or both. They are aware that places for children under one form of provision can often only be filled by making places under another form empty. This is not always easy to discuss.

One director quotes an early consultative group working well together, because 'everyone by now knows each other personally' – an example of schemes or structures having to be given time to jell. Under this authority, the first consultative group has become so warm and productive that it is being supplemented with local forums. Several directors agreed that forums work best when they are small, and when they reach the stage of subgroups having to be formed (by topic) they can become out of touch and make less impact with real policy.

Not every area appeared interested. 'We have no overall consultative body – just competition between departments for total money.' One director found a weakness in the failure to involve the housing department.

There were different views on the wisdom of voluntary organisation membership of joint groups. 'Representatives could be asked to attend a meeting, if there seemed a special reason for their being there.' One or two directors quoted the voluntary agencies being there by right, and also taking their turn to convene and chair. In one place where there was no regular voluntary participation, the deputy director present said he was unsure of, and the director had no personal experience of, the value of a PPA branch; but his department worked closely with a regional fieldworker. If PPA/SPPA representatives need a place on otherwise statutory committees, the process needs to work in reverse. One deputy director said representatives from all departments attended the PPA county committee, and he attended regional meetings and sat on appointment panels. One mixed advisory committee, convened by PPA, 'advised on finance, prepared estimates, explored the needs of the area, provided a sounding board for the PPA branch executive'.

A number of umbrella-voluntary-organisation-groups have been set up, with the intention of making statutory–voluntary consultation more possible. Inter-Vol is one, in an area where there is no voluntary representation on a joint consultative group. A voluntary committee for under-fives, already referred to, is set up legally and in receipt of grant aid for member organisations. The director thought that PPA might be more receptive of what was being tried out here, and give a sufficient period for testing out results. In another area, where the director noted the 'aggressiveness' of PPA members, there was no voluntary representation on district co-ordinating groups.

Joint consultation and the advisers' association in England

One aspect of the adoption of a constitution by this new association was its decision by a vote of 88 to 11 to make it an inter-agency body, with membership open to all working in the under-five field and appointed by statutory or voluntary agencies. (This is particularly significant, as the representation was approximately 64 social services, 8 education, 4 health, and 23 voluntary workers, and it could have formed a different type of association.) This body should have a positive role in airing different views on work of common interest, and should help to clarify the next moves in developing friendly conversation, informal and formal consultation, and policy making with budget implications. It is likely to strengthen the interdisciplinary, inter-agency groups which are in some regions now enjoying development, in others struggling into existence.

Summary

Education departments
About one-third of LEAs had posts with special responsibility for playgroups, though none did in Scotland. In southern England, many authorities made, instead, grants for appointments within PPA. Nursery advisers found that the time available for playgroups was limited, and could not offer help to individual groups. Adult education advisers, teachers, college staff and others all help, often in a 'personal' rather than an 'official' way. All Scottish regions and half the English branches use, but pay for, duplicating and secretarial services. Some authorities (two-thirds in Scotland) allow empty school premises to be used for playgroups, but teachers' reaction is mixed. Help is widely given by LEAs for playgroup training, and there has been a movement away from provision by the authority to joint planning of courses. There is generous help with fees in some areas; in others none at all. In Scotland, payment is often made to course staff drawn from SPPA

locally. Education departments also grant-aid AOs and individual playgroups, especially new playgroups. Two-thirds of respondents quoted help in kind.

It is likely that more help would be available if requested. Take-up can be much higher where the LEA appoints an interested person with time to help. Playgroups may be hesitant to approach one department when another is responsible for them; there should be, and be seen to be, more co-operation between all those concerned.

Liaison

Advisers are spending an increasing amount of time on liaison with secondary schools (regarding pupils' placements in playgroups), with other departments and health boards, and with voluntary organisations. There seems an increased readiness for co-operation, though more at neighbourhood than at decision-making level. Of respondents, five out of seven PPA counties, two out of six PPA branches and one SPPA region out of nine have some form of consultative group, though not all are optimistic about the way they work. A few authorities have made joint statements of policy. Co-operation, whether formal or informal (and both forms are necessary), needs work, and its benefits are likely to be long-term. PPA/SPPA policy stresses the need for consultative groups to consider not only the under-fives but their parents too.

Directors generally recognised a move towards formal consultation, but wondered how far it is realistic to hope to achieve agreed policy, especially when different forms of provision are in competition for the same money. There are felt to be difficulties in voluntary membership of statutory committees; specific reasons for this are not given. It is hoped that the advisers' associations, with their mixed membership of statutory and voluntary organisation employees, may give helpful leads in the development of genuine co-operation.

Questions

1 How can the community playgroup approach be more speedily incorporated into all pre-school consultation groups?

2 In what sufficiently wide forums can the differences between community and professional provision be talked through, so that they do not put a brake on full co-operation in the under-five/young family field?

3 How can communication between LEA and PPA/SPPA be improved so that playgroups and branches take full advantage of what is at present available to them?

4 Under what conditions do joint social services/work and education department appointments work most effectively?

5 What elements can be introduced into in-service teacher training to make participation of teenagers in playgroup and community work more effective?

8

Playgroups in New Towns

Background to new town questionnaire

New towns have a large population of young families with pre-school children, and arrangements which will be transferred later to the local authority to help these to settle comfortably are usually the subject of considerable thought at the planning stage. New towns in England, Scotland and Wales were estblished under the provisions of the New Towns Act, 1946. When a new town is designated, a development corporation is appointed, whose first function is to decide on policy and priorities, and to prepare a master plan for the town's development. In the earlier new towns, the role of the development corporation was more like that of a large-scale developer. In the later new towns, the development corporations have been specifically asked to consider the social planning.

The working group realised that one of the difficulties, graphically publicised in the Skeffington Report, is securing consumer participation at the time of the master plan. A small section of the available population will attend exhibitions, study, and be vocal in appreciation or criticism. The large majority will wait to find out by experience what is offered, and then be vocal and express itself 'unconsulted'. By this stage, sites have been allotted and systems of communication finalised, and it is not easy for alternatives to be incorporated. In new towns there are additional reasons for the lateness of comment, since children whose parents might be vocal two or three years later are unborn, and their parents who will have followed industry or been rehoused there have not yet arrived. Pre-school requirements need therefore to be watched over in the earlier stages of development by families already in the area, and knowledgeable about priorities of spending. This could well be seen as an area of involvement for the nearest PPA branch.

The concern of PPA/SPPA to accommodate individual and family needs, and work opportunities and the necessity for some young women to earn, remains. In some new towns these may be unusually difficult to reconcile. Work for men in light industries may be comparatively poorly paid, and work-shifts for women may be available to bring in an almost indispensable supplement, at the cost of precise organisation of the family night and day.

Where this is so, and where there are the human pressures of neighbours all furnishing new homes, there may be a widespread problem of provision for the under-fives. Some new towns have built in almost a surplus of day-care and nursery places, others very little. The playgroup, doing valuable work for large numbers of parents and young children, may be denuded of parent helpers or fee-paying children because these have to be minded elsewhere for longer hours. This is a very complex situation, and it must be accepted that some, driven by the strangeness of new surroundings, feel the need of an outside outlet not related to child-rearing. On the other hand, the playgroup provides an integrating activity and meets the need of many in the new community.

Those responsible for oversight have to see that flexible provision is available, including day nurseries and nursery units, childminders and playgroups, and mother and toddler groups. PPA recently summarised needs which it would like to stress:

1 More community playgroups and mother and toddler clubs, not only to provide for children but also to meet the needs of parents who would otherwise seek companionship at a workplace.

2 A change in the tax system so that mothers who choose to stay at home are not penalised, and other financial measures to encourage parents to postpone leaving their pre-school children in order to go to work.

3   Encouragement for working mothers to use a good childminder in conjunction with a playgroup.
4   Measures to encourage employers to offer flexible working hours or even two part-time jobs where one existed before.

The working group would add a note that, where employment opportunities spring up and the related needs of the working mother must be met, meeting these may cause problems for non-working mothers through the threat of competitive provision to recently established playgroups. The support of a strong PPA/SPPA branch or its non-existence may determine whether some, struggling through the early stages, survive.

Response to the questionnaire prepared with the assistance of social responsibility officers

The new towns replying to this questionnaire were designated in two clearly defined stages. Ten of the English and two of the Scottish new towns who replied were designated between 1947 and 1949. There was then a hiatus, with the exception of one in Scotland until 1962. The remaining seven in England and two in Scotland were designated between 1962 and 1970.

The majority of the new towns are still the responsibility of their development corporations. Two of those in the survey have completed their growth, and have become the responsibility of the local authority. The two in Northumberland were initiated by Northumberland County Council, and have no development corporation.

Altogether, replies were received from seventeen new towns in England and Wales and five in Scotland. Out of a possible total of forty three, there was a 50 per cent response. There is considerable variation in their stage of development, and a wide variation in their size and population, both original and planned. The rate of growth in a new town can be seen in one or two examples – Aycliffe (designated 1947) had 60 inhabitants before designation, and now has 26,000. Northampton (designated 1968) is planned to double its original size to 235,000. The planned eventual population of new towns replying ranged from 11,500 to 420,000. The new towns therefore, although they share similar origins, and each has an artificially planned and managed rate of growth, vary widely in geographical situation, in their stage of development, and in their size.

The proportion of children under five in the new towns replying also covers a wide range. When the towns are divided into two groups, according to their date of designation, the individual variation within the first group (1947–9) is from 6·6 to 10 per cent of the total population, and within the second group (1962–70) from 5·4 to 14·5 per cent; but overall, from the sample in the questionnaire, the older towns averaged 8 per cent of the population under five and the newer ones 8·5 per cent.

Question 1 The role of the community development officer

In the first part of the questionnaire, the new town authorities were asked how many community development officers there were, and what their responsibilities as to playgroups were. They were also asked whether there was one person in their authority who held special responsibility for playgroups, and if so, what proportion of his or her time was given to them.

This question revealed an immediate difference between the approaches in Scotland and in England. Of the Scottish new towns, only one had a community development officer. In the others, the community role belonged to the housing department, and in none of them was there one person with specific responsibility. On the other hand, in Scotland the social work department has a very positive attitude to playgroups, and in each area help for playgroups was available from the local authority.

In England, all the new towns except three had community development officers, or a team of them, responsible to a social responsibility officer. One would often have special playgroup responsibility. The exceptions were virtually completed new towns.

The answers to the question about particular responsibility revealed a difference in attitude between the older and newer towns. Three of the older towns had someone responsible and five did not. Of the more recently established towns, six had somebody specifically responsible, and only two did not. Overall, two-thirds of the English new towns had someone specially responsible. These officers were usually community development officers, but in four of the towns (two old, two new) there had been a special appointment of a play officer or play adviser responsible for the full range of children's play.

The time given to playgroups by the officers concerned varied. The play officers gave between 5 and 25 per cent of their time to this age group (no comment on the involvement of the children's parents). The time given by CDOs varied. In one authority there were three CDOs who between them gave two hours to playgroups. In another, through a job creation project, four community work assistants were giving 30 per cent of their time. While the official time was small, usually from 5 to 15 per cent of the total time, the personal involvement of the CDOs often goes further, including attendance at meetings and conferences. The fact that they are in post, often at the end of a telephone line, gives confidence in the early stages of playgroup growth.

The CDOs see their main role as stimulating and helping the development of new groups – in twelve authorities, new groups were specifically mentioned as being part of their responsibility. Only two, however, mentioned work with playgroup or branch committees as being significant. One listed 'help with publicity, fund raising, acquiring equipment, finding helpers, setting up committees and establishing training courses' – a wide range of help for the emerging groups.

In a majority of the new towns, therefore, personal support and advice are available in the early stages of a playgroup's life. There may be other stages with difficulties, and there is a more general aspect of a CDO's role. A new playgroup or branch or AO , with mothers still finding their way to a relationship with a possibly distant local authority, may derive considerable confidence by support from a CDO, or if necessary from the development board at higher level. They may need this backing when they press for a course mounted more locally, or help with fees and travelling to one more distant. As time passes the branch will be in a stronger position to represent its members, and can hope to be on well-established terms with departments by the time the development corporation hands over.

Question 2   Practical assistance: premisis, finance and help in kind

The next section of the questionnaire asked for details of practical or financial help given to playgroups.

Premises

In all the new towns premises are available for playgroups, although unfortunately no details were asked for which would enable the number of halls or rooms available to be related to the population under five. However, twelve of the twenty-two new towns said that in their forward planning they deliberately considered the need for playgroup premises. In one authority special provision is made for playgroups within the main community centres, and another new town has three purpose-built play centres with special playgroup provision. A room in a house which is the base for a CDO, available free some afternoons for mothers and young children, is often the origin of a local playgroup. Once established, it moves out into the nearest community centre. When asked what kind of premises were available, all except three authorities mentioned community centres. Seven mentioned community houses, and other local meeting-rooms. Four new towns have playgroups combined with schools, and one uses a college annexe.

The great majority of authorities, eighteen out of twenty-two, said that they took needs of playgroups into consideration when planning community premises. Of those who did not consider playgroups before building, one had to make subsequent alterations to meet the need for storage, another commented that the lack of storage had led to 'considerable difficulties . . . and conflict with other users'. Yet another new town said that 'they endeavour to provide storage, but this never seems to be adequate when built!' Planners do try, but requirements seem to overtake them. It is important for these playgroup issues to get aired in the very early stages of planning.

Finance

Help also comes to playgroups in the form of assistance with rents. The Scottish new towns are excluded from this, as help there is given by the social work department, but of the English and Welsh new towns eleven out of seventeen gave initial help with rent. Nine new towns continue this help on a permanent basis. In four, all community groups pay a subsidised rent; and in three, playgroups have rent-free premises. One other allows a rent-free year.

Starter grants, ranging from £25 to £150, are available in twelve out of seventeen new towns replying, and two more make occasional initial grants. Two of the authorities channelled their help through the local PPA branch. Again the Scottish new towns are excluded.

Criteria for grant aid varied. Four authorities specifically mentioned committee-run playgroups, two the need of the playgroup or the area. Two consulted the local authority playgroup adviser, and four sought advice from PPA.

Four authorities gave starter grants to mother and toddler groups.

When the figures are analysed according to the date of designation, the following facts emerge. Of the longer established new towns, seven out of ten gave initial grants to playgroups; four out of seven of the newer new towns do so. But when we look at the new towns which give subsidised rents, five out of ten of the early ones do so and six out of seven of the newer ones. The three new towns which offer playgroups rent-free premises were designated in the 1960s. In one early new town, the rent is now refunded by the borough council.

Help in kind

We have already seen that a good deal of help and encouragement is available from the CDOs. Other help comes in the form of printing and publicity (four authorities) and one new town reported that help in kind ranges from the use of community houses and the support of a CDO to off-cuts of paper from the print room and the plastic rings from typewriter ribbons for use as wheels, stringing beads, rattles, etc.

Five of the English new towns gave help to special groups – four to handicapped groups, and one to a play-bus.

Although only four gave financial help to mother and toddler groups, sixteen out of twenty two said that they gave moral encouragement and support. There seems a close identification – all the new towns which gave specific help to playgroups also gave help or encouragement to mother and toddler groups. Of the five Scottish new towns which did not help playgroups because of the involvement of the social work department, four gave encouragement to mother and toddler groups.

The development corporation is not the only source of help to playgroups. Help comes from a wide variety of sources, and in different ways. Eighteen out of twenty two referred to playgroups help from other bodies. Four did not answer this question. The sources varied – local authorities, local churches and youth groups, and an Urban Aid grant to PPA were all mentioned.

Liaison or duplication
Liaison then could be important to avoid duplication. We asked if the new town authority had any link with the local authority officer responsible for playgroups. Eighteen said they had, two (both Scottish, with no CDO) said no. We also asked if they had any contact with PPA. Seven said yes, and three no. In thirteen of the new towns the help given by other bodies was co-ordinated with that given by the development corporation, and in four it was not. The means of liaison were various – personal contact, consultation as necessary, regular meetings and 'via PPA or an under-fives committee'.

When we asked whom the authority would approach for advice on playgroups, ten mentioned PPA first, eight the local authority officer, and three their own play officer. It should perhaps be mentioned that CDOs have been useful members of PPA tutor courses, have sat on working groups, and tutored on PPA foundation courses. This illustrates the two-way exchange of experience which characterises playgroup work.

Question 3   The new-town view of playgroups
How do new towns themselves see playgroups?

The relevant question is: 'Does your authority envisage playgroups making a contribution to the well-being of the community and to the town's development? If so, could you indicate in what way?'

Not all the new towns answered this question, and some gave more detail than others. Thirteen indicated a positive 'yes' to the first part of the question; none said 'No'. Their way of seeing the contribution varied.

Four saw playgroups as provision for the children and, as such, necessary in a young community. One of the Scottish new towns mentioned the need of playgroups because of the lack of nursery provision; another in Scotland said that the presence of nursery schools inhibited the development of community playgroups. Four authorities specifically mentioned the valuable introductory role of playgroups in a new community, and three of these, and also three others, mentioned and expanded on the role of playgroups in community development.

A number of replies were represented in the following answer. 'The development corporation believes that playgroups have a very important role to play in the development of communities in the town. It believes that the benefits of playgroups both to children and to parents is important in its own right, but that in addition to this, playgroups have a vital "feet-finding" and "welcoming" role for families moving in to a new area. Playgroups give many families their first opportunity to identify with their new community, and as such are a vital link in the establishment of "community" in new areas.'

Question 4   Changes and developments in the form of support

The answer to the vital question 'Could you describe the ways in which support for playgroups has changed and developed in the years since your town was designated?' came in two variations.

1   *Several Authorities explained that they now gave more staffing support to playgroups,* and four particularly mentioned how

this had happened since 1973. In that one year, one district council established a playgroup adviser post; a social services department appointed a day care adviser; a district council appointed a play adviser; and, in another new town, a community development unit was started. Another new town said: 'Initially, support for playgroups was given to each individual group as it became established, and was by way of finance, and possibly by making accommodation available to the group. With the establishment of a community development unit, the help has become practical as well as financial. The community workers assist groups with their committee structure in liaison with the district council's playgroup adviser.'

2   In the other form of response four new towns spoke of *the value they attached to encouraging volunteers to take on responsibility*, their own staff then taking a back seat. Two quotations illustrate this: 'When the play centres opened, the playgroup at each centre was managed by the full time playleader. However, the passage of time plus the build-up of confidence, saw the formation of constitutionalised local playgroup committees . . . who pay their own bills, and manage their own affairs.' 'Our support to playgroups both individually and via the branch has steadily increased over the years. As the branch has strengthened we have encouraged it to take on a wider range of services to playgroups, and backed these with our own resources when necessary. The branch has responded well to this, and is now providing a more comprehensive and better quality of service than ever. The demands of an ever-increasing number of groups are very heavy, placing great stress on the active and conscientious officers of the branch.

Our final quotation illustrates the problems which an authority meets when it recognises the support most needed by playgroups, and is frustrated by lack of resources – 'Large demands on limited staff have forced the support and encouragement to become less of a human resource, and more of a financial help.'

Summary

New Towns
In the early stages of new town development there is a problem in that the consumers of pre-school provision are not yet present or vocal. It is especially important to provide for mothers who may be lonely or depressed or moving to a new, strange place.

Seventeen English and five Scottish new towns replied to the questionnaire (a 50 per cent response). Size, situation and stage of development vary widely, but under-five population is, on average, high: between 8 and 8·5 per cent. Of Scottish new towns, only one had a community development officer, but the social work department took an active and positive approach to playgroups. In England all but the nearly complete new towns had community development officers and two-thirds had a person with special responsibility for playgroups (more commonly in the newer towns). Officially only 5–15 per cent of a CDO's time was given to playgroups (though personal help went further), and this was spent on stimulating and helping the development of new groups. Premises for playgroups are available in all new towns, and four out of five authorities said that they considered the needs of playgroups when planning community premises. Storage is the most common problem. Most new towns give 'starter' grants and help with rent (more help is available in the newer towns) as well as various sorts of help in kind. Eighteen out of twenty-two development corporations said that playgroups also got help from other sources, and four admitted that this help was not co-ordinated with their own. Most had links with the local authority officer responsible for playgroups and with PPA/SPPA, and ten authorities named PPA as the source of advice for playgroups.

Thirteen new towns (not all answered this question) saw playgroups as making a positive contribution to the community, and six at least saw them as more than simply provision for children. Support to playgroups has steadily increased. Four new towns spoke of the value they attached to encouraging volunteers to take on responsibility. Some regret that pressures on a limited staff have forced them to offer more financial, less personal, help.

Questions

1 Is there sufficient two-way liaison between PPA/SPPA branch and community development officer, possibly under a different name, either in a new town, or in an outlying estate without the status of new town, or in a redeveloped city centre?
2 With the three-way relationship between branch, development corporation and local authority, what are the patterns of the financial support for voluntary AOs?
3 Do PPA/SPPA branches comment early and adequately enough on arrangements being set up for under-fives and their families? How could this be made more effective?
4 Are parents of young families represented enough on the planning committees of new town, new estate or redeveloped city centre?

9

Playgroups: Self-Help Pressure or a Strategy to Meet Need?

(from interviews with directors of social services departments)

We already have, from other sources, a picture of registration procedures and visiting, and to some degree of the structure established in social services/work departments to fulfil a legal responsibility for playgroups. These give an indication of the statutory system coming into contact with a self-grown voluntary system of support, on the actual premises of playgroups.

We did not go to directors to duplicate the build-up of information, but to try and fill out, from talk with them, the role they saw for playgroups. We also hoped that they would interpret their departments' present arrangements for giving support.

Some twenty directors of social services/work departments, mainly but not exclusively from the areas specially studied, discussed with us the development of playgroup work. Some saw it as new work, with new skills; others did not. (One reason for involving directors from further afield was to enable discussion to be free and general, without being closely identifiable.) These are some of their comments grouped under headings.

Who is responsible for playgroup policy?

Is it the director?

Some directors denied this. 'All our decisions are corporate ones.' One 'did not want to be deified'. 'Policy and therefore structure must reflect the widest possible range of opinions, and the director's role is more a co-ordinating and presenting one.' One 'delegates under-five policy to a divisional director who, with the divisional organisers, formulates this'. More than one stressed 'partnership and not a directorate'. 'Three grades of salary separate the director and the social worker in the field. So there was no imposing hierarchy, and a constant flow of communication.'

Others recognised that their own view had a strong influence. 'Of course the working party were concerned to know his views as director.' 'I prefer to put department money into . . .'. One indicated that his mind was made up in advance, and that certain issues need not be put forward. It is understandable that in a large department, with all age groups to look after, some directors' priorities would lie elsewhere. One said, 'I inherited an imbalance in favour of under-fives at the expense of over-seventies.' He was taking steps over a period of time to redress the balance.

Or staff with special responsibility?

Other directors said firmly that their share in running the enormous business of the department was on the management side, administering promptly and efficiently, on policy lines for which they took their lead from specialist staff. Lines of communication through the department, and points at which representations could be fed in, thus became very important.

Some directors felt themselves to be in close or reasonably close touch with their specialist staff. What was happening in the field could influence policymaking. This was easiest when a group of advisory staff worked centrally, and their senior was in direct touch with the deputy or even the director. Specialist members of an area team contributed views more indirectly, sometimes through the co-ordinating work of one central adviser. Or views could come, sometimes more effectively, through the line of management. It was not always easy if a generic social worker, hard-pressed from day to day, had playgroups as a small part of a workload, and no special understanding of them. It was unlikely that they would feature strongly when she talked to an area team leader, and it was quite possible, as one social worker had said, that she had never seen the director.

Against this, several directors pointed out, 'My door is open.' Anyone who felt strongly could come and speak directly, though tension could be set up along the line if this happened.

Or councillors?

The importance of councillors was stressed over and over again. A director presenting views would be carefully listened to, and could influence councillor's thinking. But where to cut and prune a budget was uppermost in councillor's minds, and they had the ultimate say on policy. Directors thought this was insufficiently recognised by voluntary organisations, who needed to think more seriously about the councillor lobby.

Does PPA/SPPA have any part?

One director stressed that a voluntary organisation had two possible ways of access. One was through the normal channels, with contact between branch and area organiser and department staff. The other was by special approach. Where the contribution of a voluntary organisation was valued, an appropriate delegation could always ask for an interview. (The importance of its being fully primed and able to state its case was underlined.) Or a branch chairman, perhaps with a TDO or other friend, could always come and make a case. There was a third line of communication – the director taking the initiative. One counted it among his priorities to get full information, at first hand, about the community. He attended, invited or not invited, any meetings or committees. Either he or his deputy sat on selection panels, took part in open forums, even sat on finance committees, familiarising the department with branch affairs as a prelude to policy. Others would not do this themselves, but saw it as part of the role of their specialist staff. This opened up a further line of discussion. If there was a real partnership between department and voluntary agency, was the 'right of a department to attend' on a par with the voluntary body's 'right to representation on a standing committee'?

Reviewing the function of playgroups

We were struck by the number of directors engaged in playgroup support reviews. One said: 'policy depends on tradition inherited, legal responsibility, and a belief in some unit for its potential contribution.' Social change as well as playgroup development since 1969 had made review inevitable, both of practice and policy. Several were engaged in a review of the whole under-five provision, some in conjunction with education departments, health authorities and perhaps with PPA/SPPA. One divisional director said that they had muddled through on existing arrangements and tradition, while accumulating experience, but now had to rationalise. In another area, 'We have to think. Once we had playgroup advisers, but they got lost with reorganisation.' It seemed, however, that most reviews were done on a basis of adapting arrangements rather than introducing bold new policy, and some were regarded rather cynically as irrelevant.

A middle-class luxury or a preventive resource?

Directors had very different views on the role of playgroups. Some still saw them as private ventures, to be regulated until full nursery provision emerged. Some believed in the mutual-support community group; of these some thought it worked in middle-class areas only, and others that it was or could be a major contribution to preventive work and young family care.

One group of views ran: 'Playgroups were fine in middle-class areas, but the department's concern was with families in real need.' The pressing needs of special client groups demanded urgent attention. Among hard-core families with problems, 'discussion about playgroups' was seen as inappropriate. Playgroups were not seen as having any preventive role. They were a part of the quality of living, to which parents could contribute if they liked. Play was valuable in its own right, and on occasion therapeutic, but day nurseries, not playgroups, were the unit relevant to intervention and treatment. 'Middle-class provision, tending to reinforce advantage, rather than compensate'. 'Child-minders had more developing potential, especially with the increase of one-parent families. They reproduce what the family does, left to its own resources.' Playgroups were 'sessional minding, safe play, stimulation for children – a convenience for mothers able to cope.'

In contrast, playgroups were seen as 'one of the best forms of prevention'. 'Playgroups were preventive, with children rather than parents or families.' 'Apart from meeting parents' aspirations for their children, they had intermediate treatment value, relieving the strain on the mother, linking the mother in a new area to a network of friendship.' 'In a two-way process, social workers referred clients to playgroups, and picked up clients referred by them.' Two said that they had to help playgroups 'so that they are there when the department wants to make use of them, in an urgent situation'.

One or two interviewers commented that they felt the picture was too rosy. Some directors were satisfied with good personal relations with a branch which was not biting into the real needs of the area, or not aware of tension points with a branch which wanted to work as a linked but independent community agency. They did not want to go deeper into what they might reasonably expect of PPA/SPPA.

Nearly all directors saw continued value in paying the fees of children at risk, and one or two saw the moment as 'ripe for a real study of the free and unfree varieties of pre-school provision'. Others specifically did not want this, expressing relief that the cut-back had prevented issues between education and social services from becoming strained. (This is the point discussed in Section 6, where the crunch-point between discussion and unilateral spending has to be negotiated.)

'Broadly preventive', was one assessment. 'Getting the child out of his environment, helping to identify battered children, and introducing ideas which sink in, through being repeated, for play in the home.' One director strongly denied that 'playgroups were for middle class, and day nurseries for workers'. They gave valued help to families with a number of young children.

Patterns, and the danger of perpetuating them

One director, who had supported two playgroups through a period when a new nursery school reduced membership, and seen them pick up again, made it clear: 'No pattern is of value in itself. All are related, for me, to bolstering the family and meeting local under-five need. Social services are not here to fight for playgroups who don't have children, but a fight could be worthwhile for a development involving parents more effectively.' He saw that the policy of providing in isolation for under-fives was becoming overproductive, and reflecting a sense of possessiveness, to which all types of agency, statutory and voluntary, were prone – 'my playgroup, my school, my families'. The general view expressed was that there were a number of types of provision – 'Sometimes playgroups were the most appropriate, sometimes not.' Another indicated that there would be playgroups so long as the public wanted them. 'They must live by the test of the collecting-box.'

Keenness was expressed for more links with childminders, who were very often isolated. These were not always welcomed by playgroups, or branches. There could be an undercurrent: 'You're paid to look after him. Get on with the job.' Another director hoped for more links between childminders, foster parents, playgroups and children's homes, 'to avoid parochialism'. If they talked more together, 'Day-nursery staff can give advice to playgroups at the point of registering, social workers can help with disruptive children referred to playgroups, social workers can learn in playgroups about breaking down barriers of isolation and getting parents interested in children's activities'. In one department, great stress was placed on 'day-conferences open to day-nursery staff, playgroups, childminders, with practical workshops. They invite councillors as an educative exercise.' Not all appeared to know of playgroup fieldwork courses with mixed membership of this kind.

Two directors had doubts whether playgroups helped children's educational development, but thought playgroup experience would help young people to become interested parents later. They did not care for chains of commercial playgroups, avoiding registration by meeting for just less than two hours, and 'drawing mini-schoolchildren with blazers and satchels' by the use of minibuses. One looked forward, in the long term to 'fully professional pre-school education'.

Most thought that the idea of playgroups with a dual role was becoming established: 'a service to children and also increasing the awareness and confidence of parents'. This could be a triple role when 'they provided also a chance for social workers and parents to see children developing at their own pace'. One, not referring to parent involvement, 'would like to see full-time day care in the hands of playgroups because of their informality'.

One of the few references to the need to work out professional–parent relationsips more fully was expressed: 'Any provision which does not get a strong groundswell of interest from the family detracts from the concept of under-fives in their families.' Another quoted: 'Overprofessional education can make mothers feel inferior and untrained, and this is apparent to their children.' 'Nothing has superseded or come up to the family in the interests of the under-fives.'

Strengths of voluntary provision: flexibility and independence

There was a constant refrain – 'The value of the voluntary contribution is its independence and too much assistance can prejudice this.' Some directors thought that considerable help on the administrative side released time and energy for fieldwork. One director who had recently refused payment to voluntary workers said he did this not through lack of appreciation of the voluntary organisation but in an attempt to preserve its independence. With paid voluntary workers, voluntary responsibility got confused, and 'too often voluntary agencies lend themselves to becoming statutory'. Many expressed the hope that playgroups would remain in the hands of parents.

It was recognised that the relationship between department and local voluntary agency is delicate and has to be worked at by both. Either, in partnership, can at different times take the initiative – prod the other to make a move. The function must be two-way, and each must know also when to stop prodding. There was more than one gentle hint that playgroups more than most voluntary organisations find it difficult to take a prod. Whether or not arrangements work is seen to depend in large part on personalities. One director had made two very practical appointments to meet the different needs and ways of working in different parts of his area. One adviser was 'a friend who happened to be a member of the legally responsible departmental staff'. The other 'was a member of staff, who was also a friend'. On occasion, they were interchangeable. At other times, using one rather than the other oiled the wheels. Another delicate situation arises from the appointment of a PPA-experienced person to a staff position. Playgroups continue to relate to 'her', and may expect more of her than, among new responsibilities, she is able to give. One director was fully conscious of this, when he appointed a whole experienced PPA group for his staff and allowed for a temporary effect on lines of communication.

Voluntary organisations were able to experiment more boldly – to do things rashly and withdraw if necessary. 'A department would be expected to know better and not indulge in rash experiments.' It was tempting but difficult for a director to try out and learn from mistakes: councillors rarely gave time for this to happen. 'Will you try this out?' a PPA Branch could be asked. 'We can't.' It was a big problem, how to keep councillors happy and yet allow for experiment and growth. One director urged PPA also to respect the need for time. If the statutory partner did undertake an experimental pattern, they should be prepared to give it a five-year try-out. Nevertheless, it remained a privilege of voluntary agencies to experiment freely.

Some voluntary agencies, and PPA/SPPA ranked high among these, had the benefit of a national and local network. Several directors said that the statutory support system had to rely on this network for communication – the branch, the county, the AO, the field worker, the course. One was not sure, and did not mind, whether in his area the network was purely local (an association of playgroups) or a local branch with the backing of a national association. The take-up of an advertised course could depend on the network, and it had to be used: it was impossible to visit some 300 playgroups.

In most interviews, mention was made of playgroups which did not choose to be within PPA. A network could be seen from outside to be exclusive – perhaps this was one of the difficulties confronting childminders thinking of making an approach. Relating to these playgroups as well as to those in PPA was one special function of the statutory support system.

Self-help as a quality of living

Directors noted a trend for playgroup work, originally within day care or even residential care, to come under the wing of community development sectors of departments. They were seen as a 'very positive community resource'. 'Playgroup initiative should come from the community.' They had an obvious value, especially in isolated rural areas or in new towns. A strong desire was expressed 'to back up self-help groupings, give scope for experimental schemes'. One reason given for the department not wanting to 'run' playgroups was that 'their real strength was in helping parents towards self-help'. They were a 'real community resource, involving all classes, developing self-assurance and the ability to state a case.' They also had a spin-off value. 'Clients turned into colleagues, and later became foster-parents, workers with the elderly, and so on.'

Again the outstanding problem from a department's point of view is that self-help activity is most difficult to encourage in the areas standing to gain most from it. An absence of playgroups leaves directors with a situation for councillors to question. Ought the development of work in these areas to be a condition of grant aid to a branch?

One director stated that self-help can be very difficult when playgroups are held in schools. A high degree of participation in a well managed professional service could be hard to absorb. 'I have considerable sympathy for headmasters,' he said. 'A self-help group on the premises presents management problems.' We were not able to make a full study of the point at which teacher training or in-service training might incorporate this aspect of 'new skills for new work'; or another, related, making the preparation for teenagers to participate in playgroup work. One director in Scotland was working through difficulties in getting social workers at area level freed and seconded for appropriate SPPA courses. Another director gave off-the-cuff training aims for social workers working with childminders and parents – aims which could be a good basis for discussion on encouraging self-help: 'Learn skills not innate. Learn methods of organising individuals and groups. Learn the variety of backgrounds and ways of living. Learn good management, with improved skills – including prolonged learning in very informal courses.'

Departments and playgroups

Talks with directors showed a varying acceptance of playgroups. The representation of some directors at interview by senior staff could be interpreted in different ways. While it was clear that in some cases a deputy director was speaking on behalf of his director, who would endorse what he said, this was not felt to be so in others. A director and deputy director could hold different views about a service developing rapidly, which might or might not include new thinking on the role of voluntary organisations. A senior member of staff with close knowledge of playgroups in his area would explain alternatives in providing for under-fives. We were aware of tension where keen workers within the department 'could feel cold-shouldered, not invited to PPA meetings, etc.' This raises the question 'Can keenness in the network and keenness in the field of statutory responsibility not encourage each other?'

Reference has already been made to the value, from the department's point of view, of allowing to PPA/SPPA the responsibility for a good bit of the advisory role, thus making demands on their own staff more workable. It was mentioned more than once, however, that department staff do not like being cast in the role of whipping-boy, having directed to them the hard-line playgroup leaders who cannot be brought to accept suggestions given within the voluntary network. They will include these difficult-to-influence cases, using the backing of authority as a sanction, but only as the exception in an overall advisory role, most of it happy and accepted. Neither do the voluntary branches and AOs feel happy about the suggestion that they be given an agency role, including legal visiting, with right of entry. This would undermine their roles as representatives of the playgroup movement. A director was therefore entitled to ask: 'So what about the hard-line cases?'

Nevertheless, the most critical directors, least able to see the role for two sets of supporters, spoke warmly for the need of a PPA presence, behind playgroups, in their area.

Most thought that playgroups would go on, their link still being with social services: 'Here, with the same department, but hopefully more community-based, welcoming parents more.' 'There would not be any take-over by my department, but it would like to keep the dominant role it now possesses.' 'Playgroups should keep within the flexible umbrella of the social services.' 'Playgroups are very cost-effective. We hope they will remain different from most voluntary organisations and strive to keep their identity and their independence.' 'Yes, the playgroup movement will remain. Linked to social services, but retaining the independence of PPA.'

There was the more occasional, alternative view – the director who preferred, as soon as possible, a fully professional service for under-fives, with the learning process for parents then looked after by adult education. Another thought that with a revival of the nursery school programme there would be a different pattern of responsibility for playgroups. Another view was: 'No agreement within my department about play-groups remaining one of our responsibilities. The likelihood is that there will be more nursery schools, fewer playgroups.'

One director considered the time ripe for a big debate on the place of the family among playgroup sponsors and participants. Two did not want social services actually running playgroups, which would diminish mother involvement. Another said, 'My department has always encouraged PPA, and will help to keep branches going, even though money is short.' 'PPA must continue to draw in young people.' 'We are concerned that PPA is an ageing organisation . . . absence of young people who would help run a playbus.'

Perhaps the biggest divergence of view which emerged from these interviews was between directors who believed that playgroups could be fully initiated and supported by and from the department and those who felt that the initiation and a good deal of support must come out of the community itself. In both cases, there was belief in playgroups, but the framework of thinking would be reflected in all arrangements made; whether advisers would be grant-aided to the voluntary body, or appointed within the department; whether the bulk of grant aid would be to individual playgroups or to the supporting organisation; whether the voluntary organisation representing playgroups and their parent members would be a partner among providers for the under-fives, with a say in policy, or an associate told in a friendly way what had been decided. Clearly, thinking about playgroups was at different stages of focus. Clearly, also, challenges were being put back to PPA/SPPA on the uneven take-up among branches of 'new skills for new work'.

Summary

Twenty directors of social services/work departments discussed the development of playgroup work. They had different views on where the responsibility for playgroups lay and the part that PPA/SPPA played in this, and many stressed the importance of the councillors' role. A considerable number were engaged in playgroup support reviews, but most of these seemed to be on a basis of adaptation of the status quo. They saw playgroups as anything from a 'convenience' or 'fine in middle-class areas' to 'one of the best forms of prevention'. Nearly all saw value in paying the fees of children at risk. The general view was that playgroups were one of a range of forms of provision. Links were needed with other forms, especially childminders.

Most recognised the dual role of playgroups as 'a service to children and also increasing the awareness and confidence of parents'. The strengths of voluntary provision were seen as independence (a delicate financial and advisory balance) and flexibility (the freedom to experiment). Directors noted a trend for playgroup work to move from a day-care to a community development category because of its self-help qualities. A big problem is that self-help is most difficult to encourage in the areas with most to gain from it.

They were happy for PPA/SPPA to take a large share of the advisory work provided that the statutory and voluntary networks could co-operate. A few direcors looked forward to a fully professional service for under-fives, but most saw a continuing and useful place for playgroups and PPA/SPPA. Within this group, views were divided between those who believed playgroups could be fully run by the department and those who now felt initiation and support should come basically from the community.

Questions

1 Playgroups are seen as fulfilling a variety of functions – a response to community needs, a family movement, an opportunity to 'educate' parents. How can these views be reconciled in the attempt to meet the needs of young families?

2 What is the best form of support for young families in areas of special need? Is there a need for a bold new policy which increases the capacity of parents to undertake adequate parenting while making use of the professional help needed and offered?

3 What is the role of voluntary organisations in pioneering new approaches? Should local authority money be offered for these purposes?

4 Do voluntary organisations have enough/too much say when policy is made in local authority departments, and are they sufficiently aware of the various channels of approach and the timing of policymaking?

5 How do PPA/SPPA see their associations in ten years time? As increasing the core work with playgroups or developing into wider community/family ventures? What effect would a wider spread have on relationships with local authorities?

Appendix A

Sample of Questionnaire for the Mother and Toddler Group Survey

MOTHER AND TODDLER GROUP SURVEY

A working pary was set up by PPA in 1975 to collect information about and report on the current position in the growth and development of the mother and toddler movement. The working party decided to make a survey of the groups with which PPA had contact to establish some idea of the pattern and variation in mother and toddler groups in England and Wales.

It was also decided that it would be valuable to know about as many groups as possible irrespective of PPA links and we hope all mother and toddler groups may be willing to help us, as the projected report should be of value to all groups.

The information supplied will be used to compile a report, distribution of which has yet to be decided by PPA but it is expected to be widely available. However, individual details of groups will not be available publicly.

*   *   *

This survey should be completed by the organiser or person who takes responsibility for the group.

Please return the completed survey as soon as possible but not later than...to your regional contact.

Regional Contact's Name ....

Address...

....

Surveys may be returned direct to Pre-school Playgroups Association at their London address marked 'Mother and Toddler Survey'.

On behalf of PPA, the working party and its chairman, Helen Blythe, thanks you for helping us find out more about the mother and toddler movement.

This space is for anything of particular interest you may wish to record for us. Details of group's 'history', equipment made by local school, or grandfathers, parents 'at risk' referred by Social Services, etc., especially personal stories (anon) which may be used in reports or publications on the value of the mother and toddler movement, or should be drawn to the attention of the working party.

Name and address of   ....
person supplying this
information (for possible   ....
follow-up).

                            ....

MOTHER AND TODDLER GROUP SURVEY

1. Name of Group ....
2. Address of Meeting Place ....
3. Where is the meeting held? Please put tick in box:
    [ ]   school (primary/secondary)   [ ]   church hall
    [ ]   community centre   [ ]   other hall
    [ ]   clinic/health centre   [ ]   private home
4. In what year did the Group start?   19
    If not known, was it more than 5 years ago?   (tick) Yes [ ]
                                                          No [ ]
5. At what time does the group usually start?   [ ] am/pm
    At what time does the group usually end?   [ ] am/pm
6. (a) How many sessions (i.e. mornings & afternoons)
        are held weekly?   [ ]
    (b) Are there evening meetings for parents?   (tick) Yes [ ]
                                                          No [ ]
    (c) Does the Group only meet in school term time?
                                                   (tick) Yes [ ]
                                                          No [ ]
7. How many (1) adults usually come?   [ ]
                (2) children aged 0–1   [ ]
                              2–3   [ ]
                              4–5 usually come   [ ]

8. How many families use the Group at present?   [ ]
9. How much does a family usually pay per meeting? [ ] pence
      (If nothing paid please put NIL)
10. Does the Group pay for rent and/or light/heating
    and cleaning?   (tick) Yes [ ]
                                                            No [ ]
    If yes how much **per meeting?**   [ ] pence
11. Does the Group receive any grant or subsidy?   (tick) Yes [ ]
                                                            No [ ]
12. Does the Group raise its own funds?   (tick) Yes [ ]
                                                            No [ ]
    If yes, how?

13. How did the Group obtain equipment? Please tick all that apply:
    [ ] gift (from whom ....) [ ] made
    [ ] on loan (from whom ....) [ ] bought
14. What play materials are provided for the children?

15. What do mothers do? [ ] sit and talk only   [ ]
                        [ ] sit and knit   [ ] Which
                        [ ] play with children   [ ] activity
    Pleast tick   [ ] listen to a talk   [ ] happens
    all that apply   [ ] mend or make toys   [ ] most
                        [ ] run the club   [ ] often?
                        [ ] help the leaders   [ ] Tick one
                        [ ] other activities   [ ] only here
                            specify ....
16. Do the children play in the room where most mothers sit?
                                                    (tick) Yes [ ]
                                                            No [ ]
17. Which best describes how the Group is run? Tick one only:
    [ ] An organiser who takes responsibility for the Group
    [ ] An organiser with a rota of mothers sharing the various
        tasks
    [ ] An informal group/committee of mothers
    [ ] An organiser with a play leader to keep watch over the
        children's play without a rota of mothers
    [ ] An organiser with a play leader to keep watch over the
        children's play with a rota of mothers
18. Who is mainly responsible for rent,   (tick one) Organiser [ ]
    purchasing toys, takings, money,   Treasurer [ ]
    fund raising, etc.   (specify) Other [ ]

19. How was the Organiser originally appointed? Tick one only:
    [ ] self appointed   [ ] Local Authority body
                                             (including Health Visitor)
    [ ] by committee   [ ] church/charity/
                                             organisation
    [ ] by informal group of   [ ] no organiser
         mothers
20. If there is an Organiser, is she paid?   (tick) Yes [ ]
                                                             No [ ]
21. Is the Group visited by:
    (tick)   Is help available from (tick)
    [ ] Social Worker   [ ]
    [ ] Health Visitor   [ ]
    [ ] Community Worker   [ ]
    [ ] Local School   [ ]
    [ ] PPA personnel   [ ]
         (Branch, Visitor/
         AO/TDO)
    [ ] Other – specify   [ ]
22. Is the group connected with a playgroup?   (tick) Yes [ ]
                                                             No [ ]
23. Is the group a member of PPA?   (tick) Yes [ ]
                                                             No [ ]
24. What help would your group welcome?

Name and Address of person   ....
filling in this questionnaire (for
possible follow-up)   ....

                                   ....

Appendix B

Membership of Working Party on Mother and Toddler Groups

(PPA regions are geographical areas of counties and metropolitan counties, based as nearly as practicable on those regional areas existing in 1973 for the HMI divisions of the Department of Education and Science)

Cath Armstrong	Southern region (from April 1977)
Helen Blythe	West Midlands (Chairman)
Moiya Codling	Southern region (until April 1977)
Mair Davies	North West region (until February 1977)
Margaret Dawson	Eastern region (until October 1976)
Joyce Donoghue	South East region (PPA Training and Development Officer)
Diana Elsmore	PPA's link with Health Visitor's Association
Jill Elphick	Northern region
Jill Faux	Northern region (PPA Training and Development Officer)
Rosemary Gibson	South West region
Christine Guedalla	Greater London region
Sue Haden	West Midlands region (until March 1977)
Diane Kirkup	East Midlands region
Delphine Knight	PPA National Adviser
Janet McAllister	Wales region
Edna Salsby	Eastern region
Dawn Stroud	Northern region (from July 1976) PPA Field Services Committee from July 1977
Ros Thunder	West Midlands region (from October 1976)
Anne Tyrer	North West region (from April 1977)
Jessie Vaughan	Yorkshire and North Humberside region

The Working Party are indebted to Joyce Donoghue who did the writing, Maureen Gray from PPA's Research Committee, Margaret Hanton and Susan Williams from PPA's Communications and Media Committee for editing. Dr David Weaver and Birmingham University for computing, Chris Jones, Elizabeth Hills and Pat Weaver for typing as well as the staff of PPA's West Midlands Regional Office for duplicating and administrative help.

Appendix C

Organisations which Responded to Requests for Contact with Mother and Toddler Groups

Adult Education Centres – 'informal community education' (not the creches for the use of the classes)
Area Health Authorities
Baptist Church
Catholic Church
Church of England – Board of Social Responsibility
Mothers' Union (especially Young Families Department)
Community Relations Commission (CRC)
Gingerbread
London Council of Social Service – Family Groups*
Health Visitors' Association
Methodist Church: Young Wives Groups
National Childbirth Trust (NCT)
National Society for Prevention of Cruelty to Children (NSPCC)
One O'Clock Clubs (GLC)
Pre-school Playgroups Association – branches and county associations
Salvation Army
Save the Children Fund (SCF)
Scottish Pre-school Playgroups Association
Social Services Departments
Society of Friends
United Reformed Church
Women's Royal Voluntary Service (WRVS)

*While some of the LCSS Family Groups filled in our questionnaire, others felt it was not relevant to their group. These groups are run for families and may or may not include members with young children.

Appendix D

Questions Regarding Oversight of Playgroups which would have been put to Health Authorities had Finance Permitted

1 What is the general policy of your health authority/board towards playgroups?
2 In particular, what is the policy of your health authority/board on the attachment of health visitors to playgroups? Do playgroups have their own health visitor or do health visitors visit playgroups on the basis of family and group practice attachment from the primary care teams?
3 Are the specialist skills (speech therapy, physiotherapy, etc.) available for children in playgroups and is access to these skills readily available? If a playgroup supervisor in consultation with the parent concerned is concerned about a child's development, does she have means of direct access to such skills or does she have to go through different and perhaps time-consuming channels?
4 Are playgroups and mother and toddler clubs run in health department clinics in your area? If community playgroups are run in premises, what is the scale for assessing rent? If not, is it likely that this facility could be considered as part of future provision?
5 Do playgroups in your area accept 'children at risk' referrals from doctors and health visitors?
6 Are there playgroups in your area used for your staff in training or as a way in which health visitors can observe children away from their home setting?
7 Do health education councils use playgroups as a means of disseminating information?
8 Is there an assessment centre for handicapped children in your area, and, in addition to the assessment of the children themselves, is there support for the parents of these children? In this context, I would refer to group therapy for families of handicapped children, information centres, community support, etc.

9   What is the policy in your area towards parents being with their young children whilst the children are in hospital? Are parents encouraged to stay with their children, particularly immediately after surgery, and is there open visiting at all times? Are there adequate play facilities in the hospitals in your area and are these run by volunteers or paid playleaders?

10 What arrangements are there for consultation with local authority departments concerned with pre-school children?

Appendix E

The Library Service to Under-Fives in one London Borough

It is generally recognised that under-fives must have access to a wide range of materials as early as possible to encourage their familiarity with words, pictures and stories, to prepare them for learning to read, to help introduce concepts such as time and space, and to develop their emotional experiences.

To begin to make materials really accessible where people are, rather than only in the library buildings, Lambeth Library Service has been developing a community approach, discussing with local groups the sorts of material they need and putting in collections which are regularly monitored to see how they are working. This has developed with the groups working with under-fives, so every playgroup, day nursery and one o'clock club has a collection of picture books and easy reading titles, related in content and size to the needs of the group. Organizations may either visit their local library and choose a batch to take or arrange for their library contact to bring or have delivered titles they need.

In addition, for many years, teams of librarians have been visiting groups regularly for storytelling sessions to encourage the use of books with children and to see how our materials work in practice. This information is fed back to the book selection meetings to enable us to buy the sorts of books that really work with children.

This team has been augmented by eight sessional storytellers, mostly local people with playgroup experience, who have had training in selecting titles for storytelling and in the techniques needed, and who function as a full part of our team supporting under-fives organisations. We have just received funding from the Inner City Partnership to increase the sessional team by another six storytellers, working in the centre and north of the borough.

Childminders are able to borrow 10–20 titles each to use at home with their children, and, since earlier this year, we have been co-operating with the Directorate of Social Services toy loan service to provide a collection to be delivered to each minder.

A large part of our work is in participating in training programmes for those working with under-fives: playgroup staff, nursery nurses, one o'clock club staff, secondary school child-care students, etc. As well as discussing child development in stages and relating that to books, we aim to look critically at books published for this age group, noting gaps (for example in first- and second-level materials) and errors in judgement (for example complex board books). We also look at the biases in published materials (the lack of multi cultural titles, racism, sexism and class bias – especially the lack of material set in towns) and look at materials which counteract these. This is an element of the courses which has come directly from demands from group workers for these sorts of materials.

We see the under-fives as a priority area, and this has been reflected in the amount of resources in money and staff time that we commit to this age group.

Appendix F

Membership of the Working Group on Oversight

England and Wales (Some members were not with us for the entire study, due to pressure of other commitments.)

Mrs Maude Henderson	Joint Chairman, Formerly National Adviser, PPA.
Mrs Milly Chadband	Formerly Chairman, Field Services Committee of PPA Convenor for the study.
Mrs Diana Campbell	Cheshire County PPA.
Mrs Margaret Hanton	Greater London PPA. Also Chairman, Communications and Media Committee, PPA.
Mrs Avril Holness	Formerly playgroup supervisor, tutor and member of Field Services Committee.
Mrs Teresa Smith	Formerly Chairman, PPA Research Committee. Member of the Oxford Pre-School Research Unit.
Mrs Marjorie Morris	Wales Region PPA.
Mrs Pat Meacock	Formerly Hon. Treasurer of PPA and Chairman of Finance Committee.

Grant-aided PPA Advisers

Mrs Marie Brogan	Training and Development Officer, PPA.
Mrs Margaret Featherstone	Playgroup Adviser under Urban Aid Project, Kent.
Mrs Wendy Moore	Training and Development Officer, also on Steering Committee of Playgroup Advisers' Association.
Mrs Joan Pitman	Playgroup Adviser, Hampshire.

Local Authority Advisers

Mrs Elizabeth Lowdon	Senior Playgroup Adviser, Newcastle upon Tyne.

Mrs Norma Sturgess   Playgroup Adviser, Nuneaton, also
                          representing the Steering Committee
                          of the Playgroup Advisers' Association
Mrs Anne Walker   Day Care Adviser, Northampton, also
                          representing the Steering Committee
                          of the Playgroup Advisers' Association
Mrs Angela Wylam   Playgroup Adviser, Rotherham.
Mrs Jean Hickford   Playgroup Adviser, Essex Recreation
                          Department.

Representing Other Organisations
Mrs Mary Bruce   Development Officer for Children and
                          Young Families, WRVS.
Mrs Maureen Fearns   Formerly Midlands Adviser for SCF.

Education Authority Adviser
Mrs Sheila Palmen   Teacher/Adviser, Cumbria.

Scotland

Scottish Pre-school Playgroups Association (SPPA)
Mrs Rosemary Proctor   Joint Chairman, SPPA Adviser, Fife
                          and Central Regions.
Mrs Pearl Chrystal   Area Organiser, Levenmouth Area.
Mrs Helen Grant   Area Organiser, Ettrick Branch.
Mrs Betty Stanger   Area Organiser, North Ayrshire.

Grant-aided SPPA Advisers
Mrs Nita Brown   Regional Adviser, Lothian and
                          Borders. Also member of SAAUFF.
Mrs Barbara Ritchie   Tutor/Adviser, Highland Region.

Local Authority Advisers
Mrs D.-A. Cairns-Smith   Pre-School Community Organiser,
                          Renfrew. Also member of SAAUFF.
Mrs Jane Gorman   Playgroup Adviser, Fife Region.
                          Member of SAAUFF.
Mrs Anita Wilding   Nursery and Playgroup Adviser,
                          Grampian Region. Also member of
                          SAAUFF and officially representing
                          them.
Mrs Nancy Hughes   Playgroup Adviser, East Lothian.
                          Member of SAAUFF.

For Product Safety Concerns and Information please contact our EU
representative GPSR@taylorandfrancis.com
Taylor & Francis Verlag GmbH, Kaufingerstraße 24, 80331 München, Germany